Let Them Eat Crypto

Let Them Eat Crypto

The Blockchain Scam
That's Ruining the World

Peter Howson

PLUTO  PRESS

First published 2023 by Pluto Press
New Wing, Somerset House, Strand, London WC2R 1LA
and Pluto Press, Inc.
1930 Village Center Circle, 3-834, Las Vegas, NV 89134

www.plutobooks.com

British Library Cataloguing in Publication Data
A catalogue record for this book is available from the British Library

ISBN 978 0 7453 4821 6   Paperback
ISBN 978 0 7453 4822 3   PDF
ISBN 978 0 7453 4823 0   EPUB

This book is printed on paper suitable for recycling and made from
fully managed and sustained forest sources. Logging, pulping and
manufacturing processes are expected to conform to the environmental standards of the country of origin.

Typeset by Stanford DTP Services, Northampton, England

Simultaneously printed in the United Kingdom and United States of
America

Contents

Preface

Proponents of crypto tend to see criticism as a product of ignorance. They'll suggest the haters and naysayers simply don't understand the workings of blockchain technology. Sceptics are accused of being shills for the global banking system or henchmen for some corrupt government. But I'm not a fan of banking. And I wasn't always a crypto sceptic. When I first came across the technology as a cure-all for international development and conservation, I was intrigued. There was something inherently subversive in crypto. It connected with my activist tendencies. I didn't fully understand the technical details back then. But I was very excited to learn and experiment with blockchain. The prospect of reimaging what money could be was like reimagining power itself.

Most people's first encounter with blockchain is through the cryptocurrency Bitcoin. But I had never heard of Bitcoin when I came across blockchain back in 2016. I was working in a peatland swamp forest in Indonesia, researching a climate finance initiative with indigenous Dayak communities who'd lost their forests to oil palm plantations. A carbon-offsetting company next door was proposing the use of a cryptocurrency called Stellar to deliver carbon credits to corporate buyers in the USA and Europe, without having to splash out on auditors or other expensive intermediaries. I'd been living in Indonesia for several years by then. During that time, every forest protection project that popped up failed to deliver anything close to what the developers originally pledged. Sometimes the failures ended in spectacular violence, with families' homes and lives destroyed to make way for conservation projects. Other times, the violence came in the form of unintended broken promises regarding things that people were relying on. I shared the belief that crypto could fix many of the bad things in tropical forest conservation. The technology could perhaps be useful to indigenous peoples trying to make their forests more profitable standing than cut down for timber and palm oil. Everyone had phones. The internet was reliable and cheap. It seemed at least possible that people living in and around tropical forests could plant trees and receive financial rewards without too much bother.

After leaving Indonesia a few years later, I collaborated with academic colleagues and designed a project rewarding citizen scientists in the north-east of England with a cryptocurrency we called Coastcoin. I encouraged the Peruvian charity, of which I was a trustee, to experiment with crypto as an alternative to expensive Western Union payments. I uncritically boosted various environmentally focused blockchain projects across Asia and Africa. I wrote about fishing companies using blockchain to try and eradicate slavery from their supply chains. Oxfam, UNICEF and other big charities appeared to be sending crypto to smiling faces on the remotest Pacific islands. Greenpeace was fundraising for Bitcoin after their bank accounts were frozen in India. Sea Shepherd was selling NFTs of cartoon cats, raising thousands of dollars to save whales in the process. What harm could it do? Perhaps crypto could save rainforests, the oceans and our climate. To me, blockchain was a revolution.

Sometimes, when we are convinced something's revolutionary, but we don't understand it fully, we often opt for the safe repetition of soundbites and plausible narratives. I decided to write this book because I had been doing just that. This book is my atonement. After many years of looking at blockchain projects across the world, from every angle – the coding, the economics, the politics, the environmental and social impacts – it is beyond reasonable doubt to me that blockchain makes everything worse. This book is my immutable message, documented for future generations. Everything else I've said – ignore it.

I've been a conservationist and international development researcher for over 15 years, mainly focused on climate change mitigation in Southeast Asia and the Pacific. But researching ostensibly humanitarian blockchain projects has been my bread and butter since 2018. The journey to writing this book has taken me from Iceland to India, from Burnley to Bali. Besides the tropical forests and remote islands, I've hung out in Bitcoin-themed cafes, crypto conferences, refugee camps, online chat rooms and lonely metaverses. As well as interviewing developers, policymakers and regular folks on the ground, I've been helped along the way by key thinkers and technical experts who've written many great books on Bitcoin and crypto. But as a geographer by training, I wanted to write something that turns people's heads towards what cryptocurrencies and blockchain experiments do to people and places. As someone who's interested in social and environmental justice, I also hope this book will act as a one-stop shop for anyone who is erroneously considering cryptocurrencies as a potential emancipatory or left-wing alternative to traditional forms of finance.

I've tried to write this for the uninitiated. You'll learn how crypto works, but the technical aspects of blockchain are not particularly important. Without exception, when you buy crypto, you're buying access to a scam. And without exception, everything that uses a blockchain would work better without one. The book is written for people interested in reclaiming our digital destinies from Silicon Valley, and replacing their capitalist innovation agendas with something that might actually lead to greater human and non-human flourishing.

The greatest challenge in writing this book has been the constantly shifting terrain on which I am writing. Crypto is like watching normal finance capitalism in fast-forward, without a pause button. Boom-and-bust cycles that would last ten years in the City occur weekly in crypto. I had the idea for this book when most cryptocurrencies were at their all-time price high. I'm finishing it during a so-called crypto ice age. There will likely be many more shocks for the crypto industry and more Silicon Valley pump projects for our consumption.

I'm not solely taking aim at the software developers and computer scientists here. There is a commonly held belief in mainstream academia that if we only had more philosophers and humanists in big tech and finance, we could avoid wrong turns. Yet it was mainly the coders calling bullshit on blockchain scams, the biggest of which were pushed by a cabal of environmentalists, development economists and moral philosophers turned Silicon Valley thought leaders for hire. As this book explains, trusted do-gooders were the biggest promoters of blockchain as a useful innovation for human development. Meanwhile, those who understood the underlying cogs and gears were pointing out the emperor's nudity.[1]

Much of this book has been informed by the excellent critique of others who've been shouting very loudly for years concerning the fraud and fairy tales coming from the abhorrent crypto industry. I've tried to include quotes and signposts to their work throughout the book. Others I've not, due to the activist and/or practice-based nature of what they do. But I'd especially like to thank Stephen Howson, Didier Mary, Inte Gloerich, Jillian Crandall, Olivier Jutel, Antulio Rosales, Xavier Balaguer Rasillo, Alex de Vries, Kate Maclean,

James Davoll and Paul Dolan, for being such important pioneers in your respective fields, while also being thoroughly decent human beings. Big thanks also to David Castle at Pluto Press for seeing promise in this project. And of course, to my family for tolerating me while I wrote it.

Introduction

The rise of crypto was commonly likened to a market mania – symptomatic of a 'madness of crowds'. There are many theories on what caused the bubble to finally pop. Some blamed the contagion effects from a collapsing cryptocurrency project called TerraUSD. Others blamed governments for abruptly ending an unprecedented era of 'easy money'. Increasing interest rates, Covid controls, and Russia's invasion of Ukraine all played a part in sobering up investor portfolios. But crypto was brought down primarily by sheer weight of fraud. Unlike previous manias for Tellytubby Dolls or tulips, most crypto projects were designed to deceive. The level of criminal fraud in crypto markets may eventually prove many times higher than any investment scandal in history.[1] While that's certainly an important part of the story, this book intends to crack open a much bigger magic trick; an idea that many people still find utterly mesmerising: blockchain technology.

Blockchain promised to revolutionise every industry. It would fundamentally change how we live, work, communicate and spend. Companies, banks and charities – even entire governments – would be replaced by blockchain technology as part of the so-called Web3 revolution. This book looks back at what really happened, when men tried to fix our global development challenges with blockchains. It looks at the delusional fanatics still trying desperately to keep the illusion alive, and charts the direction in which our digital lives are headed, unless the blockchain bubble bursts.

The list of popped asset bubbles, associated with popular delusions and irrational crowd dynamics, is very long. Historically, these bubbles were inflated through their endorsements. Popular celebrities, including the artist Jan van Goyen, helped push seventeenth-century Dutch society into a frenzy over tulips. In his 1841 book, *Memoirs of Extraordinary Popular Delusions and the Madness of Crowds*, Charles MacKay describes how many otherwise normal people were swept up in a speculative fever, spending a year's salary on rare tulips, hoping to resell options on future bulbs for huge profits. Likewise, the ballooning British South Sea Bubble of 1720 was inflated by King George I and most of his government. Even Isaac Newton lost his shirt. The Wall Street Crash of 1929 stole the fortune of Albert Einstein. Just like Tulipomania, South Sea stock and Pets.com, the recent crypto bubble was driven by trusted endorsements at all levels and a seemingly irrational speculative mania over some sort of innovation. Few seemed to fully understand what it was, beyond that it might somehow make them rich quickly. But there was also an underlying magic show. As the futurist and science fiction writer Arthur C. Clarke wrote in his 1962 book *Profiles of the Future*: 'Any sufficiently advanced technology is indistinguishable from magic.' And so, from time to time, we can be forgiven for seeing innovation where there is only an illusion.

In 1769, Slovakian inventor Wolfgang von Kempelen created such an innovation illusion: a mechanical chess-playing Turk. Kempelen was an industrialist. He'd built early versions of microphones, typewriters and steam turbines. After attending a party at Schönbrunn Palace in Austria, where a magician was performing an illusion act involving magnets, Kempelen decided to turn his talents to deception. After six months of tinkering, he returned to the palace with an automaton consisting of a life-sized model of a human head and torso dressed in Ottoman robes and a turban – the traditional costume of an oriental sorcerer. Its left arm held a long Ottoman smoking pipe, while its right lay on top of a large cabinet next to a chess board. The front of the cabinet consisted of three doors, which could be opened one at a time to reveal a complex interior of clockwork machinery.

Kempelen addressed his audience and began a demonstration. After opening and closing the doors, he invited members of the audience to inspect the automaton for any signs of trickery. The first person to play against the Turk was a courtier who, along with all the other challengers that day, was quickly defeated. Kempelen promptly took his Turk off on a sell-out tour around the great theatres of Europe, where it typically beat nearly all its opponents within 30 minutes. Famous losers included French Emperor Napoleon Bonaparte, Frederick the Great of Prussia and Benjamin Franklin.

But the Turk was a hoax. An accomplished chess master[2] sat inside the cabinet with an oil lamp, pulling strings and pantograph levers connected to a magnetic pegboard. The operator used Kempelen's early microphone to shout 'Echek!' (check in French). Smoke from the lamp would exit the cabinet via the Ottoman's pipe. Bruised opponents were usually heavily distracted by the Turk's nodding head, jerky hand and noisy cogs, which all pieced together to appear like cutting-edge technology. Players and paying audiences were also totally distracted by the many possibilities for human development embodied by a machine that seemed to symbolise all the hopes and fears prevalent at the dawn of the industrial revolution. Adam Smith's *The Wealth of Nations* was circulating at the same time as the automaton. Both works offered glimpses at an automated future under capitalism. Meanwhile, Luddites fearing their imminent irrelevance due to industrial automations were smashing newly installed looms. It wasn't until the 1830s, some 70 years after the Turk's debut, that an American sceptic, Edgar Allan Poe, suggested in his *Maelzel's Chess-Player* essay that the Turk was an elaborate scam. But by then, the once novel automaton had been relegated to a dusty corner of a museum, where it was destroyed in a fire.

This book considers blockchain innovation as an illusion. Like the chess-playing Turk, blockchain successfully tricked its audience not only because of its mysterious and often unfathomable complexity, but because of its trustworthy endorsements, the political moment in which it was presented and the possibilities promoted for serving human development.

As the dust settles in the wake of high-profile crypto fraud cases, the book won't get bogged down with deciding what crimes have been committed. I set out to answer a more interesting set of questions: How was the blockchain illusion possible? In whose interests were blockchain projects developed? Who were the victims? And why are there still so many believers for whom blockchain automation remains the 'jewel in the crown' of innovation?

Crypto experiments were rarely demonstrated to audiences of resilient and willing volunteers before being given to the sick. The economic guinea pigs were usually the poorest and least able to push back. I explain how these projects preyed on vulnerable communities to experiment with private programmable money, to appropriate land, data and resources, and to recruit new suckers. Men with blockchains sought out people suffering debt crises, war and environmental disasters – the more scarred from past colonial abuse the better. But they were rarely drawn to oppressed folks because they wanted to genuinely fix poor people's problems. For most crypto developers, poor people's only problem was a lack of crypto.

Quitting blockchain does not stifle innovation or human development, it stifles fraud, conflict and climate breakdown. But just because blockchain is terrible tech doesn't mean it will fade into obscurity on its own. The worst human inventions, from asbestos toothpaste to leaded petrol, have all hung around longer than they ideally should. Cutting our losses and moving on from blockchain requires a purge, exposing the levers under the cabinet and the deceptive motives of the men inside.

ILLUSIONS OF INNOVATION

So what exactly is blockchain? A blockchain is an immutable append-only database that first appeared with the cryptocurrency Bitcoin: a peer-to-peer system of digital cash. You may be thinking, 'but isn't all cash digital these days, what's so special about Bitcoin?' But Bitcoin is digital cash without banks, or any regulator at all for that matter. Instead of state-controlled banks mediating what payments are allowed and getting all the rewards for keeping the Bitcoin books straight, a consensus mechanism is built into a blockchain to help decide which transactions are legitimate. Blockchain consensus mechanisms vary, but the two most common are called Proof of Work (used by Bitcoin) and Proof of Stake (PoS, used by Ethereum). Bitcoin's Proof of Work mechanism uses millions of specialist machines, known as 'miners', who compete for the right to validate the transactions occurring on the network. Ethereum does away with the energy-intensive competition, selecting validators from a pool of willing computers instead. Bitcoin and Ethereum both use 'open' or 'permissionless' blockchains, that is, anyone can use them, join the network as a validator and view a full history of transactions.[3] In both cases, validators are compensated for their work with rewards of new cryptocurrency tokens. And whenever cryptocurrency is transacted, the sender pays a fee to the validator who recorded it. These transactions are validated in 'blocks'. When the block is full, it becomes read-only. After being time-stamped, it joins a chain of other read-only blocks. The validators doing the work can theoretically be anyone. But the huge resources needed to become a blockchain bookkeeper means that over half of all Bitcoins are created by just three 'pool' companies, while only the biggest Ethereum holders get the privilege of validating those transactions.

When Bitcoin was first launched in 2009, not many people were interested. Because only a few enthusiasts wanted to play the Bitcoin-mining competition, these early adopters were able to hoover up the bulk of the available tokens with standard computer hardware. With the heady rewards on offer today, the contest has heated up. And so has the project's energy use and climate impacts.

Cryptocurrencies are responsible for a huge environmental footprint. A crypto-mining machine is essentially a computer, about the size of a toaster, yet just one of them uses three times more energy than the average UK house. I explain why and how in Chapter 4. There are millions of these toaster-sized computers clumped together in climate-controlled ware-houses and shipping containers around the world, burning through a medium-sized developed country's worth of mainly fossil-fuelled energy. They run 24/7, flat out, for a year or two. Once they're burned out, mining machines can't easily be repurposed to do anything else. Around 98 per cent of these machines will end up on a dump somewhere in the Global South having never successfully mined a single Bitcoin.[4] Bitcoin alone produces more hazardous electronic waste than the whole of the Netherlands each year.

Whether Bitcoin is generating more pollution than a small village, or a big country, Bitcoin can't scale up. It can't process more than seven transactions per second. In comparison, the Visa network alone can facilitate up to 65,000 simultaneous payments globally. Visa, a company founded in 1958, can pull off an instant card transaction using pretty much the same technology they've always used, with one million times less energy than it takes to make a Bitcoin payment. And Bitcoin payments are far from instantaneous. Most payments take several hours to complete – if they complete at all.

Blockchain believers argue it's the inefficiency and waste that enables immutable, censorship-resistant security, free from government meddling. But blockchains are just software made of corruptible computer code, no more inherently secure than any other data storage infrastructure. When the Ethereum network was hacked in June 2016, a 'coordinated restart' followed to claw back the funds. The roll-back resulted in the need to create an entirely new version of the Ethereum blockchain: a so-called hard fork. The original version, which became known as Ethereum Classic, was hacked again in 2019. The hackers were able to rewrite the transaction history and make off with millions of dollars worth of other people's crypto.

Because permissionless blockchains use cryptocurrency and competitive game theory logic to incentivise validators, they all depend on profit seekers to keep the cogs turning. And without centralised regulators, they are always vulnerable to people trying to fiddle the books. Blockchains are generally considered impervious to meddling without breaking the whole thing. But blockchain security is like tying your precious things to a padlock using only elastic bands. One only need look at the investments lost to the secure hands of the world's largest cryptocurrency exchange, FTX.

All blockchain projects have a core team of software developers and other intermediaries. For example, ongoing maintenance of Bitcoin's software depends on just three individuals, while 80 per cent of all Bitcoin-mining machines come from one factory in Beijing.[5] On one rainy weekend in April 2021, one flooded coal furnace in China's Xinjiang province took out over a third of all the world's Bitcoin miners.[6] Then in December 2022, a storm in Texas slashed the mining (or 'hash') rate by around 40 per cent.[7] Nearly half of all Bitcoins in circulation are locked up in the wallets of around a thousand uber-rich 'whale investors'. Like a humpback in a swimming pool, each crypto whale can cause enormous volatility whenever they move their cryptocurrency around. Many whales can easily inflate prices of certain cryptocurrencies by buying the bulk of tokens before dumping their stock on smaller retail investors for massive profits. With the collapse of FTX, by far the largest crypto exchange today, Binance, facilitates more of the world's cryptocurrency trades than all the other exchanges put together. In February 2023, after transaction times slowed to a crawl on the Solana blockchain, a 'coordinated restart' was required twice. Turning the blockchain off and on again like this is a centralised method used by many supposedly 'decentralised' projects to go about fixing things. Crypto's core value proposition – decentralisation – is a farce.

When critics like me discuss the fraud, waste and inefficiency of blockchain, or raise concerns that no one has yet found a constructive use for the technology, we often hear screams from blockchain proponents arguing that 'it's still early days!' or 'if we had given up on mobile phones or the internet while developers were still ironing out the kinks, where would we be now?' But, aside from some minor tweaks, after 15 years Bitcoin is the same as it was when it was born.

You yourself might well be scratching your head right now, asking 'blockchain doesn't sound very useful. Why don't they just use PayPal?' The crypto journalist David Gerard gives out bumper stickers with the most common reaction he hears when telling people how blockchains work that reads: 'It can't be that stupid, you must be explaining it wrong.' So why would anyone use it? Answering this requires some sympathy for the politics of blockchain.

THE HUMANS BEHIND THE CURTAIN

In his 1980 essay 'Do Artifacts Have Politics?', Langdon Winner helps to distinguish between forms of technology that are associated with political ideas and those that only really have utility in the hands of a certain political group.[8] We can apply the same logic to digital technology too. Take the social media platform Parler; its growth was always highly associated with the far right. But its far-rightness wasn't inherent to the platform. Socialists might just as easily have found utility in it. In contrast, because the only real affordance crypto projects offer is in subverting political institutions, these projects are generally only useful for people harbouring hostilities towards those institutions. When I explain the principles of blockchain to my students, I often hear a pitch or two arguing for a specific use case that I may not have considered. But when I ask, 'so why do you need a blockchain?' the response *always* comes down to a cyberlibertarian distrust in human intermediaries or political institutions. Blockchains can't fix political problems. They only exacerbate them.

Although Bitcoin was born at the dawn of the global financial crisis, there's nothing anti-free market about Bitcoin. It's important to understand that Bitcoin was not put together in reaction to the predatory lending practices and fairy dust financial instruments which gave rise to the US subprime mortgage crisis. The real bugbear for Bitcoin's designers were governments. The 'Bitcoin Whitepaper' was posted in October 2008, just after US and UK banks were bailed out by their respective governments. Bitcoin went live in January 2009, just after the same governments kicked off plans for a second round of quantitative easing. The first data block on the Bitcoin blockchain (grandiosely termed 'the genesis block') shows the rationale behind the experiment by featuring the front-page headline from *The Times* newspaper that day: 'Chancellor on brink of second bailout for banks'. It's also important to note that nothing particularly innovative was born in that moment. Pseudonymous public-key cryptography was born in 1976. Bitcoin's 'Merkle tree' data structure was patented in 1979. The process of locking data blocks together in time-stamped chains was first developed in 1991.

Although Satoshi Nakamoto was credited with the Bitcoin Whitepaper, the project was a collaboration between a group of techno-libertarian coders, collectively known as the 'cypherpunks'.[9] The group came together in the 1990s around a shared belief in cryptography as a way to undermine governments. Key figures in the group included Timothy May, regarded as the father of 'crypto anarchy'. In his 1988 *Crypto Anarchist Manifesto*, he explained the opportunities for computer networks to allow individuals and groups to communicate and interact with each other anonymously, preventing any government's ability to tax and control economic interactions. May was a deeply private gun collector and sci-fi enthusiast who described his political philosophy as 'leave me alone and keep your hands off my stuff'.[10] He was convinced that public-key cryptography, digital cash and networked computing could recreate a virtual Galt's Gulch – the fictional capitalist paradise in Ayn Rand's *Atlas Shrugged*, where Rand's heroes go to escape government intrusion.[11] May was a close friend of Chip Morningstar who, while working with Lucasfilm in 1986, developed the world's first metaverse-styled online game called *Habitat*.

In 1987, Morningstar introduced May to the economist and entrepreneur Phil Salin, who had just established a private space rocket company and one of the world's first e-commerce businesses called Amix. While both May and Salin were libertarians, unlike May, Salin was a businessman and dogmatic follower of Friedrich Hayek. The central premise of the Hayekian philosophy went that peace and social stability could only be achieved when free market competition and pricing were left to ensure 'spontaneous order'. In his 1944 book *The Road to Serfdom*, Hayek argued that any government interventions in the functioning of free markets were a slippery slope to totalitarian control.[12] The idea went down a treat with neoliberal politicians and tax-dodging elites the world over. Margaret Thatcher famously slammed down her beloved copy of Hayek's *Constitution of Liberty* during a cabinet meeting, declaring 'This is what we believe!' But unlike Salin, May hated the idea of orderly markets nearly as much as he hated governments. While politically on different pages, May and Salin shared a dream for developing a future internet and digital money system impervious to government interference. In September 1992, May established an online mailing list to develop and share the group's cyberlibertarian ideas more widely.[13] By 1998 the group had shared the idea of Proof of Work mining, which was later cited in the Bitcoin Whitepaper. Nick Szabo circulated his ideas for 'smart contracts'.[14] Wei Dai first proposed his Bitcoin precursor, 'b-money', via the mailing list. The list had by then around 2,000 active users, including WikiLeaks founder Julian Assange. May's ideas later inspired Assange to write his book *Cypherpunks: Freedom and the Future of the Internet*. Things went quiet on the forum following the 2001 US terrorist attacks, as many anti-government movements were keeping their heads low to avoid the 'War on Terror'. Then, in 2008, the global financial landscape shook the group awake to give birth to Bitcoin.

Interest in Bitcoin was slow at first. Until in 2010, WikiLeaks released evidence documenting the killing of Reuters journalists at the hands of US airmen in Iraq. The video titled *Collateral Murder* stirred politicians in the USA to choke off any financial support for WikiLeaks. The personal Swiss bank account of Julian Assange was frozen. Under government pressure, MasterCard and Visa refused to process any WikiLeaks transactions. PayPal agreed to freeze their accounts, claiming that their platform 'cannot be used for any activities that encourage, promote, facilitate or instruct others to engage in illegal activity'. Assange was forced to turn his cypherpunk side hustle into WikiLeaks' only hope for survival. Crypto kept WikiLeaks afloat, but the fundraiser poked US lawmakers to consider a crackdown on Bitcoin.

In 2012, to reset Bitcoin's reputation for enabling criminality, a non-profit Bitcoin Foundation was established. Patrick Murck, general counsel of the foundation, testified before a US Senate committee convened to assess the dangers of digital currencies. Allowing illicit purchases on darknet marketplaces was thought to be the main use case for Bitcoin. But Murck managed to convince committee members that due to its open and transparent blockchain, Bitcoin was a terrible tool for illicit activity. It was usually possible for authorities to track every Bitcoin transaction. In 2013, simply by monitoring the blockchain, FBI agents identified and arrested Ross Ulbricht, also known by the alias Dread Pirate Roberts, for drug dealing and laundering around $200 million via his Silk Road website, the world's largest darknet marketplace. Ulbricht was handed down a life sentence without the possibility of parole. But it wasn't long before the Bitcoin Foundation itself became plagued by controversy.

The foundation's vice-chairman, Charlie Shrem, was arrested and sentenced to two years in prison for selling nearly $1 million worth of Bitcoin to drug buyers on the Silk Road. Shortly after, Mark Karpeles, then CEO of the Mt. Gox crypto exchange, resigned from the foundation's board after Mt. Gox lost 750,000 of its customers' Bitcoins and went bankrupt, causing the value of Bitcoin to crash. Despite bringing in PR experts from the Cato Institute to help the foundation deal with government regulators, Bitcoin's path to acceptability remained rocky. In June 2013, Edward Snowden, a private military contractor working for Booz Allen Hamilton, transferred classified files from his servers to a consortium of journalists evidencing a mass National Security Agency surveillance programme known as PRISM. The files proved the US government had, since 2001, been secretly collecting user data from companies such as Microsoft, Google and Apple. Snowden was charged by the USA with espionage and became a permanent resident of Russia. 'In 2013, Bitcoin is what I used to pay for the servers pseudonymously', Snowden said at a conference.[15] 'Bitcoin was the plumbing behind how I transferred the files to these reporters who frankly I couldn't trust to protect me.'

As the crypto community grew, most people with Bitcoin weren't concerned about the total privacy of their transactions. Snowden himself advocated for privacy-preserving alternatives to Bitcoin, like ZCash and Monero. While Bitcoin was designed to circumvent government surveillance, by 2014 the technology was becoming largely dependent on establishing crypto as a get-rich-quick vehicle. Luckily, a warm embrace of Bitcoin by conservative politicians and the banks was developing, pushing the price of Bitcoin to over $1,000. As Nathaniel Popper says in *Digital Gold: The Untold Story of Bitcoin*: 'There was a growing swell of voices talking about the virtues of Bitcoin that had nothing to do with whether a government could or could not track users.'[16] For David Golumbia, as anti-government activism and libertarian economics were coming together in the Bitcoin community, right-wing conspiracies were getting mainstreamed.[17] In *The Politics of Bitcoin: Software as Right-Wing Extremism*, Golumbia explains how, despite the historically rightist orientation of cyberlibertarian culture, central bank conspiracism was relatively new in those circles, gaining a foothold only with the introduction of Bitcoin and the blockchain:

> In the Bitcoin literature, as in the central bank conspiracy writings, we read that the [US Federal Reserve] is a private bank that hides its real purpose; that it steals money from some private citizens and puts it in the hands of the 'elites' that control the Fed; that the Fed itself is covertly run by a shadowy group of elites, often made up of Jews and members of English banking families such as the Rothschilds; and so on.[18]

For its more philosophical proponents, Bitcoin was the hardest form of money since the decline of the gold standard. For them, crypto was completely impervious to the hubris of central bank money printers. In promoting Bitcoin as a return to monetary metalism for the digital age, many Silicon Valley luminaries, such as influential venture capitalists Balaji Srinivasan and Marc Andreessen, as well as Jack Dorsey of Twitter, parroted the right-wing rhetoric. They pushed claims that government-backed money was inherently corrupt and unsustainable. With the dollar destined for hyperinflation,

Bitcoin was the only viable alternative.[19] To this day, many prominent so-called Bitcoin maximalists, from US radio host Alex Jones to Andrew Tate, are disproportionately sat towards the extreme right of the political spectrum. Chapter 6 of this book considers this conservative evolution of crypto ideology in more detail.

While many privacy-preserving alternatives to Bitcoin were being built from copies (or 'forks') of Bitcoin, a brand new blockchain with additional smart contract features was released in 2015. Ethereum was launched through a crowd-funding model known as an initial coin offering (ICO). Like an initial public offering of stock shares, the ICO was a way to raise money from the public by selling tokens. These tokens didn't carry with them an ownership stake in Ethereum; instead they were meant to provide access to some service later down the line, which would make them potentially valuable. Unlike Bitcoin, which was meant to be a peer-to-peer system of digital cash, Ethereum was designed as a general-purpose blockchain. Developers could use the Ethereum network to build their own cryptocurrencies, usually within five to ten minutes, with cash upfront if they adopted the same ICO funding model. Ethereum also allowed people to build so-called decentralised autonomous organisations (DAOs). The vision for a DAO was a company operating without human accountability. Ethereum also made it easy to create collections of unique non-fungible tokens (NFTs).

Whereas individual Bitcoins all had the same value – to make them work as a currency of sorts – NFTs worked more like rare stamps or baseball cards to collect and trade. With NFTs it wasn't the actual baseball card or any other image file getting uploaded to the blockchain. Because blockchains can only handle tiny amounts of data, usually only the file's web address – the location where the image could be accessed (usually by anyone, for free) – went 'on-chain'. NFTs enabled bragging rights rather than exclusive access. But with all these interesting features, crypto proponents set out to show that blockchains had uses far beyond money laundering and drug dealing on the Silk Road.

With the butterfingered Bitcoin Foundation fumbling for legitimacy, the most politically influential group of crypto advocates was being incubated within the Media Lab at the prestigious MIT university. The institute was the birthplace of 'blockchain for social good' ideas. Their outreach popularised claims that crypto would 'bank the unbanked': providing digital financial services to traditionally underserved communities. But for the powerful economists and technologists at the Media Lab, blockchain was not just about changing the money but reorganising nearly every aspect of civic life around blockchain applications. For them, 'for good' seemed to mean 'getting rid of government planning'. Everything that corrupt governments tried to centralise and control, including voting systems, birth, death and marriage certificates, parking tickets and land registries, should all be improved with blockchains.

The Media Lab was directed by Joi Ito. He would resign in 2019 following reports of financial improprieties involving the convicted child sex offender and Bitcoiner, Jeffrey Epstein. In an effort to disguise donations to the Media Lab, totalling some $7.5 million, Ito reportedly referred to Epstein only as Voldemort[20] or 'he who must not be named'. In 2015, Ito had invited Brian Forde and Jeremy Rubin to co-found the Media Lab's Digital Currency Initiative, where Gary Gensler would act as a senior advisor.[21] Gensler would go on to lead the US government's Securities and Exchange Commission (SEC): the US regulator of crypto investments. Rubin was a Bitcoin core developer. He'd worked as an intern at Jane Street Capital briefly with the disgraced FTX exchange founder, Sam Bankman-Fried. He'd launched the MIT Bitcoin Project, which offered every MIT undergraduate student $100 worth of Bitcoin to 'spur innovation and excite research in the space'. Forde had previously been a senior advisor to President Barack Obama, where he was tasked with writing the White House memo on Bitcoin. 'We needed to explain [Bitcoin] in a science, technology, and business way to understand what the real impact is here', Forde said. 'When people hear about cryptocurrency, they immediately go to "stranger danger"'. After Forde's briefing, Obama saw Bitcoin in a different light. 'He's a science and technology president, so he can more quickly grasp that than other world leaders', said Forde. As a Peace Corp volunteer, Forde saw peer-to-peer technology as a way out of poverty for people suffering from corrupt governments. In Nicaragua he established a telecommunication company enabling cheap Voice Over Internet phone calls. Forde explained:[22]

> Looking at all the conversations that I've had with leaders, once they're educated, they're much more receptive than you'd think. In some countries, it's actually changed policy, from one of absolutely banning Bitcoin to reversing that policy and not ultimately implementing it. What I saw in talking to other world leaders is they didn't have the staff that Obama had with technical backgrounds that could explain digital currency to them. Once it was explained to them, they saw the opportunity. They saw this as the second coming of the internet, and they were able to then make their own decisions.

While the MIT group lobbied governments globally with claims that crypto was an overwhelming force for good, by the end of 2017, various crypto project ICOs had raised around

$5.5 billion. But around 80 per cent of the ICOs were reportedly fraudulent, without a blockchain or cryptocurrency to speak of. Only a meagre 8 per cent ever went on to build a functioning project.[23] In early 2018, under the weight of its own grift, crypto markets crashed spectacularly. Ethereum dropped by 75 per cent. Bitcoin fell from nearly $20,000 to around $3,000 and stayed there for two years. With seemingly few working use-cases or popular guiding philosophical principles, the blockchain for social good idea was dead. To bring it back required much more capital, marketing and thought leadership – a set of vacuous rhetorical appeals to make people believe blockchain was the inevitable next step in the evolution of the internet.

WEB3: ONE GIANT LEAP IN THE DECLINE OF THE INTERNET

The idealism of the early internet was compelling. This was a new technology that would provide everyone, regardless of means, with equal, open access to the world's knowledge. Open and free, these were the basic principles of the World Wide Web, as reasserted by Tim Berners-Lee at the 2012 London Olympics: 'THIS IS FOR EVERYONE', read the twinkly lights. The highly centralised version of the internet that we have today is a far cry from that early idealism. Web3 was meant to change all that. In their *A Simple Guide to the Web3 Stack*,[24] the US crypto exchange Coinbase explains the now standard definition of Web3 as 'a trustless, permissionless, and decentralized internet that leverages blockchain technology'. This simple umbrella definition encourages us to buy into a series of epochs for the internet itself, as explained by the Coinbase guide: 'Whereas the first iteration of the commercial internet (Web1) was *read-only* for most users, and Web2 allowed users to both *read & write* on centralized platforms, Web3 gives users full ownership over their content, data, and assets via blockchains. It empowers users to *read-write-own*.'

In the aftermath of the dot com crash in the late 1990s, what set Web2 apart from Web1, according to the Silicon Valley thought leader Timothy O'Reilly, was the simple fact that those firms that couldn't embrace the Web2 monopoly doctrine went bust.[25] Web2 was a centralised internet dominated by platforms such as Facebook, Twitter, AirBnB and other similarly sized giants, packaging up users' behavioural data for their prediction products, which would all be controlled by venture capital (VC) giants such as Marc Andreessen's A16z.

There was very little lauding of O'Reilly's framing outside of VC firms. It wasn't very catchy. But A16z bought it. Andreessen had never been the most famous face of Silicon Valley. Yet in 1993, his graphical web browser, Mosaic, popularised the internet for the first time. Andreessen later developed Netscape and Microsoft's Internet Explorer browsers. According to Jathan Sadowski, '[i]t is hard to overstate the degree to which Marc Andreessen has played some kind of core role in every phase of the internet'.[26] He'd sat on the board of Facebook since 2008. He'd coached its founder and CEO, Mark Zuckerberg. Andreessen's firm invested billions in Twitter, GitHub, Skype and the many other centralised giants that made up the Web2 dream-come-true.

Rebranding blockchain as something that could smash the big tech oligopolies of Web2 was the original idea of Ethereum and Web3 Foundation founder, Gavin Wood. But it remained a niche idea until A16z staked their crypto fortunes on it. Cryptocurrencies, NFTs, metaverses and any other projects to come along with a blockchain strapped to them would form the next iteration of the web: Web3.[27] The narrative went like this: Web2 was an oligopolistic Goliath that needed to be disrupted through the introduction of new blockchain platforms, such as the cryptocurrency exchange Coinbase, the NFT marketplace OpenSea, various 'play-to-earn' gaming platforms and metaverse projects. All of which, conveniently, were funded by A16z.

Investment in 1,312 blockchain-related start-ups totalled $18 billion in 2021. The largest fund was A16z's $2.2 billion Crypto Fund III, which was announced in the aftermath of the firm's lucrative exit from their investment in Coinbase. The exchange went public in early 2021 at a total share value of $85.8 billion. A16z announced another $4.5 billion Crypto Fund IV in May 2022. It appeared, according to Sadowski, that 'in the midst of a market spiral for crypto, [A16z] was doing what can be described as VC Keynesianism: they were trying to combat a recession, or "crypto winter", by heating up the Web3 economy with continual infusions of capital'.

For the VC firms, their investment strategies followed the standard crypto 'pump and dump' playbook. It worked like this: following the 2018 crypto market crash, US regulators had reiterated that token offerings were illegal if the project and the tokens didn't pass the Howey test, a 1946 rule of thumb used by the SEC to determine whether an offering was an investment instrument. Cryptocurrencies are rarely used as currencies: they're speculative. Under the Howey test, then, most crypto projects would be judged as selling unregistered securities. Big VC firms would struggle to sell crypto investment instruments directly to the public without attracting the attention of regulators. Instead, these firms would invest in smaller start-ups that were selling unregistered crypto securities to the public via exchanges. As well as agreeing a cut of the profits, VC firms would take a large share of the project's pre-sale tokens. When retail markets opened, the firm could liquidate their position by dumping tokens on regular retail investors before they all inevitably fell to zero. This was securities fraud. But VC firms weren't committing the fraud. The 'decentralised' projects these firms were investing in were.[28]

Most of these projects offered buyers no utility whatsoever. But thanks to outreach work from folks at MIT, the Bitcoin Foundation and their deep-pocketed VC supporters, the popular perspective among journalists, academics and politicians remained that there was simply too much smoke around Web3 for there not to be fire somewhere; a non-scammy application to democratise the web, bank the unbanked or something else that they just hadn't thought of yet. To keep the smoke going, and give blockchain even the semblance of innovation, it was essential for old, trusted words to no longer mean what they used to mean; or more preferably to strip them of any meaning at all. The English language was hacked by Web3. In promoting the idea, nearly every crypto buzzword, assuredly stated with Harry Houdini levels of mental contort ing, meant something else for normal people.

Table 1 shows a few examples.

English tenses were set free to take on new meaning. Everything that *had* happened was redundant or 'legacy'. If it was Web3, it was the first of its kind. And if some vague pie in the sky idea was featured on the project's planning road map, then it was happening, right now. In the world of Web3, innovation no longer had to improve anything. In his ethnography of cryptocurrency marketplaces,[29] Simon Mackenzie described the crypto playing field like this:

> This is a space where FOMO [fear of missing out] can really kick off, where people lust after Lambos on the moon, and where chat rooms are full of overheated bluster about pumpamentals and getting in quick, so you don't get left behind. You could hardly ask for a better socio-economic

Table 1 Examples of Web3 words with English translations

Web3	English
Censorship	'Laws'
Censorship-resistance	'The authorities will struggle to prove it was our fault'
Community	'The people who we take money from' (or 'downline' in pyramid scheme-speak)
Decentralised	'We're not legally accountable for anything that goes wrong with this'
Dictatorships	'Countries with taxmen and/or laws against money laundering'
Distributed	'We're not accountable for anything that goes wrong with this. And we can't change it, even when something does go wrong'
Freedom	'We take your money' and/or 'we don't need to pay any tax'
Legacy [name any industry]	'A non-Web3 industry that everyone uses a lot and will probably continue to use for a long time'
Open	'Do your own research'
Privacy	'No refunds'
Surveillance	'Tax men'
Tokenomics	'The process we will use to take your money'
Trustless	'Do your own research'
Tyranny	'Someone else is trying to take our money' or 'tax'

structure within which to propagate scams. To cap it all off you have the anonymity and reach of the internet which makes it possible for scammers to talk simultaneously via chatrooms to hundreds – and in some cases thousands – of marks wherever they are in the world, receive their money through instantaneous transfers and leave without anyone ever knowing who or where they are.[30]

Crypto was essentially a huge platform for running various scams. And so, keeping people interested, and making 'number go up', meant constantly creating new smoke for new suckers from seemingly plausible project proposals. Scams are usually thought of as 'confidence tricks' involving a con-artist gaining the trust of a mark. But for Mackenzie, crypto was a 'grey economy' where everyone was a player: both a potential perpetrator and a victim, where, as in a high-stakes game of marbles, what distinguishes one from the other is who gets the winnings. Lana Swartz refers to the crypto game world as the 'network scam': a massively multiplayer game without a clear set of perpetrators or victims.[31] According to Swartz they are 'capitalism out of place: what gets called a scam is used to perform boundary work that delegitimates certain forms of economic activity (and exploitation) and legitimates others'.[32] All crypto projects are essentially capitalism on steroids, except nothing with any real utility is for sale. The only use for crypto is speculative marbles, but with huge costs for wider society and the environment.

Maintaining the smokescreen of legitimate economic activity requires the presence of trusted names using the same set of vacuous buzzwords as Web3 proponents. International development rhetoric is fuelling both the many elaborate project proposals for crypto fixes and the necessary appearance of legitimacy to attract new players. Thanks to the increasing levels of funding and lobbying capacity from influential crypto advocates, policymakers are continuing to embrace blockchain. In 2019, UN Secretary-General António Guterres instructed world leaders that they needed to employ blockchain to tackle what he called a global trust deficit disorder:

'For the United Nations to deliver better on our mandate in the digital age, we need to embrace technologies like block-chain that can help accelerate the achievement of Sustainable Development Goals.'[33] And world leaders listened. Every UN agency, the European Union, the World Bank and the World Economic Forum (WEF) touted the benefits of blockchain for leapfrogging legacy governance systems. For blockchain believers, the only risk to the poor in this brave new world was the risk of being left behind. As well as being pitched as the key technical enabler of the UN's ambitious Sustainable Development Goals (SDGs), transacting in crypto was being etched in stone as an absolute human right. Elizabeth Renieris described the obsession with transactional freedom among blockchain believers as mirroring the distorted free speech absolutism that more often than not resulted in silencing and endangering vulnerable groups of women and minorities.[34]

The recruitment of 'left-behind' suckers was now not only carefully rebranded as 'innovation', it was charity. Charities such as the Worldwide Fund for Nature (WWF), UN Children's Fund (UNICEF), Oxfam and Save the Children all joined in to woo the young, tech-savvy and idealistic breed of untapped crypto-rich philanthropists. The crypto narra-tive fitted neatly into these charities' neoliberal approaches to managing global challenges. Blockchain was considered ideal for sidestepping the state, attracting private finance and creating new markets for social and environmental services.

Unscrupulous celebrities, sports stars and super-rich CEOs all repeated claims of the emancipatory potential of Web3. Even vocal civil rights campaigners such as film maker Spike Lee took the bait, claiming blockchains would free those who were systematically oppressed and excluded in the mainstream economy. 'They call the dollar green', Spike Lee pointed out in a TV advert for a Bitcoin ATM company. 'But where's all the women, the black folks, the people of colour? There's a Native American on the US nickel. But people don't even stop to pick a nickel up from the sidewalk.' Old money is out, he said. Crypto is in.[35]

THE BLOCKCHAIN SCAM THAT'S RUINING THE WORLD

Based on fieldwork and interviews conducted over the last eight years, in the following chapters I aim to show how the economic margins – the war zones, dictatorships and online communities of vulnerable young people – made for ideal sandboxes to beta test blockchain experiments. Each chapter untangles a different set of social and environmental impacts caused by the blockchain scam. As traditional investors have gotten wise to crypto con tricks, Chapter 1 considers how blockchain developers shifted their attentions to 'subprime' communities around the globe. It looks at the non-governmental organisations (NGOs) who were key to spreading the blockchain gospel using cradle-to-grave campaigns and crypto literacy training. Despite promises of win-wins for everyone, the chapter explains how blockchain experiments compounded existing inequalities with the most disastrous impacts predictably concentrated at the bottom.

Chapter 2 looks at the disciples of decentralisation crusading towards new crypto Jerusalems like warlords to blood diamonds. I explain how these 'crypto colonists' have taken advantage of economic instabilities, weak regulations and access to cheap energy and other resources. I look at how they lobby weak governments, pushing for crypto to become legal tender, usually in places where people's lives and local infrastructure are tattered from pre-existing crises. The chapter charts the many failed attempts at building Crypto El

Dorado, where the biggest losers were the locals whose land and resources have been pillaged to make way for libertarian citadel fantasies. Just like every other empire, crypto colonists ostensibly came as friends with noble intentions of improving things. Chapter 3 considers the friendly sustainable development rhetoric used to legitimise crypto-colonial projects. It looks at how crypto is greenwashed to make one of humanity's most inefficient and polluting technologies appear 'sustainable' and how respected environmental organisations were complicit in the greenwashing. I'll explain how blockchain is used as a last-ditch effort to prop up failing carbon credits and conservation markets while causing huge challenges for sustainable living.

Chapter 4 looks at how charitable donors have been coaxed towards crypto to encode their donations with automated tax avoidance. The chapter also exposes how a cabal of charities, moral philosophers and respected thought-leaders have knowingly enabled and legitimised perhaps the biggest scam in human history. While the instigators of crypto scams were mainly men, Chapter 5 troubles the caricature of the 'Crypto Bro', as both a perpetrator and a victim. Focusing on liberal feminist projects ostensibly driven to save women, this chapter explores how gender was used as a strategic device to legitimise and connect crypto projects to capitalist gender norms. The chapter teases apart the entanglements between crypto culture, far-right extremism and the growing threats of violent misogyny. This violence was most glaring in the metaverse – where all the illusionary tactics of Web3 innovation come together. Despite not really existing, cryptocurrencies and NFT projects could all achieve their fabled 'utility' in the metaverse. If real jobs were thin on the ground, users could find full-time employment and training in virtual reality (VR). Chapter 6 looks at how strapping a blockchain to

VR social media platforms gave us the worst of both, making the internet a far darker place.

An anti-imperialist blockchain is impossible. Chapter 7 looks at various opportunities to regulate it away and the neoliberal interests desperate to keep it around. To tackle blockchain's full range of social and environmental impacts, discussed throughout this book, I argue that a global coordinated ban on crypto is likely to prove the most effective policy option for improving things.

This introductory chapter has explained the political ideas shared by committed crypto enthusiasts. I've tried not to dump all the technical jargon at the front. Rather, I drip feed it as we go. But the technical aspects of the blockchain scam are not the interesting part of this story. Blockchain constitutes a set of linguistic devices. But that doesn't make it harmless. In fact, it's the disruptive language of Web3 ideology that is destabilising our democratic institutions and directly undermining our ability to respond to crises. The blockchain illusion depends on gobbledygook and techno-blather. Innovations, on the other hand, rarely require much explanation. Take the electric toaster. English words don't need to be redefined to explain why anyone would ever want to use a toaster, because it's innovation. Meanwhile, to sell the utility of blockchain requires complex conspiracy jargon and a level of bamboozling that no other technology in human history has ever needed to deploy, because it's a hoax. Occasionally, crypto projects pop up claiming to use a blockchain when there isn't one.[36] But for the most part, blockchains are real, they just aren't delivering on their developer's revolutionary claims the way most people think they are.

Some argue that Web3, as the underlying framework driving blockchain adoption, could have been something else, as if the technology were somehow neutral.[37] But there is no such thing as a neutral blockchain project because there is no such thing as neutral language. Blockchain projects are all written with a very particular set of interests, anti-government hostility and trust issues in mind. All blockchain projects inevitably centralise power, rather than redistribute it or bring it down. If we embrace Web3 and allow Silicon Valley VC money to define the terms of our digital lives, then we deserve whatever innovation illusion they give us. Alternatively, a future world of real innovation, I argue, is one that dumps the blockchain scam, privileging digital democracy and equity instead.

1
Banking the Unbanked

Working projects have always been a rarity in crypto. The evidence even shows that tokens launched as part of a deliberate scam tend to trade better than genuine ones.[1] The most common scam used by crypto fraudsters is the rug pull, where developers draw in funding from investors until a critical mass is reached. The developers then do a runner, closing down the project while pulling the rug from under their investors. Where a token does finally launch, the performance of the underlying project, referred to as the asset's 'fundamentals' in stock market-speak, are often so diluted in crypto that traders refer instead to the asset's 'pumpamentals': the prospects that a 'shitcoin' will cause 'FOMO' and 'rocket to the moon'.[2] Useless Ethereum Token (UET) was a shitcoin that rocketed in July 2017, bringing in $40,000 in just three days. It's still trading today. The project's website describes it as '[t]he world's first 100 percent honest Ethereum ICO' in that it involved 'giving your money to someone on the internet and getting completely useless tokens in return'. Its anonymous creator said: 'I realised that people didn't really care about the product. They cared about spending a little bit of money, watching a chart, and then withdrawing a little bit more money. So why not have an ICO without a product, and do so completely transparently just to see what happened?'[3]

FOMO Coin also promised very little, other than nailing it as 'the next hottest shitcoin'. 'Get in before it's too late!' the project's website explained. 'We've been working on FOMO Coin for at least two hours!' Jamie Farrelly, FOMO Coin's founder explained from the get-go that his project was a good-hearted intervention. 'The current situation is nuts. I wanted to make people think a bit more about it',[4] Farrelly said.

In the regulatory abyss of crypto, responsibility for exposing the scammydocious nature of shitcoin trading to newbies fell squarely on the shoulders of self-appointed white-hat auditors. WarOnRugs was such an online vigilante, alerting people to potential crypto scams via his Twitter account of the same name. But despite his efforts, the weight of fraud grew. In a final flamboyant swansong to his cause, WarOnRugs aggressively marketed his own token, before pulling the rug out from under it. 'Since we can't do anything and there's no regulation in place, I decided to show you so you understand that you should stop being a clown and aping into anything', the Twitter account read as the scam closed. 'Hopefully after this you don't trust anyone anymore. Goodbye everyone.' A final post featured a GIF animation: a triumphant Elmo from Sesame Street, parading in front of an inferno.[5]

Even in the small number of crypto projects that weren't out-and-out scams, their marketing message to prospective buyers was the same as that used by Elmo, FOMO and UET: 'This crypto project isn't like all those other shitcoins, we're the good guys.' And when the projects were indeed fraudulent, they were often framed as virtuous interventions – an honourable Banksy-esque life lesson in cryptoeconomics. In 2022, 'Bitcoin isn't crypto' became the marketing centrepiece for the Bitcoin community. Bitcoin's mission to enlighten and civilise people with home-made internet money was framed as different from all the other crypto projects out there that were exploiting people with home-made internet money. 'Bitcoin is the original, and very different from crypto projects, which are all basically cheap knockoffs', read one article in *Bitcoin*

Magazine.[6] Like Edward Said's view of altruistic Christian missions in *Orientalism*, Bitcoiners also described their empire as unlike all the others: 'Our circumstances are special, we have a mission to enlighten, civilize, bring order and democracy, and use force only as a last resort.'[7]

SATOSHI'S CHILDREN

In July 2020, Richard Swisher and Valentin Popescu were exploring the Peruvian highlands around where I lived in the old Incan capital of Cusco. Swisher was an ex-police officer and evangelical Christian from Arizona. Popescu was a Romanian missionary with congregations across Peru. 'We came upon this village, up in the Andes, remote village', Swisher said in an interview. 'And they have a 5 percent mortality rate in their children. And the kids are dying from medical conditions related to exposure to cold, primarily through their feet.'[8] The children in Andean villages were dying at such a rate of knots, according to Swisher, because of their poor-quality socks and shoes.

Immediately, Swisher and Popescu jumped into action. With their new charitable organisation, Motiv,[9] they would teach the indigenous Quechuans how to use Bitcoin. 'We place an education hub in each community', says Swisher in a word cloud of philanthropic buzzwords: 'We call it the five Es; we *Educate*, *Equip*, and *Empower*. That helps *Emancipate* them, and then *Elevate* their community.'[10] Thanks to his community links as a church leader, Popescu was able to preach the supposed emancipatory potential of Motiv's cryptocurrency and, according to their website,[11] help to onboard thousands of new users every month from across 16 remote Andean villages. But this wasn't charity. It was the start of a sustainable 'circular economy'. The idea of a circular economy is usually thought of as one that tackles global challenges, such as climate change, biodiversity loss, waste or pollution. But in crypto, an economy is circular when someone buys and sells things other than cryptocurrency, with cryptocurrency. With the promise of future riches, Motiv's Bitcoin fix involved convincing the rural poor to invest what little real money they had in cryptocurrency, while encouraging vendors to accept it for payments; a fix seemingly divorced from infant mortality or podiatric problems.

The issue with Bitcoin is that when it goes up in price, people want to save it, spending their US dollars and Peruvian sols instead. And when it goes down in price, no vendor wants to accept it, while those sold on Motiv's sales pitch are left holding bags of magic internet beans. Motiv overcomes this chocolate teapot issue by asking users to forget real economics. Through the regressive logic of crypto, it doesn't matter if prices swing wildly from day to day relative to things you want to buy with it: 'one Bitcoin is worth one Bitcoin', as anxious Bitcoin zealots say when suckers are thin on the ground.

Jorge Cuéllar, a professor at Dartmouth University, describes Bitcoin, with its constantly fluctuating value, as a mismatch for those who don't share the same financial cushions as real-money millionaires. 'The volatility is much more real for poor people than for those pushing the crypto into these communities',[12] Cuéllar says. According to Mariel Garcia Llorens, an anthropologist at University of California at Davis, the wealthy people pushing crypto are not using Bitcoin for daily purchases; they're waiting for prices to go up before selling it to new suckers. 'Why would anyone think the poor would use Bitcoin for payments when rich people aren't?' she tells me. Sarah Oakes, founder of the UK charity Latin American Foundation for the Future, gave her perspective: 'The root causes of child mortality are complex. Grassroots organisations and local experts are best placed to design and deliver contextually appropriate solutions recognising indigenous values.'

Across South America, Christian preachers doubled as door-to-door salesmen for crypto projects. For the evangelical Christian missionary Patrick Melder, who had preached the gospel around the globe, Bitcoin was the truth and the light. Like Christ's second coming, 'Bitcoin's eventual dominance is inevitable', he said. Melder reportedly admitted that his techniques for spreading the message of Bitcoin – using children, promising riches, door knocking – were the same as those used by real Christian missionaries.[13] Melder explained to his flock that Satoshi Nakamoto's gift to humanity followed by sudden ascendance is indistinguishable from the story of Jesus Christ. In his self-published book, *The Christian Case for Bitcoin*, Melder describes how Bitcoin mining is equivalent to the work of Christ's disciples. 'In the not-too-distant future, those who adopted Bitcoin early will be immensely wealthy', Melder writes.[14] How they will then pass through the eye of a needle or kingdom of God isn't explained.

In 2012, Melder set up an art camp at a private Christian school in Panajachel, Guatemala. Since then, he's returned each summer to persuade businesses to accept Bitcoin, educate children about the cryptocurrency and encourage residents to mine it.[15] Ben Weiss, a researcher shadowing Melder's mission for several weeks, explained that marginalised indigenous Guatemalans were also Melder's primary target for recruitment. 'Four to five hundred years ago, the Spaniards came. They raped your land. They took your gold', Melder explained to a group of indigenous leaders at Lake Atitlán, Central America's deepest lake, where over 95 per cent of residents surrounding it identify as indigenous. 'It is my desire that the natural resources that you have here, which will produce digital gold – Bitcoin – will stay here in the community.' The sermon rang hollow for the group who've lost much of their customary land to a more contemporary *conquistador*: American ex-pats looking for lakefront homes. Melder himself is developing a prime patch of ancestral land for his new project dubbed Lago Bitcoin, or Bitcoin Lake.[16] It's still early days for the project but the plan involves installing noisy Bitcoin-mining machines powered by incinerated municipal waste. Melder promises it won't make a mess, and to give a percentage of his winnings back to the project's indigenous hosts as a 'decentralised basic income' to help them escape poverty.[17]

Bitcoin dogma is swallowed easiest where inequality is stark and political challenges are most complex. Economically divided cities in South Africa are growing hot spots for Bitcoin missions. Ekasi is a Bitcoin education centre and surf school-turned Bitcoin bootcamp which opened its doors in 2021. The project caters for impressionable children in a township near Mossel Bay, Cape Town. It was kicked off by a local Bitcoiner, Hermann Vivier, with funding from Paxful and the Built with Bitcoin Foundation. The non-profit worked to promote Bitcoin adoption in the Global South. Paxful was an associated kid-friendly crypto-trading app. Ekasi's surf coaches were paid in Bitcoin to encourage new poor kids into the crypto fold. 'Bitcoin is life', the recruits were told. The centre teaches adults and kids alike how to 'self-custody' their Bitcoin, taking them off the exchanges to stop them easily swapping their relatively useless crypto for more widely accepted Rand.[18] Recruits were also given metal-stamping kits to help them hammer their crypto wallet seed-phrases into steel plates.[19] The goal here was to fully remove poor kids from the traditional financial grid.

Internet penetration in the township was around 30 per cent. But instead of helping children access the internet, Ekasi teamed up with a local start-up selling children access to 'dumb phones', so they could send and receive Bitcoin without needing to go online. Meanwhile, all the township's economic ailments – the rusty internet, social divisions, crime and other persistent hangovers of apartheid, as well as rolling blackouts and power shortages – were blamed on the government. In the topsy-turvy book of Bitcoin, solutions for poverty involved swapping what little state-backed money one had for crypto. And paradoxically, the solution for energy shortages involved using massive amounts of energy to mine Bitcoin.

The Bitcoin missionaries all pay homage to their religious leader, Mike Peterson. Peterson is also an evangelical Christian and the founder of El Salvador's Bitcoin Beach, or El Zonte as the locals call it. The Salvadoran beach grab gave birth to what the other crypto missionaries refer to as the 'Basis Underlying Bitcoin Beach-Like Efforts', or BUBBLEs.[20] In 2019, Peterson received instructions from an anonymous Bitcoiner, together with a miraculous gift of $100,000 worth of Bitcoin. But again, this wasn't charity. The donor needed disciples for a new Bitcoin utopia. El Zonte would become Bitcoin Beach: a tax-free libertarian 'circular economy' where people could pay for anything, from groceries to electricity bills, using Bitcoin.

Peterson spent the next year aggressively promoting Bitcoin to the 3,000 residents of El Zonte and nearby Punta Mango village. Bitcoin would 'bring people out of poverty', he promised. It would 'change the world'. But the Bitcoin payment system didn't work very well. The town's remote location meant the internet connection was usually terrible and Bitcoin's volatility meant the groceries and electricity bills still needed to be priced in dollars. In the spiritual centre of the El Zonte development sat Hope House, an educational building teaching tourists and locals how to swap their US dollars for Bitcoin.[21] Peterson pulled together a local team led by a well-connected surfer named Jorge Valenzuela. According to the project's website, Peterson prayed for Valenzuela until he 'accepted Jesus as his Lord and Saviour'. Valenzuela went on to become a Bitcoin disciple with an aggressive sales pitch, converting thousands of Salvadoran kids to Christianity and crypto.[22]

'HYPERBITCOINISATION'

The aggressive isolating of marginalised young people from the mainstream cash economy is referred to in crypto circles as 'hyperbitcoinisation' – a marketing strategy to fulfil Bitcoin's original use case as a system of digital money. In sub-Saharan Africa, young people account for the bulk of the working poor. Young women tend to be more disadvantaged than young men in accessing work. They also experience poorer working conditions. While a greater level of incorporation of Africa's youth into the productive economy is viewed by all intergovernmental organisations as essential for more equitable human development, crypto companies have other ideas: detaching young people from that economy entirely.

Ray Youssef, the founder of Paxful and primary sponsor of the missionaries' projects, was convinced that while the traditional Bitcoiner demographic (middle-class white men) were already sold on the idea that crypto could be a viable money maker, there were still plenty of untapped and unbanked punters in Africa that needed convincing on the bumf of hyperbitcoinisation.[23] Youssef originally made his fortune selling novelty mobile phone ringtones before getting into crypto. For him, anyone not able to give him money appeared to fit the criteria of being 'unbanked'. 'You consider my first start-up. Teenagers want ringtones. They're technically "unbanked" so how do you get money from them right?'

Youssef explained. 'They usually find creative ways. But then their parents find out and then there's charge backs.'

Like every big crypto exchange, Paxful often recruited users to its trading platform through its owner's US-registered 501(c)3 non-profit, the Built with Bitcoin Foundation. Paxful's strategy of using a charitable organisation to support its profitable hyperbitcoinisation initiatives was being deployed across Africa by evangelists and exchanges; a house-to-house round-up of young people's savings into a scam. Bitcoin, after all, could never fulfil any of the functions required of a digital money system.

According to Stephen Diel, a computer scientist and co-author of *Popping the Crypto Bubble*:

[A Bitcoin] has no manifestation in the real world, produces nothing, has no assets, income, customers, cashflow or dividends. The net present value of Bitcoin is zero and can never be non-zero. It's value is purely from a form of recursive speculation, a delusion that more victims will come to speculate in the speculation thus perpetuating the scam and driving the speculated 'value' higher. It is a futures contract with an underlying [bet] on human gullibility, a bet that there will be more fools in the future to pay out present fools.[24]

US economics professor and politician Robert Reich describes Bitcoin as a modern Ponzi: a fraudulent scheme where existing investors in a non-existent enterprise are paid with the funds collected from new investors. But calling Bitcoin a Ponzi scheme is offensive to Ponzi schemes. A Ponzi involves taking from Peter to pay Paul. It's a redistributive game with the facilitator taking a cut. Meanwhile, Bitcoin constitutes a deeply negative-sum game involving huge costs for wider society and the environment. Even Satoshi Nakamoto described the value proposition of Bitcoin as follows: 'It might make sense just to get some in case it catches on. If enough people think the same way, then it becomes a self-fulfilling prophecy.'[25]

With Bitcoin, you're not a sucker. That is, as long as there are some other suckers more gullible than you. But there was a problem: Bitcoin was running out of suckers.

PIVOTING TO THE POOR

The pool of crypto buyers has historically been dominated by middle-class white men in the Global North. By the end of 2020, high-income, well-educated white men made up 80 per cent of all retail buyers. Most were Millennials and Gen Xers with an average annual income of $130,000; 70 per cent had university degrees.[26] But from November 2021, these proto-typical Crypto Bros commenced a massive sell-off. Benefiting from high digital connectivity and trading apps seamlessly integrated with online bank accounts, these traditional buyers tended to exit their positions with tidy profits, while poorer, less tech-savvy suckers got stung. The price of a single Bitcoin plummeted from a peak of around $70,000 since the 2021 sell-off to about $16,000 a few months later. Cryptocurrencies as a whole lost more than $2 trillion in paper value over that period.

With the available pool of white, middle-class men drying up, Bitcoin needed a predatory pivot to a new source of income: emerging markets in the Global South. But the swindlers would be dressed as saviours. Unlike the predatory lending practices precipitating the subprime mortgage crises, creating optimal conditions for Bitcoin at the expense of local economies was being framed as charity. For the missionaries,

Bitcoin was going to 'bank the unbanked' into the fantasy of hyperbitcoinisation.

The phrase 'banking the unbanked' was born at the dawn of 'micro-finance'. It was based on the idea that access to credit was one of the most basic of human rights and key to equitable human development. The Bangladeshi economist and entrepreneur Muhammad Yunus, who founding Grameen Bank, pioneered the concept of micro-finance in the 1980s. Yunus' idea for giving the poor access to small, low-cost loans was a big hit with international development agencies keen to mobilise private finance for development projects while also promising a return for investors. It connected seamlessly with the neoliberal rhetoric that solving global challenges could be a profitable win-win for everyone. While starting as a charitable endeavour, micro-finance schemes commonly struggled to balance their priorities for profitability and human development. Most aggressively privileged the former, with interest rates often on a par with unregulated loan sharks. But for Yunus, micro-finance schemes were special and not like all the other loan sharks. 'Poor people are desperate to find some money for survival and so on', Yunus declared. 'So, they have to borrow money. Seeing this repeatedly in the villages, I was wondering whether I can protect them from the loan sharks, because all people are entrepreneurs. And all they need is money.'[27] The UN General Assembly declared 2005 the International Year of Micro-finance. The following year, for his efforts in banking the unbanked, Yunus was awarded the Nobel Peace Prize.

While rich investors loved Yunus' neoliberal dream of helping unbanked entrepreneurs to thrive in the dog-eat-dog world of global capitalism, the scheme was often a disaster for loan recipients. The once-charitable micro-finance organisations were soon reporting record annual returns for their investors. For those falling behind with their repayments to lenders, such as Sri Lanka's LOLC bank, owned by the country's richest man, debtors were turning to loan sharks, or worse. Across much of unbanked South Asia, micro-finance loans were blamed for epidemics of suicide.[28]

If there is one phrase that deserves to be left behind in the dustbin of history, it is 'banking the unbanked'. The reason poor people do not use bank accounts is usually because they are poor. It's not in their interest to use one. The poor are poor, not stupid. The pithy financial inclusion claims peddled by crypto interests tended to ignore specificity, lumping unbanked populations together globally no matter what their local conditions. People want access to simple, safe, convenient and inexpensive ways to save and spend their money.

One reason many in the US do not use a bank account (roughly 4.5 per cent of households, or approximately 5.9 million in 2021) is because US banks have historically served people without wealth poorly. US financial services are expensive if you're poor. Insurance, savings, loans and credit cards are often withheld or subject to a poverty premium if you live in a deprived area, a practice called 'redlining'. In *The Unbanking of America*, Lisa Servon explains that for many households incessantly stung by high overdraft fees and disproportionate penalties for breaching spurious terms and conditions, banking is set up to trick rather than to serve. When poverty premiums are applied, there's little wonder these groups are giving up on banks and turning to payday loan sharks instead. But crypto proponents like Youssef may be surprised to learn that not everywhere is like the USA.

Instant free payments are the norm for Europeans. If you are legally resident in the EU, you are entitled to a free basic bank account with a debit card. Banks legally cannot refuse your application or charge fees. Personal reasons for being unbanked in France, then, look very different to those in the Philippines, where only around 23 per cent of adults have a bank account. A Philippines Central Bank study on financial inclusion in 2017 found that most people who didn't use a bank account there simply didn't have enough money to make it worthwhile. Some didn't have the necessary documentation to open one. Cryptocurrencies alone can't solve any of these problems.

BITCOIN ISN'T BANKING

When you send crypto, you're not sending money. You're sending crypto. To convert that into something useable as money requires expensive and generally unregulated intermediaries. Other than basement-dwelling cypherpunks with a deep ideological loathing for any and all intermediaries, most people using crypto opt towards easy-to-use exchange apps to trade their crypto. These all typically require a bank account, so they can't genuinely serve the unbanked. Even for the basement dwellers, swapping real banking for crypto without any intermediaries is complicated and expensive. All payments in crypto incur a transaction fee. These are typically around $2 per transaction with Bitcoin but can be as high as $60. There are also exchange fees to consider and most transactions take many hours to settle. Sometimes they are never settled, but the transaction fee is charged regardless.

Buying things with Bitcoin is tricky. Saving with it is even more problematic. Cryptocurrencies require a crypto wallet, an app that stores passwords giving access to one's funds, otherwise known as 'private keys'. They come in many forms, from hardware wallets (which look like USB sticks) to mobile or desktop apps run by online exchanges. All of these options are vulnerable to scammers, and because they're 'decentralised' there's usually no customer service number or complaints department when things go wrong. Shady exchanges frequently go bust without warning. Even when the exchange isn't brought down by necrotic levels of fraud, exchanges still regularly lose everything. Their websites conveniently go down during a liquidity squeeze. People with all the keys to the crypto bank vault also have a habit of mysteriously dying,[29] sometimes never to be seen again. Gerald Cotton, CEO of Canadian crypto exchange Quadriga, died in 2018 with $250 million of other people's crypto. His body was never found. Investigators called it 'an old-fashioned fraud wrapped in modern technology'.

Due to the domino effect caused by collapsing crypto exchanges, in early 2023, more and more crypto fans were 'self-custodying' their crypto in hardware wallets. 'Not your keys not your Bitcoin', as Bitcoin fanatics say. But the practice of self-custodying has its downsides. In 2019, three robbers disguised as policemen forced their way into the home of a well-known Bitcoiner in the Dutch city of Drenthe, torturing him with a drill in front of his four-year-old daughter until he agreed to give up the keys to his Bitcoin wallet. In April 2021, two men armed with handguns forced their way into an apartment in Calgary before torturing the owner for his seed-phrase. The UK's first Bitcoin heist took place in 2018, when armed robbers broke into the home of a Bitcoiner, Danny Aston, in Oxfordshire. The robbery was bungled thanks to the Bitcoin transfer that Aston was reportedly forced to make at gunpoint taking too long. In 2021, a 14-year-old boy in Bradford, West Yorkshire, who'd put red laser eyes on his social media profile photo (a sign that one is 'bullish' on Bitcoin) was kidnapped by three men who repeatedly hit him with a glove full of sand until he gave them access to his crypto. With no human overseer, your crypto is always at risk from hackers and scams.

Even a simple fat-finger typing error can spell the end of someone's life savings. And it's not just amateurs losing their nest-eggs in the blink of an eye. Even Bitcoin code developer Luke Dashjr – one of the three the entire network depends on – reportedly lost over $3.5 million worth of crypto from a hack involving his offline hardware wallet in January 2023.

IT engineer James Howells claimed he unintentionally binned a device with 7,500 Bitcoin on it. The loss, worth around $200 million as I write this, prompted Howells to kick-start his own mission to unbank the rundown ex-coal mining city of Newport, South Wales. 'The coins are definitely in that landfill site', Howells tells me. 'If we're successful in recovering them, I've made a pledge to the people of Newport. I'll onboard this entire area into the twenty-first century, and they can use their new knowledge to better themselves, on their own – teach a man to fish, you know? We'll uplift Newport out of the dumps!' Newport council, who operate the landfill site, have so far declined Howells' offer.

PLAYGROUND PUSHERS

For its supporters, there's no such thing as a legal age to buy Bitcoin. 'If you're old enough to appreciate it, you're old enough to buy it', so they say. Some of Bitcoin's earliest miners were minors. Some well-known Bitcoiners, such as crypto millionaire Erik Finman, got into cryptocurrencies at just twelve years old. 'The most amount I've lost in a single trade is probably around $60,000', says 13-year-old crypto trader Youssof Altoukhi. Meanwhile, twelve-year-old Benyamin Ahmed made headlines and $3.5 million in 2021 after selling a series of cutesy whale images as NFTs. With all this money sloshing around in the crypto kiddies' piggy banks, you would be forgiven for thinking it was fair play for children to trade crypto. But trading apps are generally forbidden from allowing access to under 18s. Flouting the rules, apps like Paxful allow kids to swap their book vouchers for Bitcoin. Using UK-based Solidi, children of any age can gamble up to $35 of weekly pocket money on crypto markets, according to their website. Like gambling sites, exchanges lure in punters of any age with free bets and bonuses. Where children want to gamble beyond the trading limits imposed by the exchanges, they can easily register on peer-to-peer trading apps such as LocalBitcoins. com, allowing children to transfer funds directly from a bank account without limits. Melvin Breton Guerrero, a policy specialist for UNICEF's Office of Global Insight and Policy, explains that one of the biggest challenges to consider is age verification. 'There are few safeguards in place for children when it comes to accessing crypto apps', he says. 'A child can transact using various crypto wallets, and nothing can be done.'

The connections between crypto investing, problem gambling, depression and suicide have been documented.[30] Despite all this, exposing children to crypto is commonly viewed as a worthwhile idea. According to one independent poll, 64 per cent of American parents and 67 per cent of American college graduates feel that Bitcoin and cryptocurrency should be a compulsory part of the school curriculum. Roxana Marachi, a researcher in blockchain and education, told me that 'parents are worried about their kids getting scammed and their online safety. They hope crypto literacy classes can help with that. But there's a problem. Lessons in crypto gambling are often disguised as online safety classes, coding, and STEM camps.'

In response to new demand from parents, crypto summer camps have sprung up across the USA and beyond. Crypto Kids' Camp offers trading tips to children as young as five, while ten-year-olds are encouraged to build cryptocurrency portfolios, most of whom live in deprived urban neighbourhoods. According to founder Najah Roberts, the camps are a way to lessen the wealth gap between privileged kids and underserved communities. 'It's important to catch our kids when they're young to help them open their minds to what the possibilities are', she says. The camps hope the student's enthusiasm will result in more parents being onboarded. Lessons feature more than just the usual gateway drugs such as Bitcoin and Ethereum. 'Bitcoin is awesome. That's our staple', says Roberts. 'But we have guys from projects like duacoin and skycoin, they come in once each year to make sure the kids are set up with those.' Skycoin offers zero utility and is currently worth $0.09, down from a 2021 high of $45, when many of the children bought in.

The camps were reportedly being expanded across 41 cities with premises and resources donated by local businesses and BitGive, an American 501(c)3 non-profit that solicits Bitcoin donations for charitable causes. According to Roberts, the kids' camps were working with Disney to take their lessons online. But as usual, this isn't charity. The weeklong camp costs $500 per child. But attending kids receive a laptop, a VR headset and a phone with a crypto wallet, all of which they get to keep. Those crypto wallets can also be used to store the child's favourite Disney-themed NFTs. And the phones come in handy for scrolling through Zigazoo.

Zigazoo is a TikTok-like social media app for pre-schoolers aged three years an up. 'We're trying to teach kids about digital and financial literacy', says Zigazoo founder Zak Ringelstein in July 2022. The platform teamed up with Moonbug Entertainment to sell Blippi Fan Pass NFTs to toddlers, as well as crypto collectables associated with Cocomelon and Serena William's Qai Qai's Invisible Universe project.

For parents scared about what their three-year-old might get up to with a smartphone and a crypto wallet, there's Pigzbe. The pocket-sized box is described by its developers as 'what the piggy bank did next'. As well as functioning as a crypto hardware wallet, Pigzbe also pairs with a kid-friendly version of Task Rabbit: a gig economy phone app. Family members and friends download the app, buy some cryptocurrency called Wollo, and then pay it to the child once they've success- ful completed some assigned tasks. The company's founder Filippo Yacob explains that 'Pigzbe teaches kids how to earn, save and spend, so they can grow up to do the things they really love'. So long as they love chores.

As kids become dependent on dopamine and Wollo tokens, motivating them to do jobs, or even get out of bed, requires the parent to repurchase evermore Wollo from the Pigzbe guy, before the child sells them back to him, usually at a lower price. Educating children about labour theory of value is a noble cause. But onboarding toddlers to the wild west world of crypto isn't the only way to do it. You could use a piggy bank.

Crypto is damaging people's education, not helping it. In my own classes, I hear stories almost weekly from students about their failed crypto investment strategies, sometimes involving their entire student loan instalments. Some have experimented with mining cryptocurrencies in their student accommodation where electricity is included in their rent. A 2020 survey found that around 20 per cent of university students used their loan cheques to invest in cryptocurrency rather than for daily essentials.[31] Data from the UK website Save the Student suggested the number of university student's putting at least some of their meagre loans towards NFTs and crypto had tripled by the end of 2021. Their results indicated that crashing crypto markets have not helped matters, with around 76 per cent of student investors now worrying how they'll make ends meet.[32]

The widespread losses caused by cryptocurrency markets crashing are even broader among Black investors. According to a survey by Ariel Investments, Black Americans were more than twice as likely to purchase cryptocurrency as their first investment compared to white Americans. They also tended to buy at the market's peak, and those with reduced connectivity were the ones still holding the bag as the markets crashed. Yet many American celebrities, including Snoop Dogg, the boxer Floyd Mayweather and the actor Jamie Foxx, have promoted crypto projects for Black empowerment.

In the summer of 2022, the rapper Jay-Z announced a partnership with former Twitter boss Jack Dorsey to launch the Bitcoin Academy, an initiative meant to spread the good word of crypto through free online and in-person classes. The course was kicked off at the Marcy Projects, a social housing complex in Brooklyn, where Jay-Z himself grew up. Free phones preloaded with crypto apps and data plans were given away to students. And even though attendees for Jay-Z's twelve-week course were all issued with around $25 worth of Bitcoin to trade with, Marcy residents were unimpressed. For one 24-year-old attendee, Nyashia Figueroa, the classes symbolised how out of touch the organisers were from the residents' real-life challenges. 'If you want to do something, fix this place up', Figueroa told *The Guardian*. 'We have a basketball court with no hoops. Our parks are broken up in here. [Jay-Z] should be doing more for his community, not no Bitcoin Academy.'[33]

Providing courses for folks with only periodic internet access means crypto projects can onboard people who are generally unaware of tumultuous conditions on the markets. Onboarding complete newbies also makes it easier to encourage a lasting loyalty towards any one of the thousands of tradeable cryptocurrencies. In the summer of 2022, I was invited to observe a crypto literacy class in Dallas, Texas. The audience this time was a group of around 15 pensioners living in a care home. The crypto coach, 21-year-old Owen Robertson, said he was approached by the home to help the senior citizens who were 'extremely vulnerable to scams'. More than one in ten elderly people in the USA fell victim to crypto-related fraud in 2021, with scammers cheating pensioners out of approximately $2.9 billion, according to a US Senate Special Committee on Aging. This was a safety online course. But the crypto marketing messages seeped through. 'If you really want to', Roberson explains, 'you should buy only Bitcoin, nothing else.'

WE COME AS FRIENDS

Across Africa, crypto companies were waiting outside school gates to push their shitcoins. Exchanges were particularly attracted to Nigeria due to the country's youthful population and 33 per cent unemployment rate. About 70 per cent of Nigerians are under the age of 30; 42 per cent are under 15. Exchanges were also itching to penetrate the country because of the 'poverty premium'. Since 2021, Nigeria had tight capital flight controls in place and had banned local banks from servicing crypto exchanges. But these policies didn't have the desired effect. Nigerians were willing to buy their crypto from overseas exchanges at a premium price, around 70 per cent higher than in the USA. By 2022, young Nigerians accounted for the largest volume of cryptocurrency transactions outside the USA.[34] Jack Dorsey had been flogging his crypto businesses in Nigeria since 2019.[35] Trusted global charities such as Mercy Corp were pushing Ejara, 'a unique savings offer for

Africa's unbanked and underbanked populations'. The Ejara scheme encouraged poor people to drop their life savings into a high-risk collateralised crypto bond with a $1,600 minimum deposit.[36] Crypto-related charities were hard at work funding initiatives such as Nigeria's Bitcoin Village, who were building schools using crypto donations. Meanwhile, the Fix the Money, Fix the World Foundation was translating textbooks into local Nigerian languages. The school only taught skills relating to Bitcoin. And the four books translated as of January 2023 included only Bitcoin books: *The Bullish Case for Bitcoin*, *Thank God for Bitcoin*, *Learn Bitcoin*, and *The Little Bitcoin Book*. But it was charity, nonetheless.

A favourite exchange for Nigerians was Sam Bankman-Fried's FTX. Bankman-Fried was a hit across West Africa and trusted like a saint due to his association with African development projects and the 'effective altruism' movement. 'One thing that a lot of people miss is the enormous amount of good that you can do in Africa', Bankman-Fried explained knowledgably in a 2021 interview. In November that year, he was the richest person in the world under 30. And he planned to give it all away. 'Africa is where the most underserved globally are and where there's a whole lot of lowest-hanging fruit in terms of being able to make people's lives better', he said. To snatch that lowest-hanging fruit, much of FTX's marketing energy involved conscripting campus ambassadors. For example, 19-year-old Mary from the University of Nigeria, in Enugu. She was stuck for money. Her university was empty during Covid and then closed again for eight months while her lecturers were on strike. Mary agreed to work for FTX for free, in the hope it might lead to a paid job later down the line. 'To be paid, you must have hosted a successful event', said Joseph, another FTX ambassador. Attracting a few hundred students to a recruitment event could net the ambassador around $200.[37]

As his crypto empire was collapsing in early November 2022, Bankman-Fried reached out to the region via Twitter. 'Hello, West Africa!' he tweeted, sharing the news that FTX would accept their real African currencies in exchange for FTT, a token which Bankman-Fried had conjured out of nothing in just a few hours. A few days later, FTX was underwater.

Godswill was a founding member of an organisation called FTT DAO, a community dedicated to FTT. Members proudly referred to themselves as BFFs, short for Bankman-Fried's Fans. Godswill and other local BFFs held events to promote the benefits of blockchain technology. They donated books to schools and helped flood victims in Nigeria, funding it all by signing people up for FTX accounts.[38] 'It was like we were carrying that guy on our head and going into the streets. It was like evangelism', said Godswill. 'We did it passionately, self-lessly. We had hope. And he crushed it.'

Following the collapse of FTX, it was common for ambassadors to receive death threats from the recruits they'd signed up, many of whom had dropped their entire life savings into their BFF's bank account, only for them to be swallowed up by FTX's more powerful creditors. 'I look at my phone, there's someone threatening to harm me if I don't return their money', says Elijah, a 22-year-old student and FTX ambassador. Elijah had sold everything he owned, even his bed, to pay back his recruits. 'It was still not enough', he said. For the many ambassadors suffering Elijah's predicament, dropping out of university was usually their safest option. Mary had been hosting FTX events for members of her church. Losing that connection, she felt betrayed. 'I started thinking, there are universities and high schools in America. They don't host crypto programmes the way we do in Africa, especially in Nigeria', she said.[39] 'They were using us.'

While some FTX ambassadors retreated into hiding, others joined an ambassador programme at a different exchange, such as Hong Kong-based AAX who employed similar marketing strategies in Nigeria. With AAX, student ambassadors were paid, but only if they met the company's outrageous recruitment targets, made even more demanding with collapsing market conditions. Reuters journalist Avi Asher-Schapiro told me that the AAX ambassadors he'd spoken to were expected to recruit 50 new users who would each need to trade $250 on the platform each week. They were also given a monthly target of $50,000 in trading volume.

None of the new ambassadors were paid. Their recruits again lost everything they'd invested. Jumping from FTX to AAX, the ambassadors had jumped from one sinking ship to another. Two days after FTX had filed for bankruptcy, AAX suspended all withdrawals and deleted its social media accounts. Its website and trading app also disappeared, leaving only a trail of more death threats and shattered dreams.

But AAX was not the last ship to sink. With the giant exchange FTX gone, Binance CEO Changpeng Zhao, or CZ as he was popularly known, was keen to hoover up the glut of new suckers with his ambassador programme, Binance Angels. CZ was very open about his marketing special sauce, frequently tweeting from the exchange's Africa account: 'The secret to Binance's success? Binance Angels.' According to their website: 'Angels are passionate volunteers whose belief in the transformative power of blockchain technology ignite their passion to contribute to Binance's vision: to increase the freedom of money around the world.' The Angels programme kicked off across the Global South at the same time as the Binance trading platform in 2017, as a way to grow the company's pyramid with student volunteers doing all the costly social media marketing and customer services work. In April 2023, the Angels distributed bags of rice on Easter Sunday 'to feed the 5,000' while recruiting prospective crypto investors queuing up in Lagos, Nigeria. 'Angels are the Binance missionary team spreading the word of Binance', explained the company's recruitment video. 'We are sometimes invited to special online Q&As with CZ! And sometimes you even have the opportunity to meet him in person!' Like those of FTX, AAX and all the other exchanges, the dream of one day having a job with a secure salary was always peddled. 'The possibilities are really endless', a promoter explained through a forced grin.

In 2018, the US-based crypto exchange Coinbase launched its non-profit ambassadors experiment GiveCrypto. Founder Brian Armstrong published a lengthy blog post where he argued that for cryptocurrency to gain mainstream adoption, it needed to be distributed directly to those left behind by the mainstream economy.[40] GiveCrypto would function as a direct giving organisation, distributing crypto across the world through local ambassadors. With media fanfare, Armstrong promised to deliver a total pot of $1 billion to the world's poorest within two years, while onboarding many thousands of new Coinbase users. The giveaway would make Coinbase one of the most charitable companies in the world. More charitable than Disney and Google put together. The plan was simple: GiveCrypto would 'financially empower people by distributing cryptocurrency', Armstrong said. 'Initial recipients will be people living in emerging markets, especially those going through financial crisis.'

A few months after launching GiveCrypto, Armstrong gave the reins to Joe Waltman. Like Armstrong, Waltman had little experience delivering effective humanitarian assistance. Before joining Coinbase, Waltman had co-founded a San Francisco-based veterinary services app called VetPronto. He was stumped when it came to finding the poor people needed for GiveCrypto to get off the ground. With $1 billion to spend, the clock was ticking. Waltman reportedly turned to the freelancer platform Upwork, where he scrolled across a 30-year-old student and translator in the Democratic Republic of Congo (DRC) named Christian Maloba. 'The project is likely quite different from what you normally do on Upwork', Waltman's invitation reportedly read. 'But, if it appeals to you, it could be very rewarding.' Maloba's mission was to find three people in need and set them up with a Coinbase wallet. Each poor person Maloba identified would get $100 in crypto. Maloba would get $30. He was sceptical but he needed work, and so with a click of the app, Maloba was GiveCrypto's local ambassador.[41]

He felt like a saint. Maloba was asked to invite ten more poor people to receive crypto payments. But despite Waltman's $1 billion budget, he reportedly confirmed in a message, 'unfortunately, we can't pay you more for this, but you will be able to help people in your community'. Maloba agreed. 'Since it's going to help people in need in my country. I'm still positive and hoping that I will also get something in return maybe later, hopefully.' Waltman later asked him to produce two proposals for a new hospital and a school, each with a budget and timeline. Maloba again agreed to work for free, lining up teams of local engineers and construction workers. He sent the proposals back to Waltman but was met with silence.[42] Leo Schwartz, an investigative journalist at *Fortune Magazine*, told me: 'From conversations I've had with many of these global ambassadors, there are so many broken promises. Most of them are not getting the money they're promised. It's pervasive.'

The fireworks of Coinbase's billion dollar promise to the poor was quietly folded. Four years after GiveCrypto was born, the platform had distributed around 0.001 per cent of what had been originally pledged. But before the tears had dried, Coinbase had another billion dollar poverty fix on the go.

THE CHILD CATCHERS

Coinbase was teaming up with the usual Web3 suspects, including A16z, FTX and Sam Altman – the former president of Silicon Valley tech incubator, Ycombinator. Altman was famous for getting platforms such as Reddit, Twitch and AirBnB off the ground. The team's newest project promised to bank the unbanked by giving poor people a $20 voucher and a monthly basic income payment denominated in a planned future cryptocurrency. The project also aimed to give poor people a blockchain-based digital identity document. 'Just think of it as free money, only better', sign-ups were reportedly told.[43] Apparently, unlike real money, Worldcoin would appreciate by 500 per cent. Although, as the token was non-existent, the price prediction was pie in the sky. The catch for getting free future internet money? Their retinas, faces and bodies, photographed and stored on Worldcoin's centralised database. Any human with eyes was able to join, so long as they weren't from China or the USA. It's not clear why those citizens were excluded, especially given Worldcoin's guarantees of anonymity.

Like GiveCrypto, Worldcoin relied on a network of casually employed gig workers, known as 'operators'. The operators were tasked with inviting members of their communities to stare into a camera that was dressed as an ominous basketball-sized Christmas bauble, otherwise known as 'the orb'. Becoming an operator was competitive, involving the submission of a business plan. Once in receipt of an orb, if operators signed up fewer than 500 people for two weeks in a row, they were forced to relinquish their equipment,[44] a process called 'involuntary orb return'. Getting more than 700 sign-ups for two weeks in a row made operators eligible for an additional orb. Onboarding bigger numbers usually meant working in teams, roping in local officials and school teachers, and reportedly bribing them with anything from a free lunch to Apple Airpods.[45] Rarely were questions asked about the recruits' age or capacity to consent to anything. Nor were many questions asked by Worldcoin of their operators. Setting up shop outside schools seemed a standard tactic, a fact proudly presented on Worldcoin's website.

As of early 2023, Worldcoin had over a million registered users, mainly in India, Indonesia, Kenya and Uganda. The company had promised to delete the images – one day. They hadn't said when. Edward Snowden, the former NSA contractor and crypto advocate criticised the system on Twitter: 'Hashes of the biometric data could be matched with future scans', Snowden tweeted. 'Don't use biometrics for anti-fraud. In fact, don't use biometrics for anything.'

Beyond wanting to give away free money, the purpose of harvesting massive amounts of biometric data, with little in the way of informed consent, was only vaguely understood by the orb operators. But citing a report by McKinsey Global Institute, Worldcoin's marketing materials, which they circulated in January 2023, explained the problem, and their proposed fix: 'There are over 4.4 billion people worldwide who either don't have a legal identity or have one that can't be digitally verified. We believe that Worldcoin, through World ID's privacy-preserving digital identity, has an essential role to play in solving this and other fundamental global challenges.'

The figures were misleading. World Bank data, referred to in McKinsey's report, estimated that around 850 million people globally did not have the official identification they need. But the report also detailed the economic opportunities that come from digital IDs, which would earn companies such as Worldcoin a truckload of cash. The report estimated that digital IDs would increase the host country's gross domestic product (GDP) by up to 13 per cent.[46]

Being undocumented – not having access to a birth certificate or any other ID granted by the state – is a headache. It makes owning things difficult and makes people vulnerable to slavery and homelessness. But lumping this together with 'not having a digital ID' is disingenuous. Digital ID schemes have always been intolerably hot potatoes in the UK, the USA and elsewhere, and are consistently rejected by the public because of snooping concerns. When Theresa May became the UK's home secretary, scrapping plans for a national ID card scheme was her top priority.[47] 'This bill is the first step of many that this government is taking to reduce the control of the state over decent, law-abiding people', she said. 'With swift parliamentary approval, we aim to consign identity cards and the intrusive ID card scheme to history within 100 days.'

Not having a digital version of an ID card is for most people not a human development concern. But this is Web3 problem solving in action, what Evgeny Morazov refers to as 'the metaverse mindset: If the reality doesn't exist, we'll create one by talking it into existence'. It involves talking profitable problems into existence, then building a technical solution rather than fixing the actual problem, which would be politically much more complicated and less profitable.

According to two separate investigations by *MIT Tech Review* and *BuzzFeed*, many donors of biometrics felt used by Worldcoin. And so did their prospective orb operators. Once approved, some had quit their day jobs and spent their own money on complimentary merchandise to give away. But it could take five months or more for Worldcoin to despatch orbs. Some never received their orbs at all, or they arrived with defects and software glitches. If orbs were returned for repair, they were reassigned based on operators having missed their sign-up targets. Operators often received their remunerations late, if at all, even though they were being paid in crypto, a supposedly 24/7 alternative to slow international wire transfers.

Capitalising on surplus pools of talented but underemployed young people across Africa was Electronium. Similar to TaskRabbit, Electronium allowed young freelancers to find jobs through a competitive marketplace called AnyTask. Unlike TaskRabbit, gig workers toiled in exchange for crypto. Employers could request anything from academic essays, for around $5, to chat bot services for around $10. While employers used their credit cards, sellers in Africa got a volatile token that had dropped in value by 99.07 per cent from its high of 17 cents. The principle behind Web3 solutions for unemployment was simple: if the young can't get a job paying good money, they should work for our magic internet money instead. 'It's not a case of build it and they will come. It's not just "bank the unbanked". They have to work for it', explained Electronium's founder, Richard Ells. 'And if they work for it, then we will get this circular thing.'

Across marginalised communities, crypto organisations were helping young people find jobs and all the other things they needed, in the same way the Child Catcher in *Chitty Chitty Bang Bang* helped kids find loppy pops. While billionaire blockchain developers hit the jackpot, the poor were left trapped with a bad taste in their mouths. Despite loud endorsements and cries of financial inclusion, crypto companies were simply on the lookout for new market footholds in left-behind communities in order to take from them.

For example, there is no evidence of Quechuan footwear being a significant driver of child mortality in the Peruvian Andes. Sarah Oakes explained: 'Poverty and extreme inequality drive child mortality rates in the Andes, and these can't be solved with new shoes and Bitcoin.' Banking the unbanked with crypto was like helping the homeless by selling them virtual homes in the metaverse (we'll discuss more about that particular Web3 experiment in Chapter 7). But fixing poverty with crypto was never the intention. Searching for solutions to complex development challenges with Web3 is like losing one's house keys in a dark alley, then searching for them under a streetlight where it's easier (and more profitable) to look.

The crypto organisations looked at in this chapter have all onboarded new users with the age-old tactics used by other pseudo-religious cults. As Stephen Diehl suggests, there's plenty of intermingling between crypto fanaticism and the cult-like quirks of the QAnon super-conspiracy:[48]

> Both have doctrine passed down by a mysterious unknown founder, puzzle-solving, and internet meme culture and lots of predictions about politics and economics that are completely unfalsifiable. They're both rooted in this ideology that claims to oppose a common enemy: corruption and untrustworthy intermediaries, and both see the internet as the way to finally eradicate those problems in some great apocalyptic event.

Bitcoin depends on divisive mysticism, using illusions of technological innovation and claims of magical powers to heal any political or economic ailment. Many of the crypto evangelist projects required isolating the faithful, forcing them to withdraw into fantasy. Being 'banked' into the cult of Web3 meant surrendering one's dreams in return for unimaginable riches, but only once the existing world comes to an end. Die and be reborn. Then refer 50 friends and claim a bonus.

2
The Crypto Colonists

Extorting people using crypto often involves an 'affinity fraud'. With a standard token rug pull scam, the victim is usually unknown to the perpetrator, except for their wallet address. But the affinity fraud depends on trust. It works like this. A con-artist infiltrates a group by pretending to share their values and motivations. Sometimes the perpetrator is already a trusted face. It's an old trick that predates crypto. For example, throughout the 1960s till late 2000s, Bernie Madoff's $65 billion investment scam targeted his own Jewish family members and friends as 'investors'. In 1999, Christian scammers in Arizona established the Southern Baptist Foundation to execute an affinity fraud on their worshippers. 'Your investment actually touches the lives of countless numbers, while you earn a very attractive rate of interest', the foundation's victims were told. Neither the worshippers nor the countless numbers got anything at all. Just like the Arizona church scam, crypto projects rely on seemingly shared religious values to effectively execute a con. Projects prey on faithful followers of crypto's libertarian principles, with all the spiritual iconography, promises of future riches and feelings of community that go with that.

In early 2022, a private Fijian island known as Cryptoland became the latest Mary Poppins pavement painting, offering online crypto fanatics the opportunity to jump inside and join like-minded folks in real life. 'Most of us in the crypto space, when we turn off our screens, we still live in fiat[1] environments', the project's website said. 'But what if we could improve the physical world around us to be more aligned with our passion? This is happening, it's called Cryptoland.' A promotional featurette promised investors plots of land on their crypto-themed version of Jurassic Park. Lucky new 'Cryptolanders' could ride Lamborghini taxis to their homes in the 'Blockchain Hills', access shared cryptocurrency developer spaces in the 'House of DAO' and find a girlfriend at the 'Vladamir Club'.[2] Prospective investors asked questions about life in their new Jerusalem via Twitter. 'What's the age of consent on the island?' one hopeful Cryptolander asked. 'Mental maturity should be more than enough! ;)' was the project's response. The age of consent in Fiji was 16. But it didn't matter. Cryptoland was a crypto Fyre Festival.[3] There was no Fijian island, just empty promises drawing in lonely people who'd made crypto mysticism core to their identities. The affinity fraudsters roped in the dreams of people desperate for community using seemingly shared fundamentalist libertarian values, language and crypto culture. The perpetrators also took advantage of their marks' sense of entitlement and belief in crypto as a worthy cause for colonial conquest.

The Cryptoland idea connected to another fantasy popular in crypto circles known as the 'Bitcoin citadel'. The fantasy goes back to 2013, when an anonymous Redditor, using the pseudonym Luka Magnotta,[4] uploaded a post as a time traveller from the future. He described his world as a wildly unequal dystopia divided between Bitcoin maximalists and their eternal no-coiner slaves. In his premonition, Bitcoin early adopters reside in isolated citadels as kings, while everyone else suffers the social collapse outside. This was all meant to provide a nightmare vision of a future under Bitcoin. But predictably, Magnotta's post was lauded by crypto enthusiasts. The Bitcoin citadel embodied their libertarian dreams of cosseted bunkers and private enclaves, where fortuitous crypto speculators would rise from the economic ashes of a fiat world gone mad, free to amass great wealth without doing any work, or paying any tax.

Many influential Silicon Valley venture capitalists have given careful thought to the importance of crypto for when shit hits the fan. They've been busy acquiring ships, remote islands and subterranean boltholes all powered by Bitcoin. Most of them failed, predictably, leaving only scuttled dreams and disappointed libertarian pilgrims without their promised land.

Blockchain City was supposedly being built by crypto millionaires in the Nevada desert. Then there was the Utah desert Crypto-Kingdom of Bitcointopia, an elaborate scam, which as it turns out didn't have any desert to speak of. To avoid land issues, the MS Satoshi was to be the world's first floating citadel for libertarian tax dodgers. It's now back to being a P&O ferry. Inspiration for these tech utopias came from an obscure libertarian manifesto, *The Sovereign Individual: How to Survive and Thrive during the Collapse of the Welfare State*. The book's authors, William Rees-Mogg (father of the UK's Brexit Calamity, Jacob Rees-Mogg) and the conservative financier James Dale Davidson, produced a string of disaster capitalist handbooks. But it was *The Sovereign Individual* that launched them as the spiritual forefathers of crypto ideology. The book was published in 1997 and explains how to profit from social collapse. Billionaire Bitcoiner and Seasteading fanatic Peter Thiel wrote the book's foreword. Despite being written well before Bitcoin, it makes some pretty close predictions for the ascent of cryptocurrencies. Like Magnotta's post, the book foretells a wildly unequal dystopia, where tech-savvy speculators rise from the wreckage of economic breakdown as an elite class of sovereign individuals.

BITCOIN CITADELS

In the summer of 2017, a group of wannabe sovereign individuals, in leather waistcoats and cowboy hats, stepped off their private plane in San Juan, Puerto Rico. Hurricane Irma and Maria had just departed, leaving the island a disaster zone. But the group led by Brock Pierce were there to push a recovery plan to turn Puerto Rico into a crypto capitalist utopia, which they imaginatively called 'Puertopia'. 'Wherever I went, people would follow, so when I realised that I took it as a social responsibility. If people would follow me anywhere. Let me go somewhere that could benefit from that', Pierce explained in a 2019 interview. He added:

> This is how I pitch it to people though. I tell people, 'Hey you know we have an opportunity to make the world a better place, blah blah blah blah'. And they say, 'Well it's cool, I love that you're making the world a better place, but I don't know about moving there'. And then I'm like, 'Did I tell you about the taxes?' They say, 'I'm packing my bags', because in the US if you're a crypto trader, we have to pay taxes on every transaction, it's a nightmare. So, if you're into crypto, you have to live in Puerto Rico, or you have to renounce your citizenship.[5]

Pierce was a former child actor most famous for his role in the 1992 Disney film *The Mighty Ducks*. He retired from acting at 16 and joined an early video-streaming start-up, Digital Entertainment Network (DEN). Pierce hosted hundreds of followers at his 'DEN parties' in the house where he also produced shows including *Chad's World* (targeted towards a young, gay audience), *The Chang Gang* (targeted towards a young, Asian audience) and *Redemption High* (an evangelical Christian high school drama). Pierce left the company aged 18 in the wake of child abuse allegations. In 2013, he co-founded the VC firm Blockchain Capital. As well as being an early adopter of Bitcoin, Pierce also worked with one of the first Bitcoin offshoots, Mastercoin, and co-founded the cryptocurrency Tether. He later took the reins of the Bitcoin Foundation, the non-profit set up to improve the image of Bitcoin. Most of the foundation immediately resigned over fears Pierce's child abuse allegations would further tarnish the brand.[6] Pierce maintained lofty political ambitions too. He stood as a candidate to be US president in 2021 with a promise to build 'America 2.0': a government that embraced technology and a crypto-powered universal basic income. In November 2021, with the support of Donald Trump aide Steve Bannon, Pierce confirmed he was considering a run at the US Senate seat for Vermont. But a win would force Pierce to relinquish his federal income tax-free status as a resident of Puerto Rico, so he withdrew.[7]

Puerto Rico has been a mecca for US landgrabbers ever since they first invaded in 1898. The island's economy swiftly collapsed when the incoming visionaries turned the island into a sugar plantation, giving 80 per cent of the land over to 2 per cent of the population. Land that wasn't producing profits for US sugar giants was used to test naval munitions, agent orange and depleted uranium.[8] Cancer rates in those areas remained several times higher than the rest of the country. As a fix for Puerto Rico's new-found poverty problems, the USA imposed 'Law 116', a eugenics campaign requiring the mass sterilisation of poor landless Puerto Ricans. The campaign continued into the 1960s. For those resisting the plan, the 'Gag laws' were imposed forbidding protest. Even singing Puerto Rican songs in public was outlawed. The number of Puerto Ricans fell, and not just because of the eugenics. By 2014,

84,000 Puerto Ricans were migrating to the USA each year. Meanwhile, crypto-rich investors were ready to take advantage of the exodus.

In the aftermath of Hurricane Maria in 2017, instead of financial assistance to get basic services back up and running, the USA officially declared Puerto Rico a 'Zone of Opportunity'. Crypto speculators were pulled in with tax breaks. Act 22, or 'Promoting the Relocation of Investors to Puerto Rico Act', was originally drafted in 2012 to attract US-based productive industries, bringing jobs and infrastructure development. Instead, it attracted thousands of Bitcoiners snapping up the island's prime beachfront properties on the cheap without having to pay any federal income tax or capital gains tax.

Analysis published by the Centre for Investigative Journalism in June 2021 found the influx of tax dodgers had 'barely achieved any job creation' and had a 'meagre impact on the economy'.[9] Many Puerto Ricans referred to the crypto-friendly policies as 'tax apartheid', while the mass influx of Bitcoiners was pushing up the cost of living for locals. To take advantage of Puerto Rico's crypto-friendly tax system, the law required incoming crypto crusaders to commit to buying property within two years of settling. This was great for landed Puerto Ricans. But for the majority living in the poorest US territory, life got tough. House prices ballooned, pricing out locals and prompting their departure. 'It is not logical in a country where millions of people are leaving every year, to continue laws that make it impossible [for locals] to live in Puerto Rico', said one local senator.

Puerto Rico became a perfect base for money laundering, crypto scams and investment frauds. In December 2022, Avraham Eisenberg was arrested in Puerto Rico for market manipulation and crypto frauds worth $116 million. High-profile crypto tycoons seemed to show little interest in blending in. Salil Zaveri was arrested after allegedly killing a dog that happened to interrupt his round of golf.[10] YouTube stars and NFT moguls Jake and Logan Paul upset the locals after footage emerged of the pair driving golf buggies over a beach full of baby turtles near their new Puerto Rican home.[11] 'The locals are not happy. There are always public protests during their marketing events', Jillian Crandall, an architect and blockchain researcher from New York's Rensselaer Polytechnic tells me. 'Although there are no physical walls gating the crypto utopia in San Juan, there are digital walls and gates that keep anyone out unless they are high net worth "accredited investors" and on the inside in the blockchain space.'

For the Puertopians, the locals' protests were misguided. 'This isn't about going down to Puerto Rico to make money. Although that's always a primary focus', one US crypto entrepreneur told Crandall.[12] 'It is more about the spreading of a new religion: the religion of peace, of economy, of all things that are beauty and all things that we want for this world.' To win over the locals, re-education events were set up touting the advantages of evading taxes via cryptocurrencies as a means of encouraging development and an entrepreneurial spirit. In December 2022, the crypto colonists kicked off a conference called BUIDL (a deliberate misspelling of 'build'). It was organised by the Puerto Rico Blockchain Trade Association, a group of US crypto enthusiasts led by Keiko Yoshino, with the goal of making crypto more inclusive.[13] Yoshino saw the need to launch the organisation when she noticed that crypto colonists seemed to be the only ones in Puerto Rico who cared about crypto. 'There were no women, and there were no Puerto Ricans, and I thought "OK, this is a problem"', she said. But at $250 per ticket, the conference was still way out of reach for most Puerto Ricans. And the events seemed to focus on selling cryptocurrencies to locals, rather than helping the locals reBUIDL.

According to Pierce: 'They're offering us massive incentives to move [to Puerto Rico], because they want the most important technology being developed in the world. They want it to be present.' But according to local politician Manuel Natal Albelo, that mindset was the same colonialism Puerto Ricans had experienced for over a hundred years.

SATOSHI ISLAND

Private Bitcoin citadels were springing up across the tropics, attracting crypto colonists using short-sighted tax breaks. Vanuatu was especially keen. The small Pacific Island nation, one of the poorest in the world, was in a pickle with a tiny tax base and few industries. The sale of passports was the government's largest source of revenue in 2021, accounting for 42 per cent of the country's income.[14] Despite economic upsets caused by Covid lockdowns and multiple tropical cyclones, Vanuatu was still maintaining a budget surplus thanks to its controversial citizenship-for-sale programme. Passports had gone to various North Korean defectors, an Indian politician, Vinay Mishra, who left India abruptly during a corruption investigation, and Italian businessman Gianluigi Torzi, who allegedly extorted the Vatican for $15 million. A group of six Chinese crypto scammers used takings from their $2.9 billion Ponzi scheme, known as PlusToken, to buy their new passports. They were tracked down by Chinese police in 2019 and extradited. In 2021, two South African brothers were accused of using illicit funds from their 'AI-powered crypto exchange' Africrypt to buy themselves citizenship. The brothers, Raees Cajee, then aged 21, and Ameer Cajee, 18, emailed users about a 'catastrophic hack' resulting in the loss of up to $3.6 billion worth of their customers' crypto. Police confirmed that the brothers had sold their Lamborghinis and luxury accommodation in Durban, before asking their customers not to inform the authorities as 'this would delay efforts in getting the money back'.

In March 2022, Vanuatu's approach to offering safe haven to crypto fraudsters led the EU to suspend its visa waiver agreement with the country.[15] Desperate to maintain demand for the citizenship-for-sale scheme, fewer than two weeks after the EU suspension, the country's prime minister, Bob Loughman, officially gave the green light to Satoshi Island, a tax-dodger's hideaway, promising to make Vanuatu the 'crypto capital of the world'.

The three kilometre square Satoshi Island, or Lataro Island as it was known to the locals, was 90 per cent undisturbed rainforest and home to rare giant coconut crabs. It was first developed in 2010 by Anthony and Theresa Welch, a British couple marketing the island as a pristine nature reserve. By 2017, with the crabs no longer paying the bills, the island was put on the market for $12 million. A promotional video described the 'pristine coral reef surrounding the island' as a 'marine conservation area' that 'teems with beautiful fish and coral life'.

Welch took the island back off the market when a team of Bitcoiners approached them with an idea for a profitable partnership. The team included architect James Law, who made prefab accommodation in Hong Kong, Australian crypto entrepreneur Denys Troyak, and Daniel Agius, who managed an agency selling Vanuatu passports. Together their proposed masterplan involved turning the island's rainforest, 'untouched by man', into a crypto city for up to 21,000 Bitcoiners. The home of the last giant coconut crabs would be transformed into a giant Bitcoin symbol, a centrepiece that would be 'visible from space'.

'With the full endorsement from the prime minister of Vanuatu in hand, we can show everyone that Satoshi Island is as real as it gets', the project announced in a press release. Satoshi Island described itself as a fix for Vanuatu's lack of tourism. But the incoming Bitcoin enthusiasts were expected to 'live on the island, not just visit'. To be allowed on the island required the purchase of a Citizenship NFT, 21,000 of which were minted by the project's developers. To own land on the island would also require one of 21,000 Land NFTs. But none of these expensive pretend things would actually get the tax-dodger past Vanuatu's immigration officers. Unless, that is, they had also splashed out $130,000 on a real Vanuatu passport. Prospective residents of Satoshi Island and Land NFT holders were invited to design their new modular dream home using the project's 'digital twin metaverse app'. But building anything on the island in real life would require planning permission and environmental impact assessments. As the prime minister's endorsement letter said, crypto tax dodgers would always be welcome in the country if 'they now and always will abide by the laws of Vanuatu'. The crabs were safe for the time being.

Satoshi Island's Bitcoiners weren't the first crypto colonists to court Vanuatu's government. In 2019, an Australian crypto start-up called Sempo, in partnership with Oxfam, was testing a blockchain system for delivering cryptocurrency as a response to natural disasters. The project was called UnBlocked Cash and it involved delivering $10,000 worth of crypto to 187 households and 29 local shops. Oxfam hoped the system would reduce the cost and transaction time of direct Cash and Voucher Assistance (CVA). These assistance programmes, where cash is provided directly to aid recipients, is generally considered more effective, efficient and acceptable to beneficiaries compared to in-kind assistance, such as bags of rice. CVAs give recipients a greater level of freedom to decide and meet their own spending priorities. But the UnBlocked Cash tokens could be switched on and off in a way that cash systems could not. Oxfam and Sempo had all the power to say if and when and for whom the disaster event applied. In the end, the pilot flopped. Locals didn't want crypto, even at the best of times. When disasters struck, they needed real things.

REPUBLIC OF PALAU

Three thousand miles away, the Pacific nation of Palau was also keen to sell passports and NFTs to overseas tax dodgers. Before Covid struck, the archipelago was a magnet for uber-rich tourists. Palau's population of 18,000 welcomed around 100,000 Yachties each year in search of remote, unspoilt beaches and pristine reefs. To protect the oceans for scuba-diving tourists, most of Palau's waters were designated off-limits for commercial fishing. Pre-Covid, all of Palau's eggs were in the tourism basket. But by 2021 that basket was empty and Palau's cash was drying up. Diversifying the economy without mass tourism was a pressing priority for Palauan President Surangel Whipps Jr. Like many Pacific governments, Palau was trying desperately to avoid defaulting on sizeable loans. Then in February 2022, Whipps met Brock Pierce and the other crypto colonists, before promptly starting the country's sale of digital Palauan ID cards to Bitcoiners.

I travelled to Palau in 2017. I was interested in the growth of PalauCoin, a crypto scam-token with loose links to a local politician. The scandal prompted then President Thomas Remengesau to implement a strict moratorium on cryptocurrencies. So, a few years later, many were surprised when Whipps reopened Palau's digital doors to anyone wishing to become a crypto citizen.

Palau had made a deal with a different colonial devil some years earlier. Under the post-World War II tutelage of the USA, the people of the Pacific Islands Trust Territories, as they were known – living across the Western Pacific – were forcibly relocated to make way for the US Pacific nuclear-testing programme. After the programme was suspended in 1958, Palauans voted in favour of independence from the USA in a referendum. The newly created nation drafted their own nuclear free constitution, preventing the USA from testing or moving nuclear ordinance through Palau's waters. After a few assassinations and the installation of US-backed President Salii, the USA finally got its way and in 1990 the new 'Freely Associated State' won a visa-free work and travel agreement with the USA as well as her 'military protection'. The deal was better known to the locals as 'letting the US park nuclear weapons and snatch land for military bases'.

With Palau effectively a US colony, passports couldn't be sold without annoying the colonial master. So, partnering with the cryptocurrency outfit Ripple, Binance and Palo Alto blockchain developers Cryptic Labs, Palau kicked off a digital residency scheme instead, known as the Root Name System. For $248, anyone anywhere could apply for a limited edition NFT ID card enabling them to use a Palauan business address, apply for a certificate of legal name change and open online accounts to trade cryptocurrencies. These would prove handy for Chinese and other investors whose governments didn't allow crypto trading. But like any NFT, for most people, Palau's citizenship NFTs were useless. Holders wouldn't automatically be able to reside in Palau. They wouldn't be able to open a real business there or become a citizen. As with similar announcements of blockchain game-changers, Palau's crypto partnership was light on details and heavy on the future tense. But the problem the project purported to solve was overcoming geographical boundaries that stood in the way of a 'new generation of global digital existence', also known as 'tax dodging'.

Pacific nations in financial pickles were desperately appealing to the global tax-dodging elite in search of an island hideaway. As Whipps declared: 'This is all about economic freedom. Digital nomads roaming around the world. Why not come and be a [digital] resident of paradise?' Similarly, back in 2018, Papua New Guinea signed an agreement with Ledger Atlas, a company backed by Silicon Valley venture capitalist and Bitcoiner, Tim Draper. The agreement sought to establish 'a tax-free blockchain economic zone and sandbox' administered by Ledger Atlas, obliging the government to promote crypto.[16] Despite Draper's claims that the platform would prove 'a model for all future governments', Ledger Atlas never got off the ground. Alongside Whipps, Draper was inaugurated as a 'Founding Digital Resident' of Palau. Draper had pulled the same crypto marketing move before. He was the first recipient of Estonia's e-residency programme, which became mired by crypto scams, leaving Estonia's government with egg on its face. Palau's programme soon attracted a similar clientele. Bernadette Carreon, a local journalist with Organized Crime and Corruption Reporting Project (OCCRP) explained, 'Chinese organised crime groups were moving in, building illicit online business empires, and laundering money using cryptocurrency. By offshoring their criminal activities, they avoid Beijing's ire and show their usefulness to the [Chinese Communist Party] through corrupting local elites.'

SANGO

Like most places attracting crypto colonists, the Central African Republic (CAR) was a human rights bomb site. NGOs such as Human Rights Watch and UN experts reported that Russian mercenaries had been torturing, raping and executing civilians across CAR with complete impunity for years. In 2022, one Central African out of four was internally displaced or seeking refuge abroad. To maintain control, CAR's government was completely reliant on foreign military assistance from the Wagner Group, a private military security contractor controlled by Yevgeny Prigozhin, a Russian oligarch with close ties to Vladimir Putin. Nicknamed 'Putin's Chef', Prigozhin and his covert army of convicts, otherwise known as the 'Little Green Men', were implicated in war crimes across Ukraine. Wagner were also deployed in under-the-radar military operations in at least six African nations. According to General Stephen Townsend, the commander of US armed forces in Africa: 'Wagner essentially run the Central African Republic and are a growing force in other African countries.'

According to the European Platform for Democratic Elections, crypto had been essential to Russian soft power diplomacy in CAR, enabling Russia to fund covert operations anywhere despite sanctions. As well as Russian mercenaries, Prigozhin was also overseeing the social media meddling efforts of the Internet Research Agency, an organisation prosecuted in the USA for election interference. Prigozhin's political troublemakers were being paid for their assistance using cryptocurrencies to ensure maximum off-the-books deniability. Likewise, Prigozhin's so-called grassroots organisation, the Association for Free Research and International Cooperation, was paying its 'African Agents of Influence' using privacy-preserving cryptocurrencies such as ZCash and Monero.

Making all this possible was Mara, one of several African blockchain start-ups funded by the US crypto giants Coinbase and FTX. Mara's role was reportedly to write policy and assist the Russian-backed regimes in Africa with favourable crypto regulations.[17] For CAR, that meant adopting Bitcoin as a national currency. Mara's CEO, Chi Nnadi, explained that his company's mission was to engage African governments, including those that had an anti-crypto stance such as Nigeria and Kenya, drafting licensing regimes for crypto companies to operate in their countries. Prior to founding Mara, Nnadi ran Sustainability International, a non-profit organisation that managed 'community-led solutions for solving UN Sustainable Development Goals'. But Sustainability International's goal, just like Mara's, was to help onboard the poorest and most vulnerable people in Africa to crypto. In Nigeria, Sustainability International worked to onboard illiterate rural woman; to teach them how to part with their real money using Mara's app, without being able to read. This challenge is documented on Sustainability International's website. In fact, as of March 2023, it was the only content.

As the world's second-poorest country, CAR also had plenty of rural illiterate women to onboard, and the lowest internet penetration of anywhere in the world. Only 14 per cent of CAR's population had some access to electricity. Other crypto-friendly backwaters, such as Vanuatu and Palau, had beautiful beaches and cheap cocktails. CAR, a landlocked nation where over 90 per cent of households depended on foraged wood and charcoal for cooking and heating, was nowhere near ready for crypto payments. Cryptoland was a gleaming jewel of functionality by comparison.

Mara had a tough job onboarding CAR's president, Faustin-Archange Touadera, who was not your average crypto kitty. Sixty-five-year-old Touadera's announcement of his co-written crypto law went without fireworks but still forced significant fines and/or imprisonment on people and businesses who refused to accept Bitcoin for payments. It featured a photo of a letter, teeming with typos and posted on the president's Facebook page: an odd noticeboard for such far-reaching and immediate legislation. CAR's former prime minister, Martin Ziguele, confirmed that the country's crypto law was a rushed proclamation. But Touadera claimed the disruption was necessary to 'improve the conditions of Central African citizens' and distinguish CAR as 'one of the world's boldest and most visionary countries'.

Like the fantasy islands of Vanuatu and elsewhere, Mara's bold vision involved selling 'citizenship-by-investment' packages and a 'crypto smart city'. There was also a vague plan to connect all the country's precious minerals, diamonds and hydrocarbons to a purpose-built, Bitcoin-backed token called Sango. Each $60,000 passport package could also only be purchased using the Sango token. Very few countries issue a passport with so few visa-free travel options. To attract buyers – beyond just the expected Russian tax dodgers – the country would have a crypto city, also called Sango, which would be designed and built some time in the future. CAR had expected to sell around 20,000 Sango citizenships. As of January 2023, they'd sold 26.

BITCOIN REPUBLIC OF EL SALVADOR

CAR wasn't the first country to go all in on Bitcoin and allow US crypto colonists to rewrite its laws. In July 2021, the president of El Salvador, Nayib Bukele, was approached by

27-year-old crypto investor Jack Mallers from Chicago, who wished to proclaim Bitcoin the Central American country's new official currency. Mallers presented his 'Bitcoin Law' to a barrage of fireworks and fanfare just weeks after the USA threatened to pull El Salvador's International Monetary Fund (IMF) aid package following deep concerns around civil liberties, extrajudicial killings and human rights abuses. US Bitcoin maximalists Max Keiser and Stacy Herbert joined the pilgrimage. The pair had worked as *Russia TV* news hosts before dedicating their lives to spreading Satoshi's teachings full time. Religiously dressed in trademark white suits, the pair were reported to be big investors in the crypto company Bitfinex, directly linked to the stablecoin Tether. According to El Salvador researcher Ricardo Valencia, the couple were de facto Salvadoran diplomats. Bukele's government bestowed on them the authority to design public policy that Salvadorans would eventually fund. In November 2022, Bukele established a National Bitcoin Office by executive decree – helmed by Keiser and Herbert – which all executive branch offices were to collaborate with. The office was funded by Bitfinex and reported directly to Bukele. The couple had even been granted the power to open 'Bitcoin embassies' in other territories, as they reportedly did in Switzerland.[18]

Bukele had always been an autocrat for the TikTok generation. When invited to speak at the UN General Assembly in 2019, he addressed world leaders while tweeting a selfie at the podium and announcing that future sessions should be limited to a Skype call. The president referred to himself as the World's Coolest Dictator. He tweeted prolifically and was rarely seen without a backwards baseball cap. Bukele was a long-time Bitcoiner, having reportedly used it to fund part of his 2019 presidential campaign. The campaign involved mainly populist policies pushing up spending on social services, expensive infrastructure and law-and-order crackdowns.

Upon taking office, Bukele swiftly gambled over $375 million on a nationwide Bitcoin payment system and crypto wallet called Chivo. It flopped. Chivo users were offered a $30 sign-up bonus, which most people withdrew from ATMs before deleting the wallet from their phones. According to Bukele, using Bitcoin would help Salvadorans save $400 million a year on commission charges paid to US money transmitters such as Western Union. In 2019 alone Salvadorans working overseas sent home around $6 billion, making up around 20 per cent of the country's entire GDP. But in late 2022, according to El Salvador's central bank, less than 2 per cent of international remittances were being sent via cryptocurrency wallets. Another survey found that 86 per cent of Salvadoran businesses had never carried out a transaction using Bitcoin.

To many Salvadorans, Bitcoin was an absurd proposition that had no connection to local needs. But for Bukele, Bitcoin offered opportunities to concentrate his political powers, to sidestep likely US sanctions and to fund projects without going to the IMF. The fireworks of Bukele's grand Bitcoin announcements also conveniently drowned out the screams from human rights abuses. The country had the highest incarceration rate in the world. Under a state of emergency introduced and extended four times by Bukele and his Nueva Ideas party, civil liberties in El Salvador had been suspended in the name of fighting rampant gang violence. More than 60,000 people were arrested in a summer 2022 crackdown, usually on the basis of their faded gang tattoos. Families would hear nothing. Prisons, once open to visitors and journalists, became closed shops. Meanwhile, police maintained triple-digit daily arrest quotas. The goal, as some Nueva Ideas officials publicly said, was to arrest all 70,000 gang members in the country. It wasn't clear where that figure came from. According to local human rights organisation Cristosal, at least 63 people died in detention in the summer of 2022. Perhaps unsurprisingly, by the end of 2022 around 3 per cent of all Salvadoran adults were in prison.

In February 2023, Bukele celebrated the opening of his Terrorism Confinement Centre – a so-called mega-prison with a capacity of 40,000. It was the largest prison in the world. Yet, despite swollen quotas, Bukele continued to order the release of leaders from the infamous MS-13 gang, all of whom were facing extradition to the United States. According to the Salvadoran activist Domingo Flores, the habit of releasing criminals wanted in other countries, and light-touch enforcement of digital asset crimes, was strategic. Bukele wasn't against criminals per se. In fact, El Salvador was in hot competition to sell their fantasy citadel to the worst actors in cryptocurrency. 'Bukele is essentially broadcasting, look, I didn't extradite this gang member that's accused of murdering however many people to the US. I refused to extradite him. Instead, I gave him an official guard to accompany him to leave the country in freedom', Flores explained in an interview.[19] 'So that's a lot of advertising for, yeah, for the worst kind of criminal.'

The disinterest of most Salvadorans in Bitcoin saved them from a crashing crypto market. But the government's pocketbook was looking less rosy. Its 2,381 Bitcoins were, as of early 2023, worth less than half their purchase price, losing the Salvadoran taxpayer around $50 million. Bukele still planned to issue a 'Volcano Bond' to finance the construction of yet another 'crypto smart city'. Half the takings from the $1 billion Bitcoin-backed bond would go towards buying more Bitcoin. The other half would be used for the city's infrastructure and Bitcoin mining, powered by geothermal power from the Conchagua volcano. As well as the offer of permanent residency for just three Bitcoins, foreign settlers to Bitcoin City would, of course, be free of income tax and capital gains tax.

Like all proposed crypto developments claiming to be 'smart' and 'sustainable', Bukele's Bitcoin City – if successful – would make a mess, destroying a lot of what little pristine forest the country has left. The city would also dedicate much of its resource consumption to mining Bitcoin. But El Salvador wasn't producing enough energy to meet its existing needs. By the end of 2022, the country was importing 25 per cent of its electricity from fossil fuel power plants located elsewhere in the region.

Plans for the city were recycled from a previous failed scheme, just with the standard 'visible from space Bitcoin symbol' stamped on top of it. The previous fantasy charter city was to be built by the Chinese government, needing to pinch some land for their deep-sea port on the Gulf of Fonseca.[20] As of March 2023, there were no signs of heavy machinery or Bitcoin mining at the proposed Bitcoin City site, suggesting that the dream of full-scale crypto colonialism – for now at least – was yet another failed Bitcoin fantasy.

Despite their dreams of a world without oppressive governments, crypto enthusiasts tend to support populist TikTok despots of any ideological persuasion, so long as it suits the agenda of 'number go up'. As the enthusiasts often say, 'Bitcoin is for everybody', even ISIS in Syria, the Taliban in Afghanistan, tyrannical presidents such as Abiy Ahmed of Ethiopia, Kassym-Jomart Tokayev of Kazakhstan, Vladimir Putin and Putin's wingman, Alexander Lukashenko of Belarus. They've all joined the crypto choir. In August 2021, Lukashenko was lauded by Bitcoiners when he called on his countrymen to mine Bitcoin for 'economic development and human rights', notwithstanding his own full-scale assault against civil liberties. Putin's so-called foot soldier general and populist war-criminal leader of Russia's Chechen republic, Ramzan Kadyrov, puts his faith in Bitcoin above his actual faith: 'If anyone thinks that Egyptian and Palestinian fatwas on cryptocurrencies are mandatory for Russian citizens, they are deeply mistaken', Kadyrov proclaimed to his followers via Telegram.

ETHIOPIA

The torture and killings under these crypto-friendly regimes are similar to those orchestrated under General Augusto Pinochet in Chile and Suharto in Indonesia. Like those human rights disasters, crypto-colonial reforms often required violent crackdowns on dissenters resistant to right-wing dictatorship. Naomi Klein explains this strategy in *The Shock Doctrine*. In the spirit of right-wing economists such as Milton Friedman, disaster capitalism is used as a violent system of economic shock therapy where unpopular economic reforms are imposed on populations while they're simultaneously shocked and terrorised to erase existing economic norms.[21]

Neoliberal capitalism loves a blank slate, often finding its opening during wars and natural disasters. For example, Klein shows how the Asian economic crisis of 1997 enabled the fire-sale of many state-owned enterprises to US businesses. The 2004 tsunami in Sri Lanka prompted the government to force fisher folk away from their beachfront properties so they could be sold to overseas neocolonial interests. The shock of 9/11 enabled US corporations to benefit from the imposition of free market reforms in Iraq. Crypto colonists were following the same 'shock therapy' playbook.

The crypto capitalism shock therapy was nowhere starker than in Ethiopia. Cardano's Charles Hoskinson had been awaiting his opportune moment patiently there for years.

Hoskinson co-founded Ethereum with Vitalik Buterin before leaving the project due to a dispute over management structures. 'Back in 2015, I got to a point where I said, "Hey, you know, I have the ability to do a 'cleanroom approach', where we just assume nothing exists, start from the science and first principles", and say, "Okay, with all that we know, how would we actually build a cryptocurrency if we could do it all over again"', Hoskinson said. He went on to found rival project Cardano in 2015 as a cluster of offshore entities. Unlike in El Salvador, Cardano's plan for Ethiopia was to develop blockchain architecture from the ground up. The opportunity for a 'cleanroom approach' in Ethiopia came when civil war broke out in the northern region of Tigray.

The director-general of the World Health Organisation, Tedros Adhanom Ghebreyesus, described the ensuing crises as 'the worst humanitarian, man-made disaster on Earth'. Over 600,000 were killed. Hundreds of thousands were suffering from famine. Rape was a common weapon of war and thousands of refugees were spilling into neighbouring Sudan, falling victim to people-traffickers. Roads and bridges across the region were in ruins. Electricity and telephone lines had been cut. Only 15 per cent of Ethiopians had access to the internet at the best of times. With everything under heaven in chaos, for many people it seemed a strange time to kick off the country's digital revolution. For Hoskinson, the situation was excellent.

Cardano launched a training and apprenticeship programme exclusively for Ethiopian women and girls who would be trained in Cardano's niche programming language, Haskell. The best candidates were to be offered full-time jobs as Haskell developers.[22] Cardano's coders were set to work building centralised surveillance and automated conditions to be encoded into the country's digital IDs and educational record systems, as well as various supply chain management tools. The initial plan was for Cardano's blockchain applications to be used to digitally track students' grades and academic performance across the country. The developers then hoped to expand the system to incorporate an Ethiopia-wide cryptocurrency payment system, before connecting the entire African continent together with Cardano infrastructure. As well as benefiting from being first in, Hoskinson's Ethiopia partnership pushed Cardano's ADA token to an all-time price high.

With the help of autocratic politicians, Cardano was imposing systems of economic surveillance without public debate on entire populations. This included refugees and other vulnerable groups. In Tigray, where local interests sat squarely at odds with the Ethiopian government, unruly populations were especially exposed. There were also serious privacy and data protection concerns with the logging of data carried out by those who didn't have the best interests of certain citizens in mind.

The dangers of metadata meddling were well documented. Hoskinson himself conceded the perils of blockchain-based ID schemes, saying: 'Regimes like China or Saudi Arabia have an onerous record of very significant institutional violations. There, it makes no sense to build identity solutions or blockchain solutions because there's a high probability that those solutions are going to be abused and weaponised against the population.'[23] But nowhere was the risk of weaponisation more acute than in Cardano's new sandbox. Hoskinson also suggested blockchain applications for Afghanistan even while the USA were planning to withdraw. ISIS or the Taliban seizing a sensitive database built on an immutable ledger would pose enormous risks for the personal freedoms of many Afghans. This is not an unlikely scenario. Biometric records collected by the International Security Assistance Force sold on eBay for $68 in December 2022. Data protection regimes designed to keep biometrics safe and secure can easily collapse overnight when political sentiments switch.

Rather than decentralising control to balance the risk of power abuses in Ethiopia, the Cardano network was at risk of becoming a single point of failure: if the network got hacked or went down, so would all the government's record systems. We should of course contest the underlying imaginations that shape these projects and ask in whose interests are they being built. As Ruha Benjamin has said: 'Most people are forced to live inside someone else's imagination. And one of the things we have to come to grips with is how the nightmares that many people are forced to endure are the underside of an elite fantasy about efficiency, profit, and social control.'[24]

Those escaping the chaos in Tigray as refugees into Sudan and Eritrea were far from safe, thanks to other misplaced crypto fantasies. Meron Estefanos was a Sweden-based Bitcoin activist. She claimed to help families to send cryptocurrencies in order to pay ransom demands for kidnapped refugees. 'They give [victims] a phone and they have to call their family as they are getting tortured', Estefanos explained. 'So, the families are pressurised to pay a ransom, because they listen to the torture of their daughter who is getting gang raped by five or six people. And so, you would do anything.' But making these sorts of ransom payments is illegal. The 2013 G8 communiqué on non-payment of ransoms and the 2014 UN Security Council Resolution 2133 forbids the payment of ransoms for good reason. Payment of ransoms strengthens the ability of criminal gangs to organise and carry out further kidnappings. It also enables them to grow their membership and fund military operations. 'Western Union have limited my payments to $4,500', Estefanos added. 'But today the normal ransom has gone up to $33,000. I was eventually blocked from making any payments. So now I train people in Sudan how to receive Bitcoin and how to exchange it and we managed to do it like that.'

BITCOIN BLOOD DIAMONDS

Like other empires before them, taking other people's things without asking was a brave and noble gesture for crypto colonists. Gridless – a Jack Dorsey-backed Bitcoin-mining firm – was keen to 'help' remote communities across Africa by relieving them of their surplus energy issues. It worked like this. Big international NGOs had built thousands of small hydropower plants in rural villages over the years to promote clean development in Africa. But without ongoing financial support there were few successes. Not many businesses or households could afford the energy being offered.[25] Meanwhile, for Bitcoin miners the infrastructure offered a cheap source of 'stranded energy' that would otherwise go to waste. In taking it, Bitcoin miners made a killing, while the locals usually carried on without. The crypto takeover was framed as a gift for 'sustainable development'.

During the British scramble for Africa and India in the late nineteenth and early twentieth century, similar gifts were provided. The empire used railways, ports, camps and other infrastructure to facilitate the extraction and movement of things for themselves, while hampering the freedoms of locals. Apologists for empire still like to claim that the British brought democracy, the rule of law and trains to those under her tutelage. But those trains were sold to India to make it easier to steal India's stuff. Colonial gifts are like someone breaking into your house, wheelbarrowing your stuff out via a ramp, leaving behind a bill for the ramp and expecting a kiss goodbye. The term crypto colonialism was coined before blockchain. Michael Herzfeld used it in reference to clandestine strategies used by the British to ensure that newly 'independent' countries remained strongly dependent on their colonial master, mainly through unfair trade agreements and debt. Today's crypto infrastructure – the Bitcoin-mining machines, trading apps, software and marketing scams 'gifted' to poor countries – is done with the same neocolonial motives. There are few job prospects for the locals. No useful development projects are left behind. For local people, all that's bequeathed is a headache.

Bitcoiners have also been 'helping' with wars raging in the DRC. Civil wars have been off and on (mostly on) since Belgian colonisers came to DRC a hundred years ago. Fighting over the last ten years, involving over 130 different armed groups, is continuing to kill about 45,000 people each month, half of whom are under five years old. For most industries, such conditions would write the country off as a safe investment option. But for Bitcoiners, chaos brings opportunity.

In the country's famous Virunga National Park, a European Union-funded hydroelectric plant has been constructed to encourage sustainable alternative livelihoods for war-ravaged communities. That is, jobs that don't involve joining an armed militia, poaching gorillas or illegal logging. The plant was also intended to support clean water systems. Communities would no longer need to cut down trees for wood fuel. As well as bringing cheap electricity to domestic consumers, the project was meant to feed industrial developments with clean energy in the provincial capital of Goma.

According to the park director, Bitcoiner and Belgian Prince Emmanuel de Merode: 'Every Megawatt of electricity generated empowers the community by creating thousands of jobs, 5 to 10 percent of which go to ex-combatants. When people are empowered, they have the choice to control their future and move into productive society, away from armed groups.'[26]

But, contrary to these objectives, locals' homes and businesses were never connected. Instead, rusty shipping containers littered the site, humming relentlessly 24/7, 365 days a year. The European Bitcoin miners who owned them got special access to the plant's cheap electricity.

In DRC, Bitcoin mining required just one or two workers to oversee the many container-loads of specialist machines. The park's managers claimed cryptocurrencies were funding their conservation work. But for young Congolese people, Bitcoiners were pushing them closer to their employers of last resort: as militiamen, poachers or illegal loggers. Esther Marijnen, a Dutch political ecologist who'd been working in DRC since 2013, told me that '[Bitcoin mining] is counterproductive for conservation. For all the development taking place in the park, especially around hydropower, Virunga has failed to bring widespread stability or employment. This is just another example of excluding local people from conservation projects and forcing them into illicit livelihoods.' Meanwhile, Virunga is the only UN Educational, Scientific and Cultural Organization (UNESCO) world heritage site that provides funerals for murdered rangers at such a rate: once a month on average.

BLOCKING ANTI-COLONIAL STRUGGLES

Incoming cryptocurrency miners were putting the brakes on decolonisation in the disputed territory of Western Sahara. The sparsely populated country bordering the Atlantic Ocean remains Africa's last colony. Spain sold it to Morocco in 1975 in exchange for continued access to Saharawi fisheries, and profits from a phosphate mine. Morocco then invaded, using napalm against fleeing Saharawi refugees. The UN and International Court of Justice have both stated that the indigenous Saharawi have a right to self-determination, requiring a referendum on independence. But this has been continuously blocked by Morocco who have turned to Bitcoin mining to entrench their occupation. Joanna Allan, a researcher who has been working in the region for several years, told me that 'as long as Morocco can profit from its occupation of Western Sahara, there is little incentive for it to meaningfully engage in peace talks'. In 2021, Morocco gave the green light to Soluna, a US crypto company, to develop a massive 900 megawatt energy plant and Bitcoin-mining operation in Dakhla. According to Western Sahara Resource Watch, by setting up shop in the region, Bitcoin miners were 'strengthening Morocco's belief that it can violate international law and human rights'. According to Allan:

> Crypto companies that do business with the occupiers in Moroccan-controlled Western Sahara, one of the worst places in the world in terms of civil liberties and political freedoms, undermine the human rights of Saharawis. And these activities are also legally questionable. They amount to plunder, which is a war crime. Soluna makes factual errors in the way it describes its activities in occupied Western Sahara. They claim that the [Bitcoin mining] will be in Dakhla, Morocco. But Dakhla is located in Western Sahara. Soluna is whitewashing over the crimes of the Moroccan occupation and denying the very identity of the Saharawis, who are still engaged in an anti-colonial struggle for freedom.

For the Navajo nation of New Mexico, incoming colonies of Bitcoin miners were a false solution for historic struggles against colonial resource grabs. The Navajo people experience the highest rates of poverty, crime, alcoholism, incarceration and suicide of any racial group in the USA. Located in the centre of the richest country on earth, 15 per cent of Navajo people suffer extreme poverty. Over 14,000 of the 55,000 indigenous households located on Navajo lands do not have access to electricity. The Puerco River flowing through the nation is highly radioactive. Since the 1960s, US mining giants have made a killing from the Navajo's uranium to satisfy the US nuclear weapons programme. Cancer rates for the Navajo are far higher than elsewhere in the USA. Huge piles of uranium waste make tourism, agriculture and other land-based industries unviable. Instead of remediating the land, mining firms are paying to relocate many residents away from the Navajo nation altogether. Locals refer to the relocation as a genocidal trail of tears. Meanwhile, incoming Bitcoiners continue to make a killing from the Navajo's resources that are left behind. In August 2021, the Canadian crypto-mining firm WestBlock agreed a deal to grab 15 megawatts of electricity per year from the Navajo grid. That energy would have been enough to power all 14,000 homes without a grid connection. But instead, the Bitcoin deal gives WestBlock access to subsidised electricity at less than a tenth of the price paid by other US buyers.

On the Pine Ridge Indian Reservation in South Dakota, with little access to electricity or internet access, Payu Harris has created a cryptocurrency called MazaCoin with the expressed goal of decolonising the reserve. Harris claims he wants to build a system that could deliver value to native people, starting with the Lakota – the same tribe devastated in the Wounded Knee Massacre over 100 years ago – before expanding to other tribes and reservations. MazaCoin is a cut-n-paste version of Bitcoin in almost every way, except for the reservation connection. Reportedly without the permission of any other Lakota people, Harris is working on his own Sango-like solution, tokenising then selling the tribes' natural resources, including unmined coal reserves and gold in the Black Hills. He's also storing tribal treaties, documents and historic records on the MazaCoin blockchain.[27] Harris is marketing MazaCoin across the reservation, setting his fellow Lakota people up with crypto wallets and educating them on how to invest. But the crypto 'investment opportunity' seems to be a clear-cut affinity scam. Shared indigenous values and experiences of colonialism and poverty are used to build trust and sell an asset with no value.

BROKEN PROMISES

Governments around the world were scrumming for crypto opportunities because of their implied promises of high-tech jobs and clean development. But shiny tech-industry campuses, clinics, residential skyscrapers and lots of secure jobs are a masterplan of make-believe when crypto is involved. Take the 'Binance City' proposal for Nigeria,[28] a digital economic zone which, according to its developers, would help entrepreneurs 'fast track blockchain technology' in a digital hub 'similar to the Dubai virtual free zone'. The dream of huge skyscrapers sprouting from the African desert is one that Binance used frequently to negotiate their terms for low-tax and light-touch regulation in the emerging economies where Binance did its bidding. Binance had been so fundamental to the vision of Sheikh Mohammed bin Rashid Al Maktoum that the sheikh pledged to make Dubai 'the first city fully powered by block-chain' and therefore 'the happiest city on earth'. 'Binance is building the future', read the lightshow projection against Dubai's Burj Khalifa in October 2022 after the sheikh granted the crypto company a licence to operate there. But crypto outfits weren't building anything in the deserts of Africa, besides virtual tax-havens.

Urban crypto mirages didn't get any more grandiose than Akon City, a $6 billion 'crypto smart city' promised for Senegal by the R&B 'Smack That' artist, Akon. The city, which was modelled on Wakanda – the fantasy world from Marvel's Black Panther movies and comics – would use Akon's own purpose-built cryptocurrency, Akoin. 'My goal is to build something people deem impossible. Right here in Africa', said Akon. After the project was formally agreed in September 2020, the Senegalese government set about clearing 3,000 fisher folk living happily in the proposed construction site of Mbodiene, near Dakar. According to Awar Bakala, a journalist at the OCCRP, 'there's a real need for work, infrastructure, hospitals, and universities in Senegal. And all of this is packaged within Akon City.'

Crypto was the central marketing instrument of the project from the get-go. Before launching the plans, the project's website announced an ICO called the Token of Appreciation (TOA) fundraising campaign, designed to cover the costs of launching Akoin some time in the future. The pre-sale was framed as a 'donation opportunity'. But contributors were told that for every $1 they put in they would receive four TOAs which would later all convert to Akoins, the city's official currency. Following a standard crypto rug pull trajectory, Akoin launched in September 2021 with a price of around $0.35, before falling sharply to $0.01. As of January 2023, after years of promises and plenty of fireworks, the Akon City site – given to Akon by the people of Senegal – was still grassland, leaving locals wondering about their future. But the failure didn't stop Akon from promising Wakanda II, this time to be developed, sometime in the future, on a city-sized plot given by the people of Uganda.

Explicit nods to afro-futurism in Akon's architectural plans added to the sour taste left by the broken promises.

Afro-futurism is a mix of sci-fi and social justice. The movement promotes an imaginary where the struggle for Black civil rights is over. But in the imaginative wasteland of crypto, afro-futurist landscapes – far from providing a utopian paradise for the dispossessed – invited crypto investors to a gaudy theme park. An 'African Village' with restaurants, markets and accommodation would have offered a sanitised taste of 'all corners of the African continent'. It could best be described as a theme park version of Africa, in Africa. The word 'utopia' itself means 'no place': a place that cannot exist. But, according to the futurist Monika Bielskyte, historically, 'utopias have existed. They were just utopias for the few.' Where utopian visions have evolved into places, they have proved exclusionary by default. 'They were designed by people in ivory towers, looking down at people below and excluding them', she says. Akon's failure to break ground in Senegal or Uganda was probably no bad thing after all.

THE SEASTEADERS

Patri Friedman – grandson of Milton Friedman – and the Bitcoin billionaire Peter Theil established the Seasteading movement in the belief that setting up tax-free libertarian countries should be as easy as setting up new companies. Theil explained:

These countries would mean more scientific and techno-logical progress, that is too heavily regulated by the heavy hand of our existing state. There are all these things that would be better. Different penal systems [for example]. But what I'm most attracted to is this question of whether we can do these new biomedical things.

In 2019, inspired by Theil and Friedman's ideas, US Bitcoin traders Chad Elwartowski and Supranee Thepdet, constructed a floating seastead on a small concrete spar in the Andaman Sea, twelve miles off the coast of Thailand. According to Elwartowski, living on a small, lonely spa in the middle of the ocean 'was definitely not the end goal', but rather a gateway to space. Their Waterworld was to encompass 20 connected floating platforms, which they'd christened XL II.[29] Elwartowski had a steel platform specially developed to replace the old concrete one, upon which they reportedly intended to house workmen to construct a 'Lofstrom loop': a massive gun designed to fire vehicles along a huge maglev track before ejecting them into space.[30] Thai authorities became concerned when the Seasteaders started openly soliciting from 70 other prospective investors to expand the development. And in no time at all, just as the pair were settling into their rocky new lives, the spar was intercepted by three Royal Thai Navy vessels. In occupying the spa, the Seasteaders were accused of threatening the sovereignty of Thailand. While the spa was towed back to dry land, Elwartowski posted, 'I was free for a moment – probably the freest person in the world'. But this wasn't a tax-free treehouse gone wrong. It was colonialism. To avoid Thailand's 'different penal system' (the pair face the death penalty), they currently live in hiding.

Thiel, Andreessen and Pierce had more success colonising the Honduran island of Roatán. Their exclusive crypto city called Próspera broke ground in 2020. The development embodied the same libertarian ethos as the Seasteaders, with its own laws designed to inspire tax-free, crypto-friendly innovation. Like Puerto Rico, land grabbing had a long, bloody history in Honduras. Fighting over farmland sold to international corporations led to around 150 murders and disappearances in 2008. A move to amend the country's constitution in 2013 allowed many more foreign companies to create charter cities. This escalated land conflicts further. Pushing out the locals to make way for new exclusive hotels and gated golf courses, Próspera hoped to become a mecca for medical trials that tended to be too costly to carry out where pesky regulations apply. One of the island's new residents was the biotech start-up Minicircle. The company carried out gene therapy trials. While in the USA, under the exacting gaze of the US Food and Drug Administration, trials would have cost the company millions of dollars. But in the Willy Wonka world of Próspera, human guinea pigs were reportedly shipped in after purchasing golden tickets as NFTs.[31] The chosen few were 'biohacked' in exchange for cryptocurrency. And – if the Follistatin gene therapy worked – sent home with comedically huge muscles.[32]

For crypto-colonial experiments to be successful, it didn't matter if the fantasy offered shining Wakanda skyscrapers or a filthy Kowloon city of darkness. The marks and guinea pigs were generally not drawn in by speculative greed but by a want for safe haven in a community of like-minded people free of oppression. Many of the foundational crypto-utopian ideas clearly stem from the nineteenth-century US Homesteaders movement. In having access to otherwise empty land, 'every man can have the means and opportunity of benefitting his condition', Abraham Lincoln said in 1861. A nice idea, but Lincoln's Homestead Act enabled the erasure of indigenous histories and genocide. Both the Homesteaders and today's Seasteaders are modes of the same 'clean room' colonialism. And as with all past colonial scrambles for *Terra nullius*, the biggest losers from attempts at Crypto El Dorado were the locals, whose land, lives, histories and resources were taken for citadel fantasies.

3
Green Wash Trading

In November 2021 the total market capitalisation of all cryptocurrencies exceeded $3 trillion.[1] Only a tiny fraction of Bitcoiners had ever bought anything with their crypto. But at $1.28 trillion, Bitcoin alone was worth more than the entire GDP of Spain. To make cryptocurrencies rocket to the moon like this required a fraudulent market manipulation practice known as 'wash trading': a scam in which the buyer and the seller were on both sides of the counter. Essentially, they sell themselves an asset to create the illusion of market action. The practice was banned on US regulated markets in 1936. But crypto has always been awash with wash trades. According to Forbes research, in 2022 more than half of all Bitcoin trades were fake.[2] Others concluded that wash trading accounted for at least 70 per cent of transactions on most exchanges.[3] Even record breaker NFTs, sold by the most powerful people through the most prestigious auction houses – such as Christies and Sotheby's – were subject to this sort of funny business. For several months in early 2022, fraudulent NFT trades outnumbered those considered 'organic' five to one. Self-regulated crypto exchanges can bet against their own customers using insider knowledge, or arbitrarily cancel trades whenever the invisible hand of the market isn't moving to their liking. Exchanges have no obligation to report any accurate price information. When the suckers have all gone home and the 'pumpamentals' look poor, exchanges buy their own shitcoins at whatever price they fancy, till the suckers come back.

The same magic tricks are performed by crypto companies to fraudulently pump their project's 'environmentals'. The wash trade and the green wash work hand in hand in crypto, providing the illusion of a clean and profitable investment when the opposite is true.

PROOF OF WASTE

On most days in 2022, cryptocurrencies were using the same amount of energy as all the data centres powering the world's internet. If the internet were a country, it would be the third most energy intensive in the world, behind China and the USA. This is perhaps understandable, given that in the time it takes you to read this sentence, some 650,000 people will have used Google's search engine.[4] Yet, over the time it takes you to read this page, only five people would have used Bitcoin to purchase something besides a different cryptocurrency.[5] The Bitcoin network sometimes uses as much energy as that used by the whole of Argentina,[6] most of which is generated from fossil fuels. But for Bitcoin enthusiasts, this inefficiency isn't a bug or accidental side effect. The waste is the feature.

Unlike other aspects of our digital lives, the big environmental impacts of cryptocurrencies don't only stem from temperature-controlled data centres, from which all the ones and zeros get transmitted. Crypto's massive energy demand comes from the way so-called digital gold is 'mined'. Bitcoin was designed as a system of digital money free from government meddling. There are no banks keeping the books. The job of validating transactions is instead performed by a global network of specialist machines, known as miners. These computers compete with each other for bookkeeping duties in exchange for financial rewards. Each specialist mining machine repeatedly guesses the combination to a digital lock (an automatically generated string of random digits) while validating transactions that are occurring on the network, with the winning machine bagging its owner some Bitcoins.

Since 2021 the prize for a correct guess was just over six Bitcoins,[7] with the competition restarting every ten minutes. The prize pot halves every four years until the total number of Bitcoins in circulation reaches a cap of 21 million. The theoretical cap is a nod to the gold-like scarcity and anti-inflationary quality of the asset. Over 19 million Bitcoins have already been mined, meaning the crypto contest will continue up until the year 2140. As well as receiving new Bitcoins as a reward, the winner of the Bitcoin bingo also receives all the transaction fees paid by users of the network within their ten-minute window. These fees go up and down automatically depending on how many people are sending transactions. The guess-the-number competition is known as Proof of Work: a controlled way of wasting energy, so that each Bitcoin represents the 'work' (electricity and hardware) required to make each one.

Burning through the necessary value of resources requires each Bitcoin-mining computer to repeatedly hammer out guesses for the combination, like an ever-expanding online version of the board game Hungry Hippos. The game's difficulty automatically adjusts every few weeks, depending on how many hippos are spread out around the virtual board. So, for example, if only a handful of hippos are in the game, the board is small, and the combination remains easy enough for one of the hippos to correctly guess the combination within ten minutes. When millions of hungry hippos, attracted by the heady rewards, spread out around the board, the difficulty adjusts so that the game doesn't secure a winner until the ten minutes are up. In 2009, winning the game was very easy. With just a regular laptop and an internet connection, one could regularly scoop up 50 new Bitcoins simply by not turning off one's laptop for ten minutes. Bitcoins had very little value. Websites such as Bitcoin Faucet allowed anyone to pick up five Bitcoins for free every day. Beyond niche underground forums of geeks and hackers, no one was interested in Bitcoin.

From 2011, interest in Proof of Work mining as a profitable new industry grew exponentially. Mining hardware became much more efficient. But as the game's difficulty increased, players needed to acquire more specialist hardware to keep up with the competition, requiring more and more electricity. Graphics processing units (GPUs) replaced less efficient central processing units, which were then themselves replaced with field programmable gate arrays. In 2013, Canaan Creative, a China-based computer hardware manufacturer, launched the first application-specific integrated circuit (ASIC) units for Bitcoin mining. Unlike general-purpose chips, these devices were designed from the outset to only play guess the number. The efficiency gains from ASICs could not be matched by any general-purpose devices that preceded them. Meanwhile, the prices that speculators were prepared to pay for Bitcoin also climbed, from just a few dollars in 2012 to $250 a year later. While Canaan Creative was the first, other Bitcoin ASIC manufacturers, such as Bitmain and MicroBT, came up with new versions of ASIC devices. The increasingly advanced hardware rendered any previous iterations obsolete, sometimes within just a few months.

Today, Bitcoin is secured by a global network comprising millions of tailor-made ASICs, which together play guess the number 200 quintillion times (200 followed by 18 zeros) every single second. For comparison, the world's most powerful supercomputer, the HP Enterprise Frontier, can carry out one-quintillion operations per second. In 2022 alone, Bitcoin's ASICs were responsible for emitting around 72 million tonnes of carbon dioxide. That's comparable to the annual emissions from the whole of Greece.

The second act of this environmental tragedy is that if (or when) Bitcoin is no longer a thing, ASICs cannot be put to work to find cures for cancer or calculate future weather conditions on Mars. ASICs can only mine Bitcoin. When they're burned out, usually after 18 months or so, they're scrapped. For every 100 ASIC units coming off the factory conveyor belt today, only three will go on to guess the number correctly. Retired ASICs create around 37,000 tonnes of burned-out electronic waste every year; more than the Netherlands produces. For every one transaction entered on the Bitcoin blockchain today, the equivalent of two iPhones worth of e-waste was produced. And most of this burned-out kit is being shipped illegally to its final resting place in South Asia or Africa.[8] The waste machines are often contaminated with so-called forever chemicals such as polyfluoroalkyl substances. Their use as a non-conductive coolant fluid is popular among Bitcoin miners. When improperly disposed of though, cancer rates and thyroid disease rocket. The chemicals' persistence also causes environmental problems – forever.

The higher the price, the more Bitcoin's miners are prepared to spend on replacement ASICs and the electricity to power them, so long as their costs for doing so are less than their reward. Major chip manufacturers are jumping on the crypto gravy train. NVIDIA's GPUs and Intel's Blockscale ASICs threaten to abruptly banish the network's huge stockpile of lower-spec machines to landfill, until something better does the same to them. Proof of Work is proof of waste. And the waste is by design.

SWITCHING OFF PROOF OF WASTE

Proof of Work is not the only way for cryptocurrencies to keep the books without banks. Ethereum switched off all its mucky mining machines in September 2022 and cut 99 per cent of its energy waste in the process. At that time, many crypto-currency commentators suggested that 'the merge', as the makeover was called, represented one of the most important events in the history of crypto. The merge meant the equiva-lent of Hong Kong's annual emissions were erased overnight. All that was required was a change in the Ethereum code base from Proof of Work to PoS.

With PoS, there's no need for expensive, energy-intensive processing equipment to validate transactions. Instead, token holders use their stash as a security deposit for the chance to become 'validators'.[9] Rather than competing, validators are selected. Do the job well, and the validator is rewarded with even more crypto. But if they validate fraudulent transac-tions or otherwise defy network rules, they lose their stake. This disincentive is called 'slashing'. PoS networks are typi-cally assembled around 20 machines, using a comparatively small amount of energy. During an energy crisis and climate emergency, Ethereum's switch to efficient software was good news. But Proof of Work cryptocurrencies remain the dirty elephants in the room.

In 2022, Greenpeace launched a campaign for Bitcoin to follow Ethereum down the PoS road. According to Green-peace, coding these changes would be straightforward. Only 30 people – the largest mining outfits, exchanges such as Coinbase and Binance, and code developers – would need to agree the switch. But this ignored the fact that everyone using the network would need to run the upgraded software. Chris Bendiksen, a commentator at the cryptocurrency website

CoinShares, put the chance of Bitcoin ever moving to PoS at 0 per cent: 'There is no appetite among Bitcoiners to destroy the security of the protocol by making such a move', he said.

Bitcoin is no stranger to coding stalemates. An amendment to fix intermittent congestion issues and stabilise transaction fees was proposed in 2016. Despite being a relatively simple fix, the change split the Bitcoin community, with the vast majority continuing to support the slower, more expensive status quo. Even if some users were prepared to ditch Proof of Work, the original Bitcoin network would continue in some form. The Proof of Work version would keep the name, branding, super-rich disciples, and polluting miners. The PoS offshoot would inevitably end up as just another disappointing experiment. Starting a PoS network from scratch is another option. But there is already a BitcoinPoS cryptocurrency. It's attracted few supporters.

BITCOIN'S BUTTERFLY EFFECT

Unlike a 40 Watt lightbulb that requires 40 Watts of power to make it work, Proof of Work cryptocurrencies do not have a minimum energy requirement. The Bitcoin network will function with only a handful of miners using old laptops. Neither does it have a maximum. Many otherwise seemingly sensible crypto advocates suggest that once we've exhausted the earth's energy production capacity, the competition to win new Bitcoins should take us into space. Competitive megastructures, known as 'Dyson spheres', they suggest, would completely encompass stars to secure earth's Bitcoin.[10]

If a new miner joins the competition using only renewable energy, this does not remove the energy burden from other fossil-fuelled miners. On the contrary. Joining the competition with 'green' energy increases the difficulty level for everyone. With more players, those already powered by coal in Kazakhstan, or oil in Texas, need to increase their efforts in order to compete, while belching out extra smog. This is Bitcoin's butterfly effect. With a high Bitcoin price, any additional renewable energy-powered mining makes everything worse.

Localised bans on Proof of Work can also inadvertently increase Bitcoin's overall carbon footprint. The can is simply kicked down the road. The starkest example of this Bitcoin butterfly effect can be seen in China. Before the spring of 2021, up to 70 per cent of the world's Bitcoin miners were powered by coal and hydroelectricity in China. To maximise profits, mining machines were often crammed into shipping containers, with operators ready to up sticks at a moment's notice to find the cheapest sources of energy. During China's summer rainy season, hydro power plants in the south-western provinces generated so much energy that miners could mop up the leftovers. But in the winter dry season, many miners unplugged and hit the road, heading for the coal-fired power plants scattered across China's vast northern territories.

China's government has taken a hostile stance towards crypto since 2013, when banks were prohibited from handling Bitcoin transactions. In 2019, Chinese regulators labelled Bitcoin mining an 'undesirable and highly polluting industry'. When the government cracked down in 2021, the network's use of renewable electricity drastically decreased, from 41 per cent to 25 per cent. While miners previously had some seasonal access to renewables, this was lost when miners were shooed overseas. As I write this in early 2023, the new global Bitcoin superpower is the USA, where 40 per cent of Bitcoins are now mined, mostly with gas and coal.

All Bitcoins are created equal. Green ones are not worth any more than coal-fired coins. And it's nearly impossible to verify which is which. For miners, buying renewable energy tends to be cheaper, especially outside periods of peak demand, compared to fossil fuels that are more responsive to the needs of the wider grid. But the availability of energy from renewables is usually more intermittent than for fossil fuels. All miners, running equipment to the same specifications, have the same constant energy demand and usually run their machines 24/7. Therefore, miners usually cannot exclusively rely on an intermittent renewable energy source to meet their requirements and remain profitable.

SAVING FOSSIL FUELS

Thanks to crypto, redundant fossil fuel plants are roaring back to life. In southern Montana, the Hardin coal plant was kicking into action on just 46 days in 2020.[11] The plant was due to close, until a deal was struck with Marathon, a Bitcoin-mining company, which agreed to buy the lot. In 2021 the plant's boilers fired up nearly every day delivering 115 megawatts to Marathon's onsite Bitcoin behemoth. Emissions from burning Hardin's coal soared too, increasing by more than 5,000 per cent.

The Greenidge Generation plant in Dresden, New York, was another defunct fossil fuel monster, reopened to mine Bitcoin. Located on the sleepy shores of Seneca Lake, the plant was shut down 'permanently' in 2011. Thanks to the energy-saving projects of nature loving locals, there simply wasn't enough regional demand to justify the plant's operating costs. Its owners filed for bankruptcy. After belching noxious fumes and dumping toxic coal ash into a nearby landfill for over 70 years, the plant was poised to be demolished and remediated. Then, in 2020, Greenidge rose from the dead to reportedly spew, each year, 220,000 tonnes of CO_2 from the plant's stacks, and hundreds of billions of gallons of hot water into a nearby trout stream. Billions of cubic metres of fracked natural gas was piped in and burned. The plant's emissions went from zero to the equivalent of putting nearly 50,000 new petrol cars on the road. With the plant delivering 85 megawatts of fossil fuel power exclusively for mining cryptocurrencies, Greenidge was now not a power company with a side hustle. Greenidge became a Bitcoin-mining company with its own exclusive power station large enough to heat a city.[12]

Despite the State of New York's plans to slash its greenhouse gas emissions by 85 per cent before 2050, the Greenridge Bitcoin revival was partly enabled by a local government 'upstate revitalisation grant' worth $2 million. The grant was meant to 'stimulate the region's economy and create jobs'. But the company precariously employed only around 30 people.[13] One new job for every 7,500 tonnes of CO_2 emitted each year. Research shows that for every $1 of value created for shareholders of Bitcoin companies such as Greenidge, $0.49 needs to be spent by the state on remedying the public health and environmental hangovers.[14]

For hard-up local governments struggling to fund fixes for their fossil fuel legacies, Proof of Work miners help make environmental problems go away: by setting them on fire. Until recently, the State of Pennsylvania applied a levy on companies operating coal mines to be paid into an 'Abandoned Mine Land Fund'. The initiative ensured that huge piles of toxic bituminous waste, or 'gob', created by the industry could be suitably remediated even if the operator went bust. Gob is usually a mix of low-quality coal, clay, heavy metals and other toxic nasties. Remediated gob mountains from redundant mines have in the past been turned into play parks, nature reserves or forests. But with falling demand for coal power, remediation money also fell. The federal government stepped in, allocating $11 billion towards abandoned mine clean-ups for coal-producing states such as Pennsylvania.[15] But instead of using the federal cash, Pennsylvania offered up to $20 million in subsidies every year to companies agreeing to burn gob for electricity.

In Russellton, Pennsylvania, the Bitcoin company Stronghold acquired the redundant 85 megawatt Scrubgrass powerplant to burn gob for Bitcoin. What could have been 650 acres of parkland is today a monster emitting 85,000 cars worth of CO_2. As well as planet-changing pollution, gob plants emit localised cancer-causing carcinogens, sulphur and nitrogen oxides, devastating local ecosystems. Bizarrely, despite the mess it causes, the State of Pennsylvania pays renewable energy credits to Stronghold, recognising the toxic coal waste as an 'alternative energy source'.

GREEN BITCOINS?

The Susquehanna nuclear power plant, also in Pennsylvania, had a history of 'mildly radioactive leaks'. But in March 2023, Susquehanna commenced diverting 48 megawatts of state-subsidised power from homes to Bitcoin miners. As well as through increased health concerns, locals were also paying the price for the plant's Bitcoin profits with their increasing energy bills. Dutch energy researcher and economist Alex de Vries told me that 'this isn't the safest nuclear plant in the world. But even ignoring that; locals are literally paying the price of keeping this plant open, only to see the energy end up with these miners.'

Meanwhile, in North Carolina, burned tyres were on the menu. Instead of investing in recycling infrastructure, which can be costly, Product Recovery Technology International has so far 'baked' two million tyres in huge pyrolysis ovens, purely for Bitcoin. The process of baking used tyres emits heavy metals, benzene, dioxins, furans and other persistent organic chemicals into the air; some of these compounds are highly carcinogenic.[16] Burning 25,000 tonnes of tyre oil, the scheme emits a lot of CO_2, and causes misery for those living nearby. But according to their website the company hopes to expand their Bitcoin operations, with many additional plants planned around the world.

In the small, quiet town of Murphy, North Carolina, crypto miners, Prime Rock have set up shop. 'This morning its running at 85 decibels', one resident told journalists.[17] 'It sounds and feels like you're behind a jet sitting on the tarmac and that jet never leaves. Or imagine being inside of Niagara Falls and not being able to get rid of the noise ever, like your house is dead centre of Niagara Falls.' The noise from the facility was said to be equivalent to having a hairdryer blowing full power next to your face 24/7. Residents felt hopeless. 'I don't know if there is much we can do about it right now', a resident living near the mining centre explained. 'But what we're trying to do as a community is get it out to the public that if they see crypto mines coming up in their area, they need to do everything possible to ban them and not allow those to get on their grid.' A mining facility in Adel, Georgia was generating so much noise from cooling fans and other equipment that one local resident claimed to have installed eleven layers of insulation on her bedroom wall in a fruitless attempt to block the sound.[18] 'You can hear it five miles away from here', the resident said. 'It ripples our pond from the vibration with the machines. It's literally shaking your brain.'

While residents wanted rid of them, Dennis Porter of the 501(c)(4) non-profit Satoshi Action Fund seemed to suggest the state should be paying Bitcoiners to stay. Porter was lobbying state governments across the USA to give Bitcoiners access to oil from inactive orphaned wells.[19] Orphaning usually happens when an oil company goes bust before they've plugged their holes or remediated the site. 'It's a win-win-win for everybody', Porter said. 'It's an inarguable win for the environment. It's an inarguable win for the economy. And it's an inarguable win for those states that don't have to spend taxpayer dollars to plug these abandoned oil and gas wells.' Some found the inarguable claims ludicrous. According to de Vreis, 'when Bitcoiners talk about "going green" it quite literally comes down to burning more fossil fuels'.

Bitcoiners usually argued that miners were only really interested in cheap residual energy that would otherwise be wasted. But in Iceland in 2021, I spoke to many Bitcoin miners that were being kicked out because they were outcompeting more productive industries. Aluminium processors and green hydrogen plants were also on the lookout for cheap renewable energy.[20] Even if Bitcoin's energy were produced using only otherwise unwanted renewables all the time, a resulting renewables arms race would still be an ecological disaster. Tesla solar panels and 'Megapack' batteries have been rolled out in Texas to mine Bitcoin with '100 percent renewable energy'. Over their lifetime, these panels will have a carbon footprint just one tenth that of a similarly sized fossil fuel plant. But the panels will eventually die, leaving behind tonnes of silicon tetrachloride, lead, cadmium and arsenic. On average, a solar panel, if properly maintained, can last 30 years. But even without adding Bitcoin to the mix, by 2050 the death of all the worlds existing solar panels will result in 78 million tonnes of toxic compounds. That's a pile as tall as 430 toxic Burj Khalifas. And unfortunately, solar panels can't be burned for Bitcoin.

Wind power is less carbon intensive than solar. But one single turbine requires up to 350 tonnes of steel, copper and concrete. Hydropower is still the most popular renewable option for Bitcoiners, especially those hiding in China. But hydroelectric dams devastate local ecosystems too. Across Asia, they're responsible for the extinction of river dolphins and fish species. Two-thirds of the world's major rivers are already dammed, causing forest flooding and holding back sediments and nutrients from natural habitats downstream.[21] These hydropower facilities often emit as much carbon as conventional fossil fuel power plants. In the Amazon, hydro-power facilities are over ten times more carbon intensive than coal, and 1.3 per cent of all man-made emissions come from hydropower dams. Thousands of these dams in the USA were due to be removed to help remediate their ecological foot-prints.[22] But Bitcoin is stalling progress. Bitcoin necessitates wasting energy. And there is no such thing as wasting energy sustainably.

CLIMATE CHAOS AND CRYPTO

In February 2021, a storm in the central and southern states of the USA coincided with a polar vortex, causing temperatures to drop from 5°C, the seasonal average, to −14°C. In Texas, nuclear and gas power plants failed. Wind turbines froze solid and 4.4 million homes lost power for five days. Water pipes froze. Families were forced to melt snow for drinking water however they could, and 702 people died, mostly from hypo-thermia.[23] The severe temperatures battered other states too, but only the Texas grid fell. And the disaster was not without precedent. Back when Texas first established a state-wide network of power plants and pylons in the 1950s, much of their new electricity grid was meant to only last up until the year 2000, at which point it would all need upgrading. It never was. To avoid federal oversight, the state refused to integrate with either the Western or Eastern Interconnections: massive power grids, which together covered the entire USA besides Texas. Ten years before the winter storm – to the day – a similar cold snap snapped the tottery Texas grid. Power plants failed. People died. Federal regulators recommended urgent upgrades to ensure the network's reliability in extreme weather conditions. The recommendations were ignored. With the increasing body count, in 2022 the state grid operator, the Electric Reliability Council of Texas (ERCOT) devised a new energy management strategy. To prepare for more frequent and severe weather events caused by climate change, Texas would turn to Bitcoin.

The reason given for the seemingly bizarre energy policy was 'load balancing'. Bitcoin miners promising to 'stabilise the grid' could negotiate ten-year fixed supply agreements, paying around 2.5 cents per kilowatt hour. The going residential rate was 18.5 cents. A 'demand–response program' would enable power suppliers to ask miners to shut down their operations. If they did voluntarily, ERCOT would pay the company as credits towards future power. Miners from all over the world flocked to Texas, enticed by the low energy prices and lax environmental regulation. As of early 2023, the state was home to around 10 per cent of all the world's Bitcoin miners, who together were adding 20,000 megawatts of demand to the Texas grid. That's roughly equal to the amount of electricity used by the whole of Houston.

In July 2022, a heatwave brought 'exceptional drought' conditions to much of Texas – the highest categorisation of dryness – denoting 'widespread crop loss, dead rangeland, producers not planting fields, forestry, tourism, and agriculture sectors reporting significant financial loss, and extreme sensitivity to fire danger'.[24] Fourth of July celebrations in Texas had no fireworks in 2022, due to threats of wildfires and lack of water to put them out. While Texans suffered the heat with rolling blackouts, in Rockdale, Texas, Riot Blockchain[25] – owners of the world's biggest Bitcoin-mining centre – were reportedly to receive another 1.4 million gallons for its second centre, planned for Corsicana. One local activist, Jackie Sawicky, explained to me that the additional water demand would be enough to fill two Olympic-sized swimming pools every day. The 1,000 megawatts of electricity needed would be enough to power every home in the county ten times over. 'These people are parasites', she tells me. 'Riot spoke to us at a town hall meeting. They were honest. They said, "you people have two very important things for Riot: water, and the Navarro County electrical switching station".'

According to Texas Senator Ted Cruz, Bitcoiners were there to fix the grid without the need for government interference. 'A lot of people view Bitcoin as a consumer of energy', said Cruz at an event in October 2021. 'The perspective I'm suggesting is very much the reverse, which is [using Bitcoin] as a way to strengthen our energy infrastructure.' For Sawicky, the Bitcoiners' intentions were clear: 'They're coming here to exploit the shit out of us', she said. According to her, when the Bitcoin miners set up in Texas as data centre operators, the companies qualified for tax breaks. Meanwhile, 17 per cent of Navarro County live in poverty, struggling to make ends meet with limited state support.

According to energy management services firm Voltus, miners relocating to Texas could generate up to 10 per cent of their total revenue from demand–response credits.[26] Credits would be paid to miners from the bills of residential customers who would in turn see their rates rise by 5 per cent. Ordinary Texans were being asked to directly subsidise the profits of Bitcoin miners to the tune of $1.8 billion every year. In the summer of 2022, 268 Texans without fans or air conditioning suffered heat-related deaths.[27] Over the same period, Riot declared earning $9.5 million from credits paid by Texan bill payers – cash that could have been used to fix the broken grid.[28]

If Bitcoin miners chose not to shut down when requested, they would be charged the same standard rate as residential customers. But if mining under such market conditions were to remain profitable, or if the miners had no intention in paying their bills, the grid would likely collapse. In June 2022, another Bitcoin giant, Compass Mining, was reportedly booted out of their rented warehouses in the US state of Maine for skipping bills.[29] The electricity charges allegedly came to $1.2 million. The company moved to Texas.

PREYING ON THE POOR

Crypto miners have a keen nose for cheap energy anywhere. In May 2021, police in the UK raided an industrial estate in a deprived part of Sandwell in the West Midlands. 'On the surface it looked like a cannabis set-up', a West Midlands Police Sergeant told me in an interview. 'We used our police drone to look above the property which detected a heat source, a sign of a cannabis factory.' Once inside, police discovered 117 Bitcoin ASIC machines running from an improvised connection to the electrical grid. 'The power supply had been abstracted. The persons using this industrial unit hadn't paid for the power', the Sergeant said. 'Power companies have come across a number of these. It's a learning curve for me and my team. This is not something we are used to dealing with.' The outdated machines were so inefficient that they could only turn a profit with free (stolen) energy. With record high energy prices, the improvised grid connections were raising prices for regular households.

Crises commonly form a core part of the Bitcoin miner's business model. The industry thrives in vulnerable states, geopolitical grey zones and communities in conflict. Bitcoin miners have proved a reliable geographical marker for fossil fuel-related hostilities for years. Similar to the dental plaque-disclosing tablets that were popular when I was a child, Bitcoin-mining machines are gurgled around the global energy network, sticking in dark clumps to areas of industrial decline, endemic corruption and social deprivation. In the disputed territory of Abkhazia, on the borders of Russia and Georgia, Bitcoin mining has been blamed for overloaded electricity lines and power station fires, leaving some areas without power for days. Miners were attracted by the state-subsidised energy. But these subsidies were designed to reduce fuel poverty rather than increase profitability for Bitcoin miners.

Suffering from a vague geopolitical status, the Transnistrian Republic has become a regional centre for Bitcoin mining. Situated in the borderlands between the ex-Soviet republics of Moldova and Ukraine, Transnistria remains one of the most socially deprived areas in Europe. Shortly after Moldova declared sovereignty of the territory in 1990, Russian representatives of Transnistria established a Soviet republic. An armed conflict continued till 1992, ending with a political agreement leaving the territory as an awkward appendage to Moldova, but with continuing alignment towards Russian interests. Transnistria controls the biggest power facilities in the region, with the Moldovan government forced to buy 80 per cent of its electricity via Russian cables from an unrecognised country that broke away from its control. Russian and Chinese Bitcoin miners have flocked to the country's empty warehouses, making use of the electricity subsidised by Moldovans.

Similarly, in Kosovo, much of the country's electricity in the north is drawn from the Serbian grid. For that reason, many in northern Kosovo have not paid their electricity bill in over 20 years. The free electricity has turned the region into a Bitcoin-mining hub. But in December 2021, the Bitcoin burden for the Balkans' largest coal-fired power plant was too much. Rolling blackouts started happening and a 60-day state of emergency was declared, giving the government powers to confiscate wasteful energy operations such as Bitcoin mining. Eight months later the geopolitical plaque was revealed, and armed conflict between Serbia and Kosovo erupted.[30]

After China booted out its Bitcoiners in 2021, many miners jumped across the border into the coal-rich areas of Kazakhstan. As of 2023, nearly 18 per cent of the world's Bitcoins were being mined using Kazakh coal. The country is a fossil fuel oligarchy where coal-fired power plants prioritise the interests of powerful politicians and their Bitcoiner cronies.[31] Around 8 to 10 per cent of the country's electricity – produced using Soviet-era energy infrastructure – is used to mine cryptocurrencies for businessmen such as Zhanat Berikovich. With the support of the prime minister and Almaty's mayor, Berikovich's 180 megawatt coal-powered Bitcoin-mining centre near the eastern Kazakh city of Pavlodor was planning to expand to 500 megawatts. That's in spite of what was perhaps the world's first popular uprising against Proof of Work.

In October 2021, the Kazakhstan Electricity Grid Operating Company first stated that national power consumption was far exceeding sustainable levels due to crypto-mining consumers. As Bitcoiners continued to flock to Kazakhstan from China, months of electricity rationing and rolling winter blackouts followed for ordinary citizens. In January 2022, Kazakhstan burst. Anger over government corruption and regional energy inequality erupted on the streets of Almaty City. The protest spread across the country. Russian forces were invited in by the Kazakh authorities to quash the uprising. By the time the Russians left, 213 civilians were dead. Around-the-clock operations shortly followed to capture or kill the 20,000 so-called terrorists the Kazakh government held responsible for the uprising. Meanwhile, Kazakh crypto mining continued.

Plentiful corruption and optional taxes have made Armenia an up-and-coming hub for Bitcoiners. ECOS, the organisation managing the country's Free Economic Zone in Hrazdan, hosts more than 250,000 Bitcoin miners. The energy plant supplying ECOS is owned by the Russian state-controlled gas giant Gazprom. Following Russia's invasion of Ukraine, many countries pledged to end or restrict their oil and gas imports to curtail Moscow's revenues and hinder its war effort. Meanwhile, Bitcoiners didn't care where the gas came from, so long as it was cheap.

On the other side of the trenches, Ukrainians were inadvertently helping to keep the Bitcoin price and Russian profits high. Ukraine had always been a mecca for crypto. At the height of the Euromaidan protests in 2014, the country's Bitcoin miners were so prolific that they nearly brought down the whole global network. Nearly half of all the world's Bitcoins were mined here. For Bitcoiners, Ukraine's draw card was corruption. Even after the 2014 ousting of pro-Russian President Viktor Yanukovych, widely accused of electoral and financial fraud, trust in Ukraine's financial systems never improved. And shady Bitcoiners want it to stay that way, keeping crypto regulations vague and taxes optional. Hartej Sawhney, founder of Ukraine's largest crypto firm, Zokyo, put it like this: 'I like that it's corrupt here, we get to play the game that only elites in the US play. I don't need a lobbyist. [If] I need to pay someone at the border, I can. If I need to pay politicians, I can.'[32]

MERCHANTS OF DOUBT

Crypto is ruining the planet. But thanks to the crypto PR machine, where science gets in the way of profit potential, there are merchants of doubt for hire to flip the narrative on its head. The same playbook came in handy for other industries when the science proving their destructive impact grew irrefutable. Big tobacco, oil and chemicals companies with credibility problems have all turned to image-washing experts as an alternative to cleaning up their acts. As Naomi Oreskes and Erik Conway explained in *Merchants of Doubt*, when these industries are up against the wall, to delay regulation there is no point disproving the overwhelming evidence stacked against them concerning the impacts of their products. To continue business as usual, they need only create controversy, question the science and manufacture doubt.

For Bitcoin, the job of reframing an environmentally ruinous industry into a crown jewel of environmental innovation fell upon a clique of corporate whale investors, NGOs and intergovernmental organisations. Since August 2020, the software company MicroStrategy, led by co-founder and CEO Michael Saylor, has purchased nearly 130,000 Bitcoins, worth around $2.6 billion. In early 2021, Saylor asked other business leaders to follow his lead, including Elon Musk. The Tesla boss promptly put up $1.5 billion on behalf of the electric car maker to buy 43,200 Bitcoins. Crypto markets spiked in reaction, as did crypto miners' energy demands. Meanwhile, with the endorsement of the UN, a Crypto Climate Accord was established. The accord represented an industry pledge committing the entire crypto community to a net zero emissions target, using renewable energy generation, 'Proof of Green' carbon accounting and climate offsets by 2040.

The same month the accord launched, the International Energy Agency also released a report stating that over 50 million tonnes of CO_2 emissions had been avoided thanks to Tesla and other electric vehicle producers. Good news for Tesla. Except that, in 2021 alone, Bitcoin was responsible for nearly twice that amount. In response to these reports, a Twitter storm of climate-conscious Tesla fans urged Musk to rethink his Bitcoin buying. To appease the critics, Tesla withdrew Bitcoin as a payment option. But the move roiled cryptocurrency markets, which immediately shed $366 billion in value in a single day.

For Saylor and Musk, their crypto fortunes depended on controlling their critics. They needed to reframe the Bitcoin energy debate. For Bitcoiners, the Crypto Climate Accord had been a move by unpure crypto projects such as Ripple and Ethereum. Ripple had never needed miners, and in September 2022, Ethereum eventually transitioned away from them. The accord was effectively a non-proliferation treaty on Bitcoin mining. To combat it, Saylor and Musk convened a Bitcoin Mining Council.

Unlike the Crypto Climate Accord, which aimed to provide a centralised strategy for delivering cleaner cryptocurrencies, the apparent remit of Saylor and Musk's Council was to act as the industry's public relations mouthpiece. According to Saylor, the group's goal was not to change Bitcoin. 'You don't need to fix it. There's nothing wrong with it', he said.[33] The objective was to 'shape the narrative' and 'defend Bitcoin against uninformed and hostile energy critics'.

Because Bitcoin-mining outfits move about haphazardly between war zones and geopolitical grey areas, while depending on a competitive spirit of secrecy, estimating the network's energy use at any one time is subject to uncertainties. Bitcoin uses more energy than medium-sized countries, so country comparisons are popular. As of late 2022, the Cambridge Centre for Alternative Finance showed Bitcoin using more electricity than Belgium. The independent Digiconomist platform, compiled by Alex de Vries, showed the network oscillating between the Czech Republic and Argentina. While both platforms share their methodologies online, the Bitcoin Mining Council got its numbers from a quarterly self-reported survey circulated among its members, which altogether, they claimed, controlled half the world's Bitcoin hash rate. The underlying specifics of this were not publicly shared. But based on the council's survey, 60 per cent of Bitcoin's energy was being supplied by renewables, including nuclear. Meanwhile, peer-reviewed research described how Bitcoin's renewable energy share fell from around 40 per cent in 2020 to 25 per cent by 2022, as miners stopped using Chinese hydro and moved elsewhere.[34] While Bitcoin miners have self-reported year-on-year increases in green mining, third-party evidence appeared to show the opposite: Bitcoin's environmental performance continues to decline.

The crypto industry's greenwashing campaign found strong support among fossil fuel companies keen to use Proof of Work to boost their profits. According to *Bitcoin Magazine*, Shell Oil had agreed to sponsor the Bitcoin Conference in Miami for at least two years. Crusoe Energy had reportedly been recognised by the World Bank for its 'innovations', capturing residual gas and burning it for Bitcoin mining.[35] Traditionally, with limited local customer demand, oil companies would flare off the methane gas emitted from oil wells. With Bitcoin, energy giants such as ConocoPhilips and Exxon have reportedly followed Crusoe's lead.[36] But the only difference between setting fire to methane and setting fire to methane for Bitcoin is that the latter makes the oil industry much more profitable, slowing transitions to cleaner alternatives.

Fossil fuel interests have always set the stage for climate policy while tackling hostile energy critics. Exxon reportedly ploughed millions into climate change research in the 1970s and 1980s – resulting in spookily accurate climate predictions – before spending similar amounts on greenwashing, lobbying and cover-ups.[37] BP was the first to popularise the neoliberal idea of 'individual carbon footprints', while Shell pushed the deflective term 'nature-based solutions'. Bitcoiner oil giants, such as Shell, Exxon and ConocoPhillips, were all founding members of the International Emissions Trading Association (IETA), an oil industry lobby group who – according to a top executive at Shell – wrote much of the Paris climate agreement.[38] And while fossil fuel companies were helping to reframe the crypto industry's energy debate, IETA members also saw opportunities for blockchain innovation to greenwash them.

CRYPTO CARBON

In 2019, I was invited by the UN Environment Programme (UNEP) to present the findings from my research project looking at the promises and pitfalls of blockchain for tackling climate change.[39] Around 40 software engineers, ecologists and other academics gave their advice at the meeting in Washington, DC. After two days, each impartial scientific expert agreed that blockchain was unlikely to offer any improvement to already existing approaches to managing energy and climate change. At the end of the meeting, the UNEP's new position on blockchain seemed clear: 'This technology is key to innovations in energy and climate change.'[40] UN bodies and the World Bank, with help from the IETA, appeared to set about strapping a blockchain to every failing market-based mechanism they had for environmental management. In their view, everything from biodiversity loss to ocean plastics and deforestation could be managed more profitably by selling cryptocurrencies, rather than fixing the actual problem.

Climate change would be fixed with a cryptocurrency called Chia. The World Bank and IETA had chosen Chia for their new 'Climate Warehouse' shop, because of the network's eco-friendly credentials. Chia allowed anyone with spare hard drive space to become a 'Chia Farmer'. The network was marketed as 'the green cryptocurrency' because instead of requiring a constant turnover of ASIC mining machines, Chia used a so-called Proof of Space and Time (PoST) system that relied on farmers constantly downloading as many digital lottery tickets as they could fit on their hard drives. When Chia was unveiled in mid-2021, it was possible to win the PoST lottery with just a few terabytes of disc space. But just two weeks after launch, global demand for hard drives soared. The problem became particularly acute for solid state drives, which have a limited number of uses before they break. The network achieved decentralisation, just like Bitcoin: by wasting energy and hardware. But instead of chewing through ASICs, which can only mine Bitcoin, Chia was attacking digital infrastructure that could have been used for something better.

Climate Warehouse was a plan to bring all the world's carbon credit markets under one roof. It didn't matter that carbon credits hadn't achieved any emissions reductions in over 25 years. For the IETA's fossil fuel and cryptocurrency interests, anything else besides carbon markets was bad for their bottom line.

Crypto and carbon credits are like peas in a pod: they're both fantasy assets, ripe for fraud.[41] Carbon trading was born in June 1999, when the IETA, led by BP, convened its first formal meeting after the signing of the Kyoto Protocol at the International Petroleum Exchange in London. Their objective was to push a plan for business-as-usual pollution, with free market magic providing a cost-effective pretence of sustainability. In 1987 – to save life as we know it – the world came together to decisively ban ozone-depleting chlorofluorocarbons (CFCs) at the Montreal Conference. Ten years later, fearing a similarly heavy-handed approach to fossil fuels, the world's neoliberals stormed the Kyoto summit to establish a profitable set of market-based alternatives.

An EU report found that 85 per cent of carbon projects had a 'low likelihood' of delivering any emissions reductions.[42] But the IETA's idea of making climate action profitable for fossil fuel interests was working. In February 2022, for example, Australia's Karoon Oil purchased around half a million carbon credits to make their oil-drilling project in Brazil 'carbon neutral'. Karoon's oil would produce 6.3 million tonnes of CO_2. The producer of these credits? The Shell Oil company. Meanwhile, Shell remained committed to exploring for new sources of oil and gas and still does not have any plans to reduce the overall amount of oil and gas it produces. Though sometimes profitable, these projects have always been a 'worse-than-nothing solution' for climate change.[43] Clearing forests of indigenous communities to make way for carbon projects has often forced these communities into destructive livelihoods, such as poaching and illegal logging.

WORSE-THAN-NOTHING SOLUTIONS

Offsets are cheap. But for tackling climate change, they are ultimately meaningless. Today, the price of offsetting a lifetime's worth of pollution is less than the cost of your average bouquet of flowers. It is easy to offset 581 tons of fossil fuel smoke, about as much as the average European generates in 80 years, for $30. Some third-party-validated outfits offer the same service for just 40 cents.[44] Blockchain technology was key to innovations in energy and climate change. Meanwhile, because no globally coordinated action has ever taken place to tackle the market drivers of climate change – overconsumption – man-made emissions are rocketing. More than half of all our CO_2 emissions have occurred after 1997, when carbon markets were first established as humanity's corner-stone mechanism for tackling climate change. But for the free market fundamentalist architects of international climate change agreements, blockchain could fix everything. In the traditional spirit of Web3, climate crises simply needed to be built around the solution. And if those problems didn't already exist, they could be talked into existence. For the UNEP, World Bank and IETA, the problem with carbon credits wasn't that they were all made of fairy dust. The problem was they weren't profitable enough.

In 2021, I visited the Rimba Raya forest reserve in Indonesia. A carbon credit, representing a single tonne of CO_2, had been produced here and sold as an NFT for $70,000. At the time, millions of credits from the same project were trading on carbon markets for less than $20 each. The NFT sale had been organised by SavePlanetEarth, a company based 7,000 miles from Rimba Raya, in a garage in Bradford, UK. SavePlanetEarth's idea involved purchasing carbon credits, then minting them as NFTs, before reselling them for a profit with cryptocurrency. Using NFTs like this would allow traders to speculate on future climate sentiments.

Normally, when someone offsets their emissions with certified carbon credits, the purchased credits are 'retired' from a registry. Once retired, it shouldn't be sold again. This prevents polluters from claiming to have offset their emissions before reselling the same credits to another polluter. But thanks to the magic of blockchain, minting NFTs was enabling carbon credit markets to become completely divorced from reality.

SavePlanetEarth was not the only carbon cowboy to get in on the act. Others cropped up almost weekly, all claiming to be 'the first blockchain marketplace for carbon'. In November 2021, the Bitcoin billionaire and reality TV star Mark Cuban was reportedly investing $50,000 every ten days in a cryptocurrency called Basic Carbon Tonnes (BCTs). Each token allegedly represented one tonne of avoided emissions and they were being issued by a project called Toucan Protocol. BCTs could be locked up, or 'staked', on a sister project called KlimaDAO. For doing so, KlimaDAO promised up to 35,000 per cent annual percentage yield.

To make their tokens hold water, the project acquired over 22 million of the cheapest carbon offsets from the largest carbon credit registry, Verra. Much of these offsets came from dubious 'zombie' projects, which even Verra agreed were so detached from reality they were no longer legitimate.[45] Verra sold them anyway. But in May 2022, the registry cancelled all sales to crypto traders. According to Verra, carbon trading with BCTs was like trading ghosts.[46] Retired credits were potentially being used to offset emissions over and over again.

KlimaDAO's response was defensive, dismissing Verra as a 'legacy intermediary'. They stated in a press release:[47]

We will continue to work with our constellation of partners to further develop the on-chain carbon market. The beauty of DeFi [Decentralised Finance] is that anyone can build novel applications and integration with existing platforms. On-chain carbon is here to stay and will continue to serve its purpose as both an offsetting instrument and as an environmental asset.

KlimaDAO's tokens have dropped in price from $3,700 last year to $3. But in November 2022, the UN Development Programme (UNDP) still sang the project's praises. Their #Web3for2030 report dedicated several pages to explain how 'KlimaDAO is helping to achieve the SDGs'. Meanwhile, analysis of on-chain data showed that Mark Cuban had made almost $2 million in profits from the failed project.[48]

In May 2022, billionaire businessman Adam Neumann made his debut launching a carbon credit cryptocurrency called Flowcarbon. Neumann was the disgraced CEO of the co-working office space company WeWork. His project's underbonnet was described by Verra's chief legal officer, Robert Rix, as 'mind frying'. 'Carbon credits themselves are abstract intangible things based on counterfactuals of things that you can't actually see – emissions. And then crypto is another layer of abstraction on top of that', he said. Like SavePlanetEarth, Flowcarbon's offsets were not being retired. The project's developers argued that this allowed their offsets to 'retain full off-chain value'. Despite being ultimately meaningless for action on climate change, Flowcarbon raised $70 million in start-up capital, mainly from big polluters such as Samsung and VC firm A16z.

GARBAGE IN, GARBAGE OUT

The problem crypto carbon projects professed to fix was the disintermediation of greedy or untrustworthy third parties such as Verra. To achieve this, some carbon projects turned to blockchain 'oracles'. These software programmes were used to connect real-world forest monitoring to smart contracts on a blockchain. GainForest, for example, was a Microsoft-funded project developed by Switzerland-based researcher David Dao. His project provided smartphones to volunteers recruited from rural villages in the Philippines. These villagers were rewarded with a cryptocurrency called Filecoin for taking photos and mapping the locations of the trees they'd been tasked with planting. But using humans and oracle devices like this often resulted in what software engineers call the 'garbage in, garbage out' dilemma. If data are entered incorrectly, either deliberately (by a bad actor) or mistakenly (due to human error), conflicts cannot easily be resolved 'on-chain'. More often than not, mistakes are never resolved, and so: garbage in, garbage out. This raises the question: what's the point in using a blockchain?

'We can't value what we can't measure', GainForest frequently tweeted. But measuring things often made everything worse. Even when forest monitors did a grand job, real-world conditions quickly changed from what was recorded on the blockchain. In July 2022, data collectors working for the Dutch crypto carbon outfit Land Life destroyed far more forest than they purportedly 'saved' in Zaragoza, Spain. Five villages were evacuated and a railway line was closed after equipment operated by Land Life sparked a wildfire. The fire destroyed 14,000 hectares of forest. It was the second wildfire attributed to the company that month. Meanwhile, the company raised $3.5 million for their carbon trading efforts.

It wasn't just problems with carbon markets that crypto companies claimed to fix. A Canadian enterprise known as Plastic Bank was offering poor people cryptocurrency to clean up after some of the world's worst plastic polluters. The organisation sold the collected plastic to other companies, greening their image in exchange for real cash. Plastic Bank claimed to have prevented millions of kilos of plastic from polluting the ocean. One of the company's brand partners, SC Johnson's Chairman and CEO Fisk Johnson,[49] said: 'We want to help recover plastic equal to the amount we put into the world, through innovative recycling and recovery programs. In this way we can neutralise our environmental impact and, at the same time, do some good in communities that have excessive plastic pollution.'

When I visited Plastic Bank's collection depot in September 2022 – sandwiched between two wellness spas in the trendy Balinese town of Canggu – the profit-driven Web3 logic of the project was clear. Rather than encouraging polluters to find alternatives to plastic, Plastic Bank would provide green washing services using crypto. And thanks to SC Johnson, Bali remains a place with 'excessive plastic pollution'.

TACKLING CRYPTO'S CLIMATE DISASTER

Blockchain is not helping but rather cancelling out real environmental wins. The European Parliament, for example, has approved a new law banning the sale of petrol and diesel cars from 2035. The law is designed to speed up transitions to electric vehicles. The global takeup of electric vehicles is estimated to have prevented 50 million tonnes of CO_2 so far. That's about half of Bitcoin's emissions for 2022 alone. Accelerating efforts with carbon capture technology is completely futile with crypto in tow. Nineteen direct air capture facilities are currently in development globally. The largest carbon capture and storage facility captures 40,000 tonnes of CO_2 each year. That's like taking 20,000 cars off the road. But the facility would need to run for 1,875 years to offset just Bitcoin's emissions for a single year.

The environmental consequences of crypto were no surprise to early Bitcoiners. The man who received the first Bitcoin from Satoshi Nakamoto in 2009, Hal Finey, voiced his concerns about Bitcoin's inevitably huge CO_2 emissions via Twitter just two weeks after their experiment kicked off. Finey died in 2014, just before the full environmental calamity of crypto became clear.

Taking effective environmental action is tough when profit potential is high. The outcome of Finey and Nakamoto's blockchain innovation mirrors that of leaded petrol and CFC developer Thomas Midgley Jr. Even the Romans knew that lead caused neurological problems in kids and should be left alone. But in 1923, Midgley Jr of Standard Oil (now Exxon) discovered that adding lead to petrol prevented engine 'knocking'. Midgley named his new toxic substance 'ethyl', avoiding all mention of lead in his reports and advertising campaigns. Today, thanks to Midgley's technology, millions of people die each year from lead exposure, the same fate as many of Midgley's co-workers. Midgley later went on to invent CFCs. Like Finey, he died years before the climate-changing impacts of his invention threatened mass extinction.

Leaded petrol was only eventually banned because doing so would have a minimal impact on corporate profits. By the 1990s, most car engines no longer needed leaded petrol to run properly. Likewise, we already have better alternatives to Proof of Work. But despite the climate breakdown, Bitcoiners are resistant to change, because they profit from that breakdown.

4

Bad Samaritans

Nearly every large charitable organisation was drawn to crypto as a lucrative fundraising opportunity. Many saw it as an experiment to test potentially more efficient ways of providing assistance to their local beneficiaries. Transparency was also a key selling point. Donors could set conditions on their donations and track the impact it was having. Meanwhile, the charity's job could seemingly be outsourced to computer code. It was an ideal fit for utilitarian donors, as they were able to calculate which causes would provide the biggest bang for their buck. They could guarantee charities wouldn't mess with the donor's bottom line. For charities and beneficiaries, meanwhile, the impacts of digital automation were less desirable. The illusion of unmediated giving enabled a power shift. Humans with expertise and accountability were swapped out for anonymous crypto hobbyists and bad Samaritans.

These bad Samaritans were blockchain developers. Using other peoples' problems, they set out to sell new suckers a range of Web3 snake oils. For crypto projects, their new charity partners weren't only needed to bring in the loot. Without the presence of image-washing aid agencies and seemingly legitimate good causes, the blockchain scam would have collapsed a long time ago.

'BITCOIN FOR GOOD'

Like many wacky religious cults, crypto enthusiasts celebrated a calendar full of annual festivities. Genesis Day celebrates the birth of Bitcoin (3 January). Penis Day takes place each year on 28 January. The celebrations go back to the peak of the ICO boom of 2017, when a cryptocurrency start-up called Prodeum promised to 'revolutionise the fruit and vegetables industry', allowing environmentally conscious people to track the provenance of their food on the Ethereum blockchain. But then one fateful Sunday, slick visuals were replaced on the project's website with a completely blank screen, but for one word scrawled in small-font nihilism: 'penis'. It appeared the developers had performed a good ol' exit scam, leaving duped investors with nothing. Then there's Pizza Day. This goes back to 2010, when software developer and Bitcoin miner Laszlo Hanyecz sent someone 10,000 Bitcoins to buy him two Papa Johns pizzas. Later, Hanyecz would be ridiculed in an annual crypto celebration taking place every 22 May. The Brazilian city of Porto Alegre went on to officially add Pizza Day to its municipal festivities calendar. Articles would be published annually in crypto news outlets announcing the present value of those 10,000 Bitcoins ($240 million as I write this). In doing so, Pizza Day was a dog whistle message to Bitcoiners to always hold and never use their crypto. But there's a paradox here. By using his Bitcoins, Hanyecz showed it was possible for make-believe internet money to have real-world value. Without the pizza purchase, the community of Bitcoin early adopters, including Hanyecz, would be sitting on piles of worthless crypto beans.

Hanyecz's purchase is commonly recognised as the first time Bitcoin was used as a payment method. But the Papa Johns pizzas were actually sold for US dollars to Hanyecz's acquaintance, who arranged the delivery in exchange for Bitcoin. It wasn't until June 2011 – following the blockade of WikiLeaks by Visa, MasterCard and PayPal – that Julian Assange proved Bitcoin could do things without pesky payment providers.

With no other options, WikiLeaks appealed for donations in Bitcoin and would go on to fight another day. Assange later commented that he made a 50,000 per cent return on his otherwise useless Bitcoin holdings as a direct result of the WikiLeaks crypto appeal. But not everyone in the Bitcoin community was happy. One of the last posts Bitcoin's creator, Satoshi Nakamato, wrote before he disappeared made a direct reference to the emerging story of WikiLeaks. He wrote in 2010:

> The project needs to grow gradually so the software can be strengthened along the way. I make this appeal to WikiLeaks not to try to use Bitcoin. Bitcoin is a small beta community in its infancy. You would not stand to get more than pocket change, and the heat you would bring would likely destroy us at this stage.

Similar to Hal Finey's warning that Bitcoin would be an environmental disaster, just before vanishing from forums forever, Nakamoto warned: 'WikiLeaks has kicked the hornet's nest, and the swarm is headed towards us.' But for Bitcoin whales, such as Assange, if no one was doing something good with crypto, it was all just environmentally toxic money-laundering tokens. With such a public image, Assange predicted, the price would crash, and the regulatory hornets would be compelled to stamp it out.

Assange's fears were rooted more in conspiracy theory than an understanding of how global financial regulators operate. Yet to preserve the Bitcoin movement past its 2017 necrosis of criminality, another anonymous whale (or whales) going by the name of Pine took another hit for the Bitcoin team. 'I'm going to remain anonymous', Pine said, 'because the point of the Pineapple Fund is not me. If you're ever blessed with a crypto fortune, consider supporting what you aspire our world to be.' The Pineapple Fund was a crypto giveaway of 5,104 Bitcoins donated to 60 charities. But these weren't worthless pizza Bitcoins. By 2017, this was nearly $100 million. In December that year, with ICO exit scams breaking out everywhere, a *New York Times* annual round-up explained how the Pineapple Fund was the only good thing to happen in crypto in 2017: 'Whoever Pine is, he or she seems to have found a way to convert Bitcoin into something actually useful.'

The Pineapple Fund kicked off an exciting new fundraising opportunity for charities. Accepting donations from new crypto cash cows, many advertised the tax-dodging benefits of donating via crypto-giving platforms. Crypto giving was sold as more 'tax-efficient' compared to selling the crypto – usually attracting capital gains tax – and then donating the after-tax proceeds. Payment intermediaries such as the Giving Block gave charities the ability to accept crypto donations while connecting them to networks of whales. Thousands of non-profits signed up, covering nearly every charitable cause. And then came NFTs.

NFTS FOR GOOD

Gifting digital art, like real art, was a favourite for philanthropists struggling to manage their tax liabilities. The value of an NFT wasn't connected to its brilliance, beauty or physical form, making NFTs a breeze to overvalue. Digital art was also far easier to wash, trade and cheaper to frame. Crypto-Punk7804, for example – a pixelated blue face smoking a pipe – sold for $7.5 million. NFTs, like in traditional art markets, are commonly valued based on their price history. With crypto, all transactions are visible to anyone using a blockchain explorer. But it's not possible to tell the difference between a legitimate trade and someone just moving NFT tokens between their own wallet addresses.

This sort of market manipulation wasn't only occurring on the periphery. In January 2022, the former US first lady, Melania Trump, auctioned an NFT image from her 2018 state visit to France. The piece sold for $180,000. The lucky winner? Melania Trump.[1] In March 2021, 'Everydays: The First 5000 Days' smashed the record for the most amount of money paid for a single digital image. It was the first NFT to be auctioned by Christies, selling for $69 million. The single jpeg file featured a large digital mosaic composed of images that the artist, known as Beeple, had already released online, one a day, since 2007. The buyer reportedly hadn't even looked at it before handing over his crypto. 'It didn't need a preview', he said. 'This is going to be a billion-dollar piece someday.'[2] The mastermind behind the purchase was later revealed as the crypto entrepreneur Vignesh Sundaresan, who had, according to the journalist Amy Castor, purchased the piece to boost the reputation and value of his own crypto investment scheme, Metapurse.[3] Beeple himself reportedly owned a percentage of the total supply of Metapurse tokens. Following the Christie's sale, the tokens' value went from 36 cents per token to $23. The very obvious conclusion observers reached was that none of this was about the art at all.

Even after NFT markets crashed in 2022, tax-dodging services emerged to ease the sting. It worked like this. Say you purchased an NFT in 2021 for $1 million. Then in 2022, you and everyone else realises NFTs are nothing more than a worthless numerical entry on a blockchain. You still need to find someone willing to take it off your hands before you can claim it as a loss on your tax assessment. Lucky for you, projects such as Unsellable would buy your NFT for around one cent (plus a small fee). 'This tool really helped me unload those embarrassing early NFT hype investments. Should shave about $1,000 off my tax bill', a supposed user wrote in a testimonial blurb on Unsellable's website.[4]

Ex-Twitter CEO Jack Dorsey sold his first ever tweet as an NFT for just under $3 million. The money went to Give-Directly. While a bog-standard crypto kitty would set you back around $60 in 2017, a cartoon drawing of a cat-turtle named Honu from the same collection raised $25,000 for Sea Shepherd. There were various cartoon apes selling for $850,000, with the money going to Virunga National Park. In February 2022, WWF joined the crypto circus with its Tokens for Nature collection. But before the fundraiser had even started, the project sparked a backlash from environmentalists online, pointing out the collection's massive carbon footprint.

Crypto consultancy firms such as LibraTax, exchanges such as Coinbase and crypto-fundraising platforms such as BitGive offered advice to the super-rich for tax-efficient NFT giving.[5] To them, tax men were a corrupt constraint on the relationship between donors and beneficiaries. But this framing of the state as a corrupt entity has meant many poorer countries have struggled to raise enough tax revenue to fund even the most basic services, such as healthcare and education. Tax dodging by the uber-rich also disproportionately squeezes the middle class and younger generations.

While the proportion of charitable giving from big philanthropic foundations was on the rise, tax-starved social services and stagnating wages meant young people were donating less. The myth of youth apathy has often been peddled by charities to deflect attention away from the more obvious issue of youth poverty. Young people who may have given regularly to charity are not supporting their preferred causes, often because they just can't afford to.[6] According to the Charities Aid Foundation, nearly 60 per cent of the UK public cut their level of charitable giving in 2022, rising to 70 per cent for younger people.

[INSERT BAD THING] FOR GOOD

For every cause, there was a coin. Happycoin was a Ponzi scheme that gave away 2.5 per cent of its takings to mental illness charities. Similarly, Elongate token was a Ponzi scheme that donated up to 3 per cent of funds raised to a range of good causes. The Elongate project was inspired by a Musk tweet following reports claiming that he had sexually assaulted a flight attendant.[7] The good causes partnered with Elongate included other pyramid schemes that gave away funds to good causes, such as Angel Protocol. Angel, according to their website, provided 'simplified endowments that empower charities to have funding, forever'. Angel donors were encouraged to pledge funds to their favourite charities using a stablecoin called Terra. This would increase in value – forever, somehow – and act as a perpetual endowment. Instead of donating funds directly to a charity, the protocol promised to issue them an annual yield. With the tag line, 'give once, give forever', Angel opened its donation box in April 2021. By 'forever', it turned out, they meant one year. Terra was exposed as a scam and crashed. The project's South Korean founder, Do Kwon, went into hiding, and in May 2023, was arrested in Montenegro for attempting to use forged travel documents.

Crypto giving was an easy way to onboard new users to crypto projects. The Bitcoin Water Trust, as its name suggested, was a 'crypto native fund'. The charity planned to raise 100 Bitcoin, which they promised to hold until at least 2025. Thanks to the Bitcoin twin whales Cameron and Tyler Winklevoss, the trust's first 50 Bitcoins were match-funded. After 2025, the charity hoped to distribute the Bitcoins to local water projects without converting them. For local partners to benefit, they'd also need to consider jumping on the Bitcoin bandwagon.

In February 2023, Mercy Corps Ventures launched their second Crypto for Good Fund: $1 million was up for grabs to projects proposing 'blockchain fixes for underserved populations'. Meanwhile, UNICEF launched their CryptoFund, offering grants denominated in Bitcoin and Ethereum to projects using data-driven solutions for 'the most pressing challenges facing children and young people'. Awards went to projects helping babies in India suffering neonatal sepsis and health care charities in Mexico. Even though real money would have been far more useful, grant recipients were forced to only spend the donated cryptocurrency in its native form, without converting it to local currencies. This would be particularly challenging for recipients in the Global South where internet access was low. But even if charities tried to break the donor's rules and save lives with real cash, international exchange restrictions made it impossible for local partners in 'high-risk' countries to cash out legally.[8]

For the Human Rights Foundation (HRF) the line between crypto advocacy and their stated charitable aims was barely visible. According to its original mission statement,[9] the purpose of HRF was 'to unite people – regardless of their political, cultural, and ideological orientations – in the common cause of defending human rights and promoting liberal democracy in the Americas'. HRF's founder and president was the Venezuelan film producer Thor Halvorssen. Despite the foundation's staff writing near weekly articles in *Bitcoin Magazine*, highlighting the environmental benefits of crypto mining over gold mining and 'petrodollar' oil wars, HRF had its fingers in all the polluting pies. One of Halvorseen's most famous works was his gold-mining movie, *Mine Your Own Business*.

The film was made in partnership with Gabriel Resources, a Canadian gold outfit, which aimed to turn a Romanian UNESCO world heritage site into a tailing pond of cyanide waste.[10] The *New York Times* dubbed the film 'the world's first anti-environmentalist documentary'.

The filmmakers went on to create pro-fossil fuel propaganda, including *FrackNation* and the climate change-denying documentary *Not Evil, Just Wrong*. HRF's chairman, Russian chess grandmaster Garry Kasparov, was also an ardent crypto fan who expected Bitcoin to replace the dollar within a decade.[11] But the group's most vocal Bitcoiner was its chief strategy officer, Alex Gladstein, who wrote prolifically for *Bitcoin Magazine*. Hosting Bitcoin's annual conferences in Miami, Ghana and Amsterdam, he stood in warm embrace with Leopoldo López. In 2002, using his own armed police force, López was a key figure in the failed right-wing military overthrow of Venezuela's President Hugo Chávez. López's actions were described by Amnesty International as some of the most serious human rights violations perpetrated during the short-lived coup. López is Thor Halvorssen's cousin.

Gladstein authored *Check Your Financial Privilege*, a book detailing how people in poor countries are using Bitcoin to shield themselves from 'government abuse' (otherwise known as tax). Much of HRF's grants fund projects designed to recruit new Bitcoin users in war-torn parts of the globe, as well as the development of new Bitcoin privacy features. HRF had reportedly received funding from big Bitcoiners such as Peter Thiel and right-wing organisations such as Donors Capital Fund. The donor-advised fund also granted money to Islamophobic and anti-gay groups, including some that Norwegian white supremacist Anders Breivik cited as inspiring his beliefs.[12]

THE OXFORD MAFIA

Giving crypto and NFTs away, like any form of philanthropy, has become a modern-day mode of paying medieval catholic indulgences. Countless bad apples have been celebrated for far longer than they deserved, thanks to their gifts to good causes. As well as tax dodging, crypto has allowed self-proclaimed visionaries to ensure their indulgences align directly with their preferred dreams for the future. And wherever Bitcoiners made a mess of things, there were a band of Oxford academics willing to accept their indulgences, in return for some big-picture longer-term perspective.

Longtermism was an excellent philosophy for any everyman-for-himself Bitcoin devotee. According to Oxford philosopher Nick Bostrom, longtermism goes beyond simply tackling myopias in policy making, or the need for caring a bit more about future generations. What mattered most for longtermists such as Bostrom – commonly described as the 'father' of the idea – was prioritising humanity's long-term potential in the cosmos over relatively petty problems currently suffered here on earth. Maximising humanity's reach involves subjugating nature, maximising economic productivity, engineering a superior posthuman species, colonising the universe, and ultimately creating an unfathomably huge population of conscious beings, living rich and happy lives, in or outside computer simulations.

For longtermism's disciples, existential threats were rarely imminent, but were far more likely to impact conscious beings living in the distant future. These included for example, issues with an artificial intelligence (AI) gone rogue, or an omnicidal government or group weaponising modified viruses. As far as the longtermists were concerned, everything else should be fixed on the cheap or with an AI some time in the future (so long as it doesn't go rogue). Essentially, longtermists cared deeply about the welfare of millions of potential future rich people living on other planets, while the lives of actually existing poor people were expendable. For Bostrom's followers, indigenous peoples and policymakers who didn't pine to live in the cold inhospitable emptiness of space, but instead aspired for society living in frugal abundance and conviviality with nature; well, that sort of thinking costs lives.

Bostrom, who in 2005 founded Oxford's modestly named Future of Humanity Institute, analysed the risks of delayed technological development. By his calculations, for every second we delay colonising the universe, hundreds of trillions of lives would be lost. To save lives, Bostrom proposed a range of measures, including the 'freedom tag': a recording device worn around the neck, bedecked with multidirectional cameras and microphones that monitor the wearer from cradle to grave. The gismos would guard us against those dabbling in DIY biohacking, triggering Armageddon with biological weapons or otherwise risking humanity's onward celestial expansions.[13] Such a move would be cost-effective too, said Bostrom. The entire world population could be continuously monitored at a cost of less than 1 per cent of global GDP. Bostrom also considered 'dysgenic pressures' into his calculations. 'Blacks are more stupid than whites', Bostrom once said on an extropian community message board.[14] 'I like that sentence and think it is true.' Bostrom then used an offensive slur beginning with 'N'. 'It seems that there is a negative correlation in some places between intellectual achievement and fertility', he argued. 'If such selection were to operate over a long period of time, we might evolve into a less brainy but more fertile species.' He later apologised for coming across as racist.

In a 2003 paper, Bostrom posited that advances in computing power will allow future generations to run a vast number of highly detailed simulations of their forebears. If this eventuality occurs, Bostrom claimed, 'then it could be the case that the vast majority of minds like ours do not belong to the original race but rather to people simulated by the advanced descendants of an original race'. On the basis of this paper,[15] Elon Musk was so committed to Bostrom's ideas that he pledged millions of dollars to the Future of Life Institute, a longtermist organisation co-founded by billionaire Bitcoiner and Skype founder Jaan Tallinn. Shortly after, Musk handed over the keys to his philanthropic foundation, worth $5.7 billion, to fellow longtermist, Bitcoiner and Russian high-stakes poker star Igor Kurganov.[16]

In the 2000s, drawing on ideas from the moral philosopher Peter Singer, a small group of Oxford academics, including William MacAskill, Hilary Greaves and Toby Ord, wanted to show how reason and evidence could be used to determine which cause areas should be prioritised for long-term impact. They called this school of thought the effective altruism (EA) movement. It was a big hit with Bitcoiners. Although the movement's ambitions seemed noble, as with most things crypto lovers cosied up with, it devolved into a steroid-pumped techno-fundamentalist version of whatever brought in the most cash. 'Do the most good that you can with your money', was the EA mantra, widely translated among crypto donors as 'create as much profit as possible'.

For effective altruists, there was nothing wrong with being a cut-throat billionaire, managing a hedge fund of fossil fuel stock options, or pushing crypto Ponzi scams on desperate people. 'Being a billionaire is not immoral', Singer said, 'so long as you don't die a billionaire'. The counter-intuitive logic behind this idea was known as 'mission hedging'. Take solving climate change. The Oxford longtermists argued that strategic divestment from profitable forest-chopping fossil fuel companies was like cutting one's nose to spite one's face. Far better to invest more money in the most profitable fossil fuel companies, then use some of your new spondoolies for forest conservation and carbon offsets. The movement was particularly attractive to Bitcoiners, because generating vast sums of untaxed wealth from crypto scams could be framed as the pinnacle of altruism.

The EA culture was hostile towards women. Several said they had experienced misconduct ranging from harassment and coercion to sexual assault within the community. An article published in February 2023 described a 'cult-like' culture of polyamory.[17] One women recalled being groomed by 'a powerful man' nearly twice her age who argued that 'paedophilic relationships were both perfectly natural and highly educational'. Another described an experience with an influential EA scout whose role included picking out promising students and funnelling them towards coveted jobs. After he arranged for her to be flown to the UK for a job interview, she recalled being surprised to discover that she was expected to stay in his home. She told *Time Magazine* that when she arrived, he told her that 'he needed to masturbate before seeing me'.[18] 'It puts your safety at risk', one Indian student wrote on the EA community message board, adding that most of the access to funding and opportunities within the movement was controlled by the frontmen. Women who complained were labelled as 'bigoted against polyamorous people'. Another said that complaints would 'pollute the epistemic environment', and was a 'net-negative for solving the problem'.

As the baby-faced frontman of the EA movement, MacAskill was also the celebrated author of *Doing Good Better*. For him, economic and technological stagnation was at least as significant a threat to humanity as climate change. For MacAskill and Co., worries about waste and plane pollution were 'just not that big a deal'. Responsibility for repairing the climate could be shifted onto future generations, so long as present generations stop delaying technological innovation. MacAskill did, however, argue that coal mines globally should be closed as soon as practicable. We'll need that coal to rebuild things once civilisation collapses, he said. Many big Bitcoiners got onboard. Elon Musk called MacAskill's philosophy 'a close match' to his own, while Peter Thiel, Sam Altman and Sam Bankman-Fried have also expressed diehard longtermist beliefs. For them, longtermism allowed time and space to be contorted in whatever way they liked to ensure maximum value. Luckily, the human development these celestial gymnasts were striving for also made them the richest people on earth, forever.

Émile P. Torres, author of *Human Extinction: A History of the Science and Ethics of Annihilation*, told me that for him, longtermism was one of the most influential ideologies that few people – outside of elite universities and Silicon Valley – had ever heard about. 'Much of it is like scientology, but dangerous', he said. 'I've come to see their worldview as possibly the most dangerous secular belief system in the world today.'

But the UN is embracing these ideas. In 2023, the UN General Assembly planned to host a 'Summit of the Future' to bring longtermist ideas to the centre of their decision making. They propose a Declaration on Future Generations and a United Nations Special Envoy to ensure that policy and budget decisions consider impacts for far future generations.[19]

By 2021, MacAskill had secured around $46 billion in committed funding, almost entirely thanks to the group's supporters in the crypto industry. MacAskill co-founded the Center for Effective Altruism and an Altman-backed non-profit called 80,000 Hours, which together became known as Effective Ventures. Thanks to MacAskill, Oxford University was the epicentre for longtermist ideas and new crypto industry cash. In 2021, Effective Ventures purchased Wytham Abbey, a palatial 25-acre Tudor estate just outside Oxford. Money, which no longer seemed an object, seemed to increasingly get reinvested in the community, rather than causes. Like the Berkeley Mafia – the group of influential economists who worked to force free market capitalism in Indonesia throughout the 1960s – or Milton Friedman's Chicago Boys, EA's Oxford Mafia set out to create their own economic miracle. And just like those previous disruptive miracles, those at the bottom would pay the price for crypto.

Back in 2018, Ben Delo was one of the first crypto entrepreneurs lured into the EA fold. As a fellow Oxford graduate and one of Britain's youngest billionaires, Delo was an easy catch. The 35-year-old founded BitMEX, a cryptocurrency trading company that facilitated more than $600 billion in trades in 2018. BitMEX's value was estimated at $3.6 billion, with Delo holding 30 per cent. Delo was reportedly inspired by MacAskill to pledge his fortune to the EA movement.[20] But in the meantime, Delo would set his sights on accruing as much crypto cash as possible.

After registering BitMEX in the Seychelles tax haven, Delo was indicted and pled guilty to US Bank Secrecy Act violations, receiving a 30-month probation sentence and a $10 million fine. Despite his commitment to the EA movement, the records highlighted Delo's questionable ethics. According to California court documents he and his co-founders were described as: 'Serial offenders when it came to disregard for the rule of law, as they have demonstrated both by their fraudulent misconduct in their dealings with Plaintiffs and their brazen indifference towards the authority of courts and regulators.'[21] When asked about the differences between various global regulatory authorities and those in the Seychelles, they reportedly responded: 'the Seychelles were a more friendly jurisdiction for BitMEX because it cost less to bribe Seychellois authorities – just a coconut – than it cost to bribe regulators in the United States and elsewhere'.[22]

The outcome of the BitMEX debacle left the Oxford Mafia unperturbed. Despite leaving many investors out of pocket, for the EA crypto community, Delo's actions were a victimless crime. As they say in crypto, 'you can't cheat an honest man'. Delo's BitMEX cash was the product of ill-gotten gains anyway. And besides, MacAskill had other crypto cash cows on the go, the fattest of whom was Bankman-Fried.

INEFFECTIVE ALTRUISM

Bankman-Fried was one of the lucky EA proteges picked out and funnelled towards a highly coveted job. He was reportedly persuaded to give away his Brewster's billions in 2012, when MacAskill convinced him to pursue an 'earn to give path'. Until then, Bankman-Fried was leaning towards becoming an academic. 'That was sort of the point at which I started to think in a more principled way about what I should do with my life', Bankman-Fried later said.[23] He was offered a job at the New York proprietary-trading firm Jane Street Capital, along with many other like-minded followers of MacAskill. Jeremy Rubin, the co-founder of MIT's Digital Currency Initiative, also had a short stint at Jane Street the same year. And like others, Bankman-Fried was later convinced to get into crypto to get filthy rich, for charity's sake.

Bankman-Fried made his first crypto killing in his twenties doing Bitcoin arbitrage tricks between US and Korean markets, profiting from the so-called kimchi premium. He founded two crypto-trading companies called Alameda Research and FTX, alongside the FTX Future Fund, a grant and investment-making organisation to 'improve humanity's long-term prospects'. Bankman-Fried said it would distribute up to $1 billion in 2022, for longtermist cause areas.

From 2018, MacAskill and other senior EA figures were warned repeatedly that Bankman-Fried's business practices were unethical. He was duplicitous and negligent in his role as CEO of Alameda Research. He was accused of having inappropriate sexual relationships with subordinates as well as refusing to implement even the most basic risk management practices. But MacAskill reportedly rejected the concerns as rumours.[24] Meanwhile, MacAskill's public endorsements enabled Bankman-Fried to accrue a net worth of somewhere between $16 billion and $24 billion. He purchased a castle in the Czech Republic and a $250 million property empire in the Bahamas, where he relocated FTX for tax purposes.

In late 2022, MacAskill intervened in Musk's Twitter takeover plans, offering Bankman-Fried's services as his 'collaborator' to make the platform more aligned with EA's charitable principles. 'You vouch for him?' Musk asked MacAskill. 'Very much so!' MacAskill replied. 'Very dedicated to making the long-term future of humanity go well.'

No one outside of his inner circle really seemed to understand how Bankman-Fried made so much money. But still, he was frequently described as 'brilliant'. Despite attending business meetings remotely while playing computer games, the VC firm Sequoia Capital described him as 'a genius' having 'achieved the status of legend', while Yahoo Finance said: 'Bankman-Fried is perhaps the most pioneering young entrepreneur of our time.' As it turns out, much of his money was of the home-made internet variety, otherwise known as FTT tokens.

As I write this, Bankman-Fried is facing charges of 'fraud, conspiracy to commit money laundering and conspiracy to defraud and violate campaign finance laws',[25] which carry a maximum sentence of 115 years. Prosecutors described FTX as 'possibly one of the biggest financial frauds in American history'. Just a few months earlier, MacAskill had been celebrating the launch of his book, *What We Owe the Future*, in which he argues: 'History is littered with people doing bad things while believing they were doing good. We should do our utmost to avoid being one of them.' The celebratory dinner was reportedly organised and hosted by Bankman-Fried.[26]

'You can't cheat an honest man', as they say in crypto. But on the FTX downline were thousands of broken lives. The Ontario Teachers' Pension Plan invested and lost $95 million in FTX. Much of the $160 million pledged to more than 110 non-profits by Bankman-Fried's longtermist Future Fund became subject to bankruptcy clawbacks. Not to mention the thousands of young people FTX left for dead in West Africa. As well as helping crypto companies defraud some of the poorest people on earth, the Oxford Mafia's development interventions caused many other human development headaches.

Because of the cold utilitarianism guiding their giving strategies, EA folks generally prioritised long-term challenges to future populations over warm fuzzy connections with real people. Hedgehog hospitals and orphanages rarely featured on the EA community's Christmas list, while malaria prevention was the most popular cause for crypto givers. Based on the EA calculator, malaria was devastating for future population growth, while the fix was good value for money. The cost of one mosquito net was less than a dollar. And distributing them required no specialist medical training or expensive infrastructure.

In the summer of 2022, I spoke to project managers in Malawi at Ripple Africa, a UK charity working with local governments and fishing communities. Much of their work revolved around dealing with the aftermath of massive mosquito net campaigns from EA-affiliated organisations. The nets were causing ecological devastation and malnutrition; challenges that required lots of expensive medical training and infrastructure. One project officer told me:

> It's the most frustrating thing. We work in villages where literally MILLIONS of these nets have been distributed, with no education. It's not uncommon for us to work with villages where more nets have been given than there are people, yet not a single household are using nets. Their homes and sleeping places are not built to hang nets. So they use them for storing produce or for farming. And of course, for fishing. We find discarded fishing nets made of several thousand donated bed nets. Locals who are given lots of malaria nets will often sell them to the fishermen. So there's this underground industry going on.

Just like the Web3 solution for tackling climate change with offsets, the EA approach to malaria prevention was cheap but ultimately meaningless. 'Our idea is simple: you just can't think with tick boxes', Ripple's rep told me. 'You cannot bring lasting change without building trust and you've got to have boots on the ground. Or it will always lead to unintended consequences.'

Guessing the fate of future humans distributed among far-flung star systems, when even the distribution of nets was being botched, says a lot about the EA calculator. But not all Oxford academics believed in the direction MacAskill and Co. had taken things. Oxford Professor Amia Srinivasan argued:[27]

Effective altruism, so far at least, has been a conservative movement, calling us back to where we already are: the world as it is, our institutions as they are. MacAskill does not address the deep sources of global misery – international trade and finance, debt, nationalism, imperialism, racial and gender-based subordination, war, environmental degradation, corruption, exploitation of labour – or the forces that ensure its reproduction. Effective altruism doesn't try to understand how power works, except to better align itself with it. In this sense it leaves everything just as it is. This is no doubt comforting to those who enjoy the *status quo* – and may in part account for the movement's success.

Crypto scammers such as Delo and Bankman-Fried were not the first big-name Oxford donors to be indicted. The Sackler family, whose OxyContin opioid painkillers killed more than half a million people, maintained strong philanthropic connections with Oxford University, even as other institutions cut ties. Megan Kapler, an activist at Prescription Addiction Intervention Now – a campaign group set up to target the Sacklers' 'toxic philanthropy' – said: 'For institutions to maintain the Sackler name is to be complicit in their death toll, full stop.'[28] Responding to calls for returning funds from dodgy donors – including a petition organised by Oxford's students – the university's vice-chancellor seemed to defiantly blame cancel culture.[29]

Web3 and EA philanthropy tessellated so neatly because they were both deeply conservative ideologies. Together they would come up with innovative new ways of profiting from problems while keeping everything the same, all with an illusion of radical disruption. As Michael Saylor said in November 2022: 'Bitcoin *is* effective altruism.'

CHARITY WITHOUT CHARITIES

In the world of Web3, there was no clear line between charity and business as usual. 'It's an appealing framework for billionaires', Rhodri Davies, author of *What Is Philanthropy For?*, told me. 'If you are somebody who has made a lot of money, you see yourself as exactly the best person to determine how money should be most rationally distributed in the world, and you'd be doing a disservice to the world if you didn't.'

Crypto allowed the uber-rich to fulfil their obligations to humanity without charities and tax men getting in their way or taking their money. But the wealthiest advocates of crypto tended to take a bizarre position on what constituted worthy causes. The Winklevoss twins invested millions in start-ups aiming to bring back woolly mammoths and Tasmanian tigers. For Musk, the companies that made him the richest man on earth – SpaceX, Tesla, Neuralink and The Boring Company – were all selfless acts of kindness:

Tesla is accelerating sustainable energy, which is philanthropy. SpaceX is trying to ensure the long-term survival of humanity as a multi-planet species. That is love of humanity, you know? Neuralink is trying to help solve brain injuries and existential risk with AI: Love of humanity. Boring Company is trying to solve traffic, which is hell for most people.

Thiel also had a collection of selfless causes on the go. He reportedly channelled millions into parabiosis start-ups.[30] The grisly practice involved surgically connecting individuals so that they share a bloodstream. The objective is to transfuse blood from a younger person as a means of improving health and potentially reversing ageing. Thiel's philanthropy funded the Methuselah Foundation, a forever young non-profit that aimed to make '90 the new 50 by 2030'. Brian Armstrong also pledged his Coinbase holdings to start-ups and charities 'working toward radical extension of human health-span using epigenetic reprogramming'.[31]

The crypto-giving practices of Bitcoiners tended to reflect their far-right political orientations. In the 2022 US elections, Thiel's investment in hand-picked far-right candidates shaped the narrative for the entire election. Meanwhile, Bankman-Fried dropped $93 million into politics. 'All my Republican donations were dark', Bankman-Fried said, referring to political donations that were not publicly disclosed. 'The reason was not for regulatory reasons, it's because reporters freak the fuck out if you donate to Republicans. They're all super liberal, and I didn't want to have that fight.'[32]

It wasn't just Bitcoin billionaires displaying fondness for far-right libertarian causes. In January 2022, a series of protests and blockades, known as the Freedom Convoy movement, took off after a Covid vaccine mandate was imposed on Canadian long-distance lorry drivers. By February, Canada's President Justin Trudeau invoked an Emergency Measures Act. The government's new powers aimed to stop organisers receiving public donations and tackle the major disruptions caused by the blockades. But Bitcoiners moved in, with campaigns like 'HonkHonkHodl', 'Freedom Convoy 2022' and 'Adopt a Trucker', raising nearly $1 million worth of crypto. With every wallet address blocked by police, new crypto addresses were set up and communicated via social media to keep the Covid conspiracy efforts going. But according to research by *The Intercept*, the majority of donors to Canada's 'Freedom Convoy' were American, including hundreds who were also members of the Oath Keepers, a far-right paramilitary organisation.

Stewart Rhodes, the Oath Keepers' founder, was the first insurrectionist to be charged with seditious conspiracy following the US Capitol riots.[33] Much of the funds were handled by a Bitcoin crowdfunding platform called Tallycoin. Big Bitcoin donors to Tallycoin included the Kraken exchange CEO, Jesse Powell, who reportedly sent a whole Bitcoin to the cause.[34] 'Fix the money, fix the world', Powell said. 'Mandates are immoral. End the madness. Honk Honk!' The crypto-fundraising tactics were repeated in the Netherlands in June 2022, when right-wing Bitcoiners turned their attentions to helping Dutch farmers protesting government regulations to control greenhouse gas emissions.

Bitcoiners showed limited motivations for funding a safer world. With their investments dressed up as charity, the war in Ukraine was an ideal opportunity for crypto platforms to profit from both sides of the conflict. Within hours of Russia's invasion in February 2022, crypto exchanges around the world were onboarding thousands of Russian punters in financial pickles and desperate Ukrainians seeking refuge elsewhere. The California-based exchange Kraken announced that it would donate $10 million to Ukrainians opening new Kraken accounts. Bankman-Fried promised $25 to each Ukrainian on FTX. At the same time, most exchanges were committed to non-compliance when Ukraine's government asked the exchanges to cut Russians off from their wallets. Binance justified its stance, stating: 'Crypto is meant to provide greater financial freedom for people across the globe. To unilaterally decide to ban people's access to their crypto would fly in the face of the reason why crypto exists.'

With the help of crypto exchanges, Russians continued to evade international sanctions. According to the crypto consultancy firm Chainalysis, pro-Russian paramilitary groups, including Rusich – a branch of the Wagner Group

– raised millions of dollars in cryptocurrency donations. Rusich's crypto addresses were circulated across their social media accounts without attracting any regulatory action. Alexander Zhuchkovsky, a sanctioned Russian national, used social media to solicit crypto donations for the Russian Imperial Movement, a 'Specially Designated Global Terrorist group'. Zhuchkovsky also posted support for Project Terricon, which was soliciting crypto donations to support Russian militias in Donbas. Terricon explicitly stated on their website that they were using crypto due to the imposition of sanctions while also selling NFTs for fundraising. But thanks to high-profile crypto-giving campaigns, including a fundraising arrangement between FTX and the Ukrainian government, conservative politicians, and regulators in Europe and the USA, were convinced Bitcoin was a blessing for their Ukrainian allies. $60 million was raised through a campaign run by the Potemkin village of FTX. After that village collapsed, many questions remain unanswered: where did those funds end up? Were they used to buy a castle, or penthouse in the Bahamas, or for political lobbying in the USA? Perhaps we will never know.

With all the crypto-sponsored wars and Covid conspiracies going on, Thiel planned to wait out the impending apocalypse in his bunker in Wanaka, New Zealand. He reportedly bought his New Zealand citizenship after 'living' there for twelve days. Normal people are required to live and work in the country for at least 3.5 years. In 2016, Worldcoiner Sam Altman revealed his arrangement with Thiel, where in the event of some kind of social collapse scenario they would both get on a private jet and sit out the collapse in Thiel's Bilbo Baggins bolthole.[35]

Democratic institutions were generally an annoyance for crypto billionaires. Thiel used some of his billions to intervene in other people's court cases and settle old scores. In 2016, after the gossip blog *Gawker* mentioned that Thiel was gay, Thiel retaliated by financing wrestler Hulk Hogan's lawsuit against the website over its posting of a Hogan sex tape. The suit, which resulted in millions of dollars in damages being awarded to Hogan, forced *Gawker* out of business, with Thiel taking a healthy cut for his litigation financing.[36] As Thiel said, 'it is far easier to change the world when you don't have to constantly convince people and beg people and plead with people who are never going to agree with you. Technology is this incredible alternative to politics.'

THE GIVING DAOS

The rapid ascent of crypto giving appears somewhat inversely proportional to a fall in public trust towards charities. In 2018, thousands of Oxfam supporters ditched the charity follow- ing allegations that senior staff had hosted sex parties with local prostitutes in Chad and Haiti. In the same year, over 200 abuse cases were reportedly committed by Oxfam and other UK charity shop workers.[37] The UK government refused to consider any applications for funding from Oxfam following allegations of abuses by its field staff in DRC.[38] The conser- vation charity WWF was also on the ropes after a *Buzzfeed* investigation alleged they were funding military training for national park guards across Africa. The report revealed that guards had raped and murdered local indigenous people. WWF was also embroiled in arms deals with a rebel army in CAR.[39] To bypass dodgy charities, blockchain promised a rev- olutionary shift to algorithmically secured change-making, with DAOs.

Using smart contracts, DAOs are meant to function like lead- erless VC funds, with an added bonus of zero liability towards investors when things go wrong. Upon signing over their

assets, investors get issued roles, voting rights and other priv-
ileges within the organisation. Their decisions are recorded
and/or executed automatically, depending on the outcomes
of votes. Voting rights are usually allocated based on relative
governance token holdings. One token equals one vote. It's
similar to shareholder voting rights in a traditional centralised
company, the only difference being that overall accountability is devolved to anonymous token holders. Or rather, no
one. Today there are thousands of DAOs. But back in April
2016 there was only *the* DAO, a project that raised over $139
million worth of Ethereum. In June 2016, a hacker siphoned
off a third of all the DAO's takings, representing about 5 per
cent of the global supply of Ethereum, which today would be
worth around $11 billion. The price of Ethereum promptly
crashed. To patch things up again, Ethereum's core developers pressed pause on the entire 'decentralised' blockchain,
rewound the transaction history to a point just before the
hack and 'hard forked' the blockchain. The original (hacked)
version was renamed Ethereum Classic.

Since the hack, DAOs have evolved from just being investment vehicles to fulfilling other functions. There are DAOs
that run play-to-earn gaming guilds. There are DAOs that run
Ponzi schemes. In September 2021, a DAO was launched with
the sole aim of buying an original copy of the US constitution
at a Sotheby's auction in New York. The document was one of
only eleven printed copies and the only privately owned copy.
To prevent the document falling back into a private collection
a group of developers set up ConstitutionDAO. Their objective was to crowdfund and place a bid of around $40 million
worth of Ethereum, before demanding the document be displayed in a public place. Because ConstitutionDAO's total
treasury was completely transparent, competing bidders knew
exactly how high they would need to bid in order to win the

auction. ConstitutionDAO lost. But once ConstitutionDAO's failure became clear, the messy process of organising refunds to investors gave away the centralised and unautomated nature of the organisation.

Multiple DAOs fundraising for pro-choice organisations popped up in the summer of 2022 after the US Supreme Court overturned the constitutional rights of women to seek an abortion. The core contributors to ConstitutionDAO turned their attentions to ChoiceDAO, raising $1 million worth of crypto in 26 days. CowgirlDAO sold NFT art to raise $3 million for abortion access. UnicornDAO, led by the Russian Pussy Riot performer Nadya Tolokonnikova, launched another NFT collection to support seven pro-choice groups.[40] Tolokonnikova also co-founded UkraineDAO to raise money for the Ukrainian government's war effort. The group raised over $8 million by auctioning NFTs of Ukraine's flag. The project aimed to issue buyers with tradeable shares in the DAO called 'LOVE tokens'. Token holders would be able to vote on future sales of the project's NFTs. The founders urged owners to keep hold of their LOVE tokens as a 'reminder of our world's ongoing humanitarian needs'. Doing so would also inflate the tokens' price. As with FTX, questions were asked as to where the money ended up. While UkraineDAO were promising to give 100 per cent of donations to Ukrainians in need, co-founder Alona Shevchenko was allegedly siphoning off tens of thousands of dollars for her own salary.[41]

DAOs sometimes offer a novel feel-good factor to a cause, allowing networks of activists to crowdsource quickly. But they epitomise the challenges of replacing politics with technology. Most DAOs operate just like a joint-stock corporation, only without the legal backing. Token holders can vote on certain issues – decided by whoever set up the organisation – on the basis of one token, one vote. Decentralisation in such a system has little to do with progressive democratisation. As James Muldoon says: 'On-chain governance could give every member a vote on some issues, but it leaves most of the real work hashed out by unaccountable actors setting up the processes and writing the code.'[42]

SURVEILLANCE PHILANTHROPY

Despite the fraud and failed schemes, there remained a presumption across the world of Web3 that computer code superseded all other knowledge and skill sets. Humans, meanwhile, were cheats and couldn't be trusted. According to David Golumbia, everything important to humanity, according to Bitcoiners, is reducible to code, while nothing else could possibly be as complex as the sophisticated programming languages used by coders. The implication of such a computer-centric point of view is that other sets of technical expertise, and trust-building 'soft skills' – essential for effective charity work – are seen as corrupt, compromised and illegitimate. Meanwhile, criticism of crypto is only valid when it comes from those who code. All forms of non-crypto expertise are rejected.[43]

For crypto proponents, so-called experts should be replaced with a platform. For them, 'boots on the ground' were colonial boots in Toyota Land Cruisers. Explaining to prospective donors on *BBC News* in 2019, Jon Duschinsky, founder of Giftcoin, a crypto-giving platform that claimed to be 'decolonising philanthropy', stated that the crypto-giving revolution was 'shifting power away from the charities and non-profits, back to the beneficiaries and the donors. Because we've got this kind of idea that 'we know best'. It's a colonial vision of philanthropy and social change. We're completely shattering that.'

Giftcoin promised to give 'experts' the boot while putting the billionaires back in the centre of the giving experience.

The project's white paper stated, '[if] a project falters or fails, the funds not yet released can be returned to you as the donor to be donated to a new project'.[44] According to their website, they'd partnered with eight charities – including one of the UK's largest charitable trusts, English Heritage – in addition to collaborating with Charity Checkout, a platform available to 2,000 registered charities. Giftcoin enabled donors, who were not in-the-know about the local realities of those in need, to define what constituted success and failure for any set of complicated development outcomes. But this 'donor knows best' approach raises questions around who should enact a vision for success: local people, charities, or the donor? And who gets to regulate development projects, and how? Donations through Giftcoin, though cost-effective and tax-efficient for the donor, became highly conditional and inflexible for local projects.

Similarly, for the developers behind the Giveth crypto-giving platform, charities and development professionals were just 'unnecessary layers of bureaucracy'. Giveth was founded in 2016 to bypass traditional inefficiencies while encouraging ordinary folk to set up and fundraise for their own campaigns. Giveth also offered a 'TRACE' feature, which allowed donors to give to campaigns and see how projects were using funds. If the donor didn't like how the funds were used, they could reject those spending decisions and the funds would be returned. But far from removing development professionals from the messy humanitarian puzzle, platforms such as Giveth were just replacing charities with a surveillance platform, usually controlled by well-meaning, yet ultimately unaccountable communities of crypto enthusiasts.[45]

Aidcoin was another crypto platform aiming to be the 'preferred global method for charitable giving'. Using smart contracts and the DAI cryptocurrency, donors were able to give, track and manage how their funds were being spent by recipients. The platform incentivised recipient charities to pay their in-country service providers in Aidcoin, in order to improve transparency in the tracking process. Large international NGOs accepted donations from the platform in DAI, including WWF and Cool Earth. The platform also received endorsements from celebrity backers, such as Kate Moss and Vivienne Westwood.

For donors wishing to help the poor make better life choices, Humanity Token added a further layer of surveillance to the mix. The project kicked off in 2018, enabling donors the ability to restrict those in need from buying anything the donor didn't want them to have. Eligible goods and services included, for example, food, shelter, health care and professional courses, while cigarettes and alcohol would be off-limits to those who made the 'poor life choices' that caused their 'challenging life conditions'. According to the platform developer's website, to ensure the poor were behaving in the interest of the donor, the beneficiary's behaviour would be tracked with information analysed for better support.

CAPTIVE AUDIENCE

Crypto was always billed as open, transparent, freedom money that couldn't be stopped by governments or banks. But in the world of crypto giving, that freedom was usually highly controlled by someone completely divorced from the on-the-ground realities of development challenges. Development assistance should be delivered in meaningful partnership. A 'beggars can't be choosers' approach usually ends badly. But with crypto-giving platforms, donors could load their pledges with conditions. Meanwhile, locals wanting to tackle the structural root causes of issues would be stumped if doing so would impact the donor's bottom line. To help donors track the impact of their crypto donations, on-the-ground surveillance included novel monitoring and impact evaluation features. GiveDirectly and blockchain start-up OmiseGo, for example, distributed cryptocurrency donations to vulnerable families in Uganda as unconditional grants.[46] However, in order to evaluate the impact of their donations, the organisation reportedly monitored recipients' salivary cortisol levels using an oral swab test as a measurement of relative stress levels. Basic income grants were unconditional: they didn't require repayment.[47] But crude, invasive and humiliating hi-tech surveillance conditions seemed to be imposed on people who couldn't push back.

It wasn't just fast and loose Crypto Bros experimenting on the bodies of the poor. By partnering with legitimate aid agencies, crypto companies no longer needed to painstakingly recruit new users. The agencies would force crypto on a captive audience. UN agencies have been experimenting with biometric data for decades, in the form of gait and facial recognition, fingerprint scanning and voice samples. But by 2022, every major intergovernmental agency was incubating, researching or piloting a cryptocurrency grant-giving system integrated with biometric data. The World Food Programme's Building Blocks initiative, for example, was a platform for distributing cash-for-food aid to refugees. Using a system called EyePay, the refugees could access an Ethereum wallet and digital ID connected to their iris. Sensitive and personally identifiable information for some of the most vulnerable people in the world was being generated and made accessible across agencies. This inevitably introduced greater risk of data breaches. And breaches happened. In 2021, the biometric data of thousands of Rohingya refugees collected by the UN

High Commissioner for Refugees (UNHCR), was shared by accident with the Myanmar military junta.[48]

Iris data was collected from over 500,000 Syrian refugees in Jordan,[49] almost 40,000 of whom were housed at the Azraq camp. The UNHCR there claimed: 'The system helps to enhance the efficiency and accountability of food assistance, while also making shopping easier and more secure for refugees.' The main reason agencies were so keen to adopt solutions such as EyePay was because these systems were cheap. Agencies saved money from transaction fees associated with real-money cash transfers.

Digital anthropologist Margie Cheesman, who visited Azraq, explained that the project seemed to be built around orientalist gender stereotypes. Muslim men were often falsely portrayed as coercive towards women, who in turn needed to be empowered and protected using crypto wallets and biometrics. In reality, it was the machines the women feared more than their controlling husbands. Women were scared that frequent scanning was damaging their eyes.[50] 'It's all the time for the salary and the food and every time we want to buy bread too', one woman said. 'My eyes burn after I scan them, it's too much.' The fact that no one seemed to be in charge of the money system caused anxiety too. Paper receipts were important to the women, who conceptualised money as a tangible physical asset. 'When they talked about "receiving my salary", they meant having the cash in their hands – not the digital value in their [crypto] wallet', said Cheesman.

The winners in all these experiments was clear: early bird crypto investors. UNICEF's CryptoFund, the Bitcoin Water Trust, UNHCR's EyePay, and every other crypto-giving project, all involved buying cryptocurrency from those early investors, before giving it to captive audiences with few other options. When they did, crypto prices went up and so did the token's legitimacy.

Lots of people with good intentions were driving the pursuit of unmediated crypto giving. But they were usually out-numbered by bad Samaritans. After an earthquake flattened western Syria and northern Turkey in February 2023 – killing over 50,000 people and displacing 1.5 million – aid agencies burst into action. And so did thousands of crypto scammers. Websites and Twitter accounts popped up, such as the Turkey Earthquake Relief fund, which included emotive images alongside crypto wallet QR codes. There was no easy way to check the campaigns' legitimacy. The fraudulent crypto-giving strategies were exactly the same as those used by real charities. Unmediated giving, it seems, would always be a road to hell, paved with crypto.

5
Bloke Chains

Key to the success of most crypto con tricks were recognisable faces. Without these trusted celebrity endorsements, the scam was just too obvious. But celebrity crypto promoters tended not to add value in the way you would normally expect. Take George Clooney and George Foreman. Both are arguably more famous now for their successful endorsements of kitchen appliances than for whatever it was they were doing before promoting their respective brands. Sales rose after the Georges endorsed their products, and the value of their associated companies also went up. That's normal. But in crypto, celebrity endorsements were an excellent predictor of token values crashing. This is because celebrity crypto promoters served only to attract retail investor liquidity (real money), which enabled token developers and early institutional investors to cash out and make a killing. For example, when Elon Musk proclaimed Dogecoin to be 'the future of money' on *Saturday Night Live* in May 2021, the price of Dogecoin more than halved almost immediately, from 64 cents to 30 cents. Dogecoin continued to drop until bottoming out at just four cents.[1] A month later, boxer Floyd Mayweather, reality TV star Kim Kardashian and NBA star Paul Pierce all promoted a project called EthereumMax, only for the token's price to tank almost immediately following their respective social media posts.[2]

Celebrities tended to sacrifice their followers into pump and dumps and Ponzi scams indiscriminately. But other promotions were much more targeted and nefarious, sometimes drawing marks into a close mentoring relationship with their idolised con. There were messy gender dimensions at play in promoting crypto frauds. Where young, insecure and vulnerable men were the target, promoters exploited their crisis of masculinity. Where women were marked, they were framed as 'left behind' by traditional male-dominated finance. Using liberal feminist rhetoric, women were offered the opportunity for economic empowerment. Pink-washed projects, fronted by powerful female faces – ostensibly driven to save women – would legitimise the industry. But the opportunities for retail investors were an illusion. The only winners were a tiny minority of Crypto Bros.

THE 'CRYPTO BRO' CARICATURE

Risky investment behaviours are celebrated in crypto, mirroring the worst excesses of traditional stock trading. Trading crypto is usually promoted and normalised using an alpha male archetype. Prudence and care are framed as feminine attributes. Sceptics are labelled 'no-coiners' or 'soy boys', associating vegan diets with low testosterone and gynecomastia. The latter is in reference to Bitcoin's carnivore culture. Unsurprisingly, just like in the world of traditional finance, crypto has a diversity problem. In the UK, more CEOs of FTSE 100 companies are named Peter than are female. In the USA, there are more Johns than women leading Fortune 500 companies. Meanwhile, women make up only 13 per cent of cryptocurrency buyers globally.[3] All of this sounds unfair, and probably means something structural is going on. But crypto is a highly destructive scam. Getting more women involved is like putting lipstick on a pig.

But lipstick is a commonly used device for addressing financial corruption. Back in 2008, rather than blaming the global financial crisis on unfettered free market capitalism, maleness and masculinity were popularly condemned. This was exemplified by EU Finance Minister Christine Lagarde's statement: 'If Lehman Brothers had been "Lehman Sisters", [the] economic crisis clearly would look quite different.'[4] Crypto, like Wall Street, is perceived as a high-risk boys club, where men look out for each other and exclude women. The term 'Crypto Bro' is commonly used to describe the white, tech-savvy men dominating the crypto industry. And the high-profile scammers do seem to fit this archetypal image. In 2019, Jeffrey Skilling and Lou Pai – inventors of the pump and dump scam and executives of collapsed US energy giant Enron – were reported to be launching a blockchain company just a month after leaving prison.[5] John McAfee and Jeffrey Epstein were also keen crypto promoters. But framing these individuals as 'Bros' problemitises crypto as an exclusive group of men; a problem to be fixed through the inclusion of women.

'Bro', for neoliberal feminists, is a strategic term. Take the myth of the 'Bernie Bro'. The term was used by supporters of Hillary Clinton during the 2016 Democrat presidential primaries. It was a derogatory term used to suggest that followers of Bernie Sanders were against women's empowerment. Bro-ing gets used mostly to promote a particular brand of 'lean-in' corporate feminism, while preventing anything truly emancipatory or post-capitalist from happening. The strategic idea of the Bro is really just a nebulous collection of whichever male caricatures suit liberal feminist arguments.

Liberal feminists often frame crypto's Bro problem by rooting it in the myth of men's biological pre-disposition towards risk taking and technical past-times. Discrimination towards women in technical fields is thus fatalistically explained away through men's techy autistic traits. Jordynn Jack, in *Autism and Gender*, suggests that cinematic portrayals and amateur psychological diagnoses of influential male tech developers, such as Bill Gates (Microsoft), Satoshi Tajiri (creator of Nintendo's Pokémon) and Mark Zuckerberg (Meta), have reshaped definitions of Asperger's syndrome. The stock character of the male computer geek cements popular associations between autism, digital technology and hyper-masculinities. This narrative thus appears constructed through a gendered rhetorical landscape, where the nerd's computer skills and/or hatred towards women are understood as products of 'extreme male brains', caused by excess testosterone, and through reactions to trauma inflicted by emotionally absent 'refrigerator mothers'.[6]

While the Crypto Bro alpha male carries similar traits to his Wall Street counterpart, there are many other boys clubs in crypto with their own gender performances and symbolism. Camilla Russo, in her book *The Infinite Machine*, explains how the creators of Ethereum rejected Bitcoin's alpha male image by adopting boxing kittens and unicorn llamas as their spirit animals. While Lamborghinis, beer-pong and side-events hosted in strip clubs were central to Bitcoin annual conferences, cute costumes, stage dancing and rainbows were more common sites at Ethereum's annual Devcon events.

But Ethereum's subculture, like Bitcoin's, still displayed oppressive and colonising views towards women's bodies. In January 2022, reflecting on the gender pay gap, Ethereum's co-founder, Vitalik Buterin, suggested that '[s]ynthetic wombs would remove the high burden of pregnancy, significantly reducing inequality'. The comment was widely praised in the crypto community. 'If there aren't enough people for Earth, then there definitely won't be enough for Mars 🤔' Elon Musk replied. Ethereum's other co-founder, Gavin Wood, is also famed for expressing unsavoury views towards women. He reportedly penned a blog post reflecting on having sex with a preteen girl who was dying of AIDS. Wood claimed it as a piece of creative writing.[7] Crypto's gender performances are diverse. But they are all ultimately toxic. And the cartoonish branding of various 'meme token' projects hides their scammydocious motivations. Unlike Bitcoin's aggressive branding, Dogecoin and its spinoffs, such as Floki and Babyfloki, all featured cute shiba inu puppies. Beyond that, they all did the same thing. They were all cryptocurrencies requiring the same energy-intensive, competitive mining process. None of them had any real-world utility, beyond being speculatively traded on the same exchanges. Pumping the value of any of these tokens required recruitment from the same pool of suckers.

'Bro' implies fraternity. But there is no meaningful fraternity in crypto because it is a greater fool game. That is, one person's gain is followed by many other players losing. Tokens have no intrinsic value, meaning the only way to profit from them is to ensure an ever-greater number of fools are recruited into the pyramid, or 'community' as its referred to in crypto. Where crypto entrepreneurs claim to be helping young men, they will sure as hell be taking from them, while putting recruits to work to find new suckers.

WE ARE ALL GOING TO MAKE IT!

In February 2022, Randi Zuckerberg – the sister of Mark Zuckerberg – released a Twisted Sister remake titled #WAGMI (We're All Going to Make It). The music video tried to turn the table on the alpha male investor versus female regulator contest. While a trio of backing dancers shouted and jigged to various crypto meme acronyms, bearded middle-class men in suits are seen giving cautious investment advice. Zuckerberg responds shouting 'No! You "paper hands" are all worthless and weak!' In contrast to her brave, diamond-handed backing singers.

Zuckerberg tweeted that her aim was to explain crypto jargon to newcomers. 'All the acronyms and phrases can feel super intimidating at first. Hope this video is a fun 2-minute crypto lingo-101 lesson that speaks to the spirit of women in Web3', she said. But by the summer of 2022, crypto prices had tanked by over 60 per cent, resulting in all but the earliest early adopters not making it. Trying to restore some enthusiasm, and rope-in cash from female newbies, Zuckerberg released another song, called Ethereum – a remake of David Guetta's Titanium – explaining NFTs, DAOs and DeFi. Zuckerberg's cringe-fest campaign was reportedly part of a $1 million rebrand for crypto exchange OKCoin. Taking on influential female tech personalities like Zuckerberg would, according to the company, help the exchange reach into an untapped market while resetting the company's image.[8] The company's founder, Mr Mingxing Xu, also known by Star Xu, was arrested in 2020 by police in China on fraud charges. Xu had been arrested before in 2018, also in connection with fraud, after a group of investors claimed they incurred big losses due to a system crash they alleged Xu orchestrated. Luckily, celebrities were prepared to pick up the pieces, providing useful distractions from the crypto industry's sleights of hand.

In February 2022, actress Reese Witherspoon reportedly offered her celebrity endorsement to the World of Women NFT collection. Witherspoon's media firm specialised in helping creative projects find a female audience. World of Women launched in July 2021, with 10,000 images of women in various garb to 'celebrate the diversity of women'. The most expensive – a purple-faced portrait of a lady in a tuxedo known simply as Woman#5672 – sold at auction for around $750,000. Female crypto newbies were all very diverse, but they were all ultimately pigs for the slaughter. Following Witherspoon's endorsement, as with all celebrity crypto promotions, the collection's price fell 90 per cent. Trusted celebrities entering into promotional partnerships with crypto firms that most people had never heard of before were leaving their fans naked to significant financial risks. These promoters weren't educating their fans about the wonderful world of Web3. They weren't 'giving back to the community' – a vacuous phrase commonly used in crypto promotions. Promoters were essential for defrauding fans.

The industrial scale scumbaggery of crypto markets was made especially obvious in January 2022. OpenSea, the largest online NFT marketplace, announced that over 80 per cent of the NFTs minted through its creation tool were spam, scams or otherwise fraudulent. One of the company's bosses, Nate Chastain, was indicted in June 2022 on allegations of insider trading and charged with wire fraud and money laundering. It's alleged that he secretly bought NFTs from collections which he had personally chosen to feature on OpenSea's home page. He then sold the tokens at a profit as they were being featured.[9]

Using sites such as OpenSea, anyone can start collecting NFTs, usually without having to give personal identifying information. Often all you need is a cryptocurrency wallet – such as Metamask or imToken – linked to an NFT marketplace site. Some sites don't even require an email address to set you up. Just give your account a name and a password and Bob's your uncle, you're a digital artist empowered by Web3. But due to the ease of entry, pseudonymity and the sheer saturation of NFT marketplaces, profitable pieces must stand out from the crowd. Take the OpenSea featured Heaux Collection, for example: a set of 69 racist, anti-feminist archetypes depicting 'women of the world'. Gamer Heaux 3.0 (a nod to the online #GamerGate misogyny campaign)[10] features a girl breastfeeding Yoshi, the dragon from Super Mario World. A Japanese Heaux breastfeeds an octopus. Jewish Heaux carries a bible stuffed with $100 notes. Safari Heaux is semi-clothed in leopard print and carries a spear. OpenSea says in its terms of service that it will host 'controversial' NFTs in the name of 'openness', but many of the site's Hitler-themed NFTs stretch beyond that generous designation. The Floydies NFT collection uses the image of George Floyd, the 46-year-old man murdered by a policeman in the US city of Minneapolis in 2020. In a poke to the #BlackLivesMatter movement, Floyd is mocked wearing various tasteless outfits, with some selling for around $12,000. 'Owning a Floydie is a great way to express yourself and your beliefs', reads the creator's OpenSea bio.

Thanks to the pseudonymity of NFT minting, it's very difficult to verify that sellers of digital artworks are who they say they are. For example, Fame Lady Squad was a collection of NFTs featuring 'strong and independent woman of the NFT community striking a note for female empowerment'. But the three female developers of the multi-million-dollar project weren't independent women at all. They were a gang of Russian men.[11]

It's also nearly impossible to know how (or if) an NFT seller came to legitimately 'own' the work. Anyone can right-click and save a file before minting and selling said file as an NFT. Sellers can fabricate the provenance of the piece, or just masquerade as the artist. Dead people's artworks frequently become the 'property' of digital art traders. Qing, for example, was a successful Japanese anime artist and a four-time open heart surgery survivor. In December 2019 she tweeted: 'Got diagnosis today. Stage 4. Doc says I got about a year, or a year and a half left … ' She included a piece of original artwork: a girl being consumed by an inky shadow. Towards the end of her life, Qing's artwork revolved around her terminal illness. In one piece titled Flowering Wounds, small flowers sprout out of bandages on a girl's arms. Qing messaged her followers on Instagram explaining how she liked to pretend her blue and purple bruises were 'little galaxies'. She passed away in February 2020. Her brother Ze Han, also an artist, exhibited Qing's most famous pieces online. Despite being free for any of Qing's followers to download and enjoy, her work quickly started to appear on NFT marketplaces from sellers claiming to be Qing or her brother. Stealing the art was 'just a morally shitty thing to do', Ze Han stated in a tweet.[12] 'So, please stop profiting off of my dead sister.'

For hard-up women juggling paid work and unpaid caring responsibilities, NFTs and crypto trading can be an attractive proposition. No doubt thanks to campaigns such as Zuckerberg's and Witherspoon's, the interest in crypto among some women has grown. The cryptocurrency exchange Gemini suggested that women in 2022 made up 47 per cent of their target market. According to the crypto exchange BlockFi, 92 per cent of the women they surveyed in the USA knew how to buy crypto, with 24 per cent already owning some. But like the crypto greenwash numbers, the pink-washing stats usually failed to match up with more impartial datasets. Yet they showed that, just like multi-level marketing (MLM) schemes, women were becoming an increasingly important target market for crypto promoters. According to MLM expert Máire O' Sullivan at Cork Institute of Technology, vulnerable young mums are most at risk from these promotions, 'allured with requests to support the businesses of their friends'. They're promised an easy way to make money while spinning all their many plates at home.

Crypto, like MLMs, also offered the appeal of finding community among fellow investors. Potentially lonely periods during early motherhood could be filled with 'education' on how to turn mum's side hustle into a 'successful business', while getting support from others in the 'community'. This often resulted in vulnerable people being targeted by the allure of making easy money from passive income. And just as with more formalised MLMs, recruitment of new crypto investors focused far more on the promises of 'number go up' than selling a useful or high-quality product. The cult of crypto is very similar to the cult-like mentality of MLMs, with crypto-mums encouraged to cut the haters, no-coiners and naysayers from their lives.

Anyone can buy into crypto – that is true. But only the lucky few make it out with their shirts. Meanwhile, those least able to afford it can lose everything. Anna Sorokin was the convicted con-artist featured in the Netflix series *Inventing Anna*. She cheated many people into giving her hundreds of thousands of dollars. In June 2022 she explained how she's abandoning her German heiress persona to get into NFTs and crypto.[13] There is no sorority among the women of WAGMI, because crypto is a pyramid scheme. The only way to swim is to scam.

PINK WASHING

Connecting high-risk crypto projects to women's political struggles makes crypto investing appear prudent, with women legitimising and normalising the industry. These sorts of marketing devices are not unique to cryptocurrencies. Symbolic gestures of corporate solidarity are common in the fossil fuel industry. Fracking companies in the USA support breast cancer charities with drilling rigs spray-painted pink. Shell Oil added an apostrophe to their forecourts, becoming She'll Oil for International Women's Day. Meanwhile their Bitcoin-mining machines and toxic fracking fluids contaminate the air and groundwater with cancer-causing compounds.[14] Across the world, oil companies have been implicated in sexual assault and trafficking of women from indigenous and marginalised communities, while at the same time spearheading seemingly charitable initiatives in support of these same groups.[15] The tobacco industry has also worked to offer an illusion of care for women by positioning their carcinogens within the feminist movement. Just like cigarettes, crypto is being promised as a woman's 'torch of freedom'.

Alexis Henshaw suggests that advocates of blockchain-based development have little interest in emancipatory alternatives to neoliberalism. Their mission is deeply conservative, to keep everything the same, including oppressive class structures and conservative gender roles.[16]

UN-Women has been running blockchain hackathons since 2017. Olivier Mukuta and his team were among the first winners. Their cryptocurrency was designed for women whose controlling husbands were prone to mismanaging the family budget. 'We came up with VipiCash as a solution', said Mukuta. 'I can send money to my aunt or family and friends and lock it in to a specific service, like school fees or groceries. The money can only be managed by my aunt because she knows best what is good for the children.'

The idea of financial technology as an empowering torch of freedom for women depends on a set of age-old, gendered myths and feminist fables. As Andrea Cornwall says, women too often appear in policy narratives as both heroines and victims: 'Heroic in their capacities for struggle, in the steadfastness with which they carry the burdens of gender disadvantage and in their exercise of autonomy; victims as those with curtailed choices, a triple work burden and on the receiving end of male oppression and violence.'[17] This rallying call is stirring, but according to Cornwall, it doesn't reflect the complexity of most women's and men's experience. But this is Web3 problem solving in action. All manner of crypto scams can be benevolently imposed when ignoring the actual complexity of people's lives.

SpankChain, CumRocket and Nafty were examples of cryptocurrency projects marketed specifically to online sex workers, by men who knew best what women needed. According to SpankChain – an in-browser cryptocurrency payment platform for the adult entertainment industry – traditional payment providers systematically decline service to pornographic websites, 'leaving room for shady companies to come in and fuck [women], with fees'.[18] SpankChain was envisioned by Ameen Soleimani, a ConsenSys software developer. The company had partnered with WWF to build a crypto-giving platform.[19] With the UN, they built blockchain-based digital ID systems for victims of child trafficking.[20] With the success of SpankChain, Soleimani was reported to have pitched the idea of starting a separate department at ConsenSys specifically for 'dark and evil' projects, where ventures such as SpankChain could be incubated and run. Soleimani hoped that SpankChain could grow to become the 'PayPal of porn'.[21]

In December 2020 and August 2022, crypto payments allowed PornHub to give a middle finger to intermediaries such as PayPal.[22] Following requests from multiple payment processors, the adult website reportedly rejected calls to delist 'child rape videos, revenge pornography, un-consensual spycam videos of women showering, violent racist and misogynist content, and footage of women being asphyxiated in plastic bags'.[23] PornHub instead turned to cryptocurrencies for premium subscriptions, raising demand and prices for crypto on some exchanges.

Since the Covid lockdowns of 2020, the number of registered content creators on the adult subscription platform OnlyFans grew to 1.5 million. Users of OnlyFans have to be over 18 years old. But UK police have accused the site of failing to prevent some underage creators from appearing in and selling their pornographic videos. One investigation found a 14-year-old girl selling explicit content. She'd used her grandmother's passport to falsely verify her age. In 2021, the platform toyed with the idea of removing sexual content following pressure from regulators and payment providers. They later U-turned. But some creators, fearing future regulatory interference with OnlyFans, have turned to crypto-first alternatives such as Wetspace. The platform's founder, Allie Rae, worked as an intensive care nurse until hospital bosses discovered that Rae had been moonlighting as a pornographic content creator on OnlyFans. 'WetSpace will be a place where creators don't have to worry about big banking restrictions and payouts', said Rae.

Wetspacc models offer a 'Girlfriend Experience'. Fans, or 'simps', can request one-on-one experiences with their favourite creators, paid for exclusively in cryptocurrency. But the experience is not as quid pro quo as it seems. A similar arrangement plays out in the 2002 film *Catch Me If You Can*. Frank Abagnale (played by Leonardo DiCaprio) meets a seemingly savvy sex worker Cheryl (played by Jennifer Garner) in a hotel. They agree a price of $1,000 for the night. To Cheryl's surprise, Frank sets off towards the hotel reception desk with a $1,400 cashiers cheque. To save questions being asked by the hotel proprietors as to why Frank would want to cash a cheque at 3 am, Cheryl suggests she give Frank the $400 difference in cash and have the cheque signed over to her. The cheque however is a worthless forgery, a fact lost on Cheryl until she tries to cash it the following day. Frank meanwhile gets the cash, and the whole night with Cheryl, before disappearing. Wetspace may seem like a savvy option, but by enticing women and girls into crypto, online platforms such as Wetspace don't empower sex workers. They merely line the pockets of the token's early investors (with real money) while everyone else is left holding dodgy cheques.

FORTUNE FAVOURS THE BRAVE!

Young men were the target market for big crypto advertising campaigns, from New York's Times Square to London's Underground. 'Fortune favours the brave', explained Matt Damon during one of several crypto-related ads during the 2021 Super Bowl. Sports stadiums were particularly popular venues for targeted advertising towards men. The Singapore-based cryptocurrency exchange Crypto.com was relatively small. But in 2021 alone the company reportedly spent around a billion dollars on sports ads. That's similar to the entire advertising budget of Microsoft or Apple. The exchange kicked off 2022 paying $700 million to change the name of Staples Arena in Los Angeles to Crypto.com Arena. They paid $175 million to sponsor the Ultimate Fighting Championship, $100 million on Formula One, $40 million to become the exclusive cryptocurrency trading platform of FIFA Qatar World Cup and $25 million on the Australian Football League, as well as individual deals with the Philadelphia 76ers, Paris Saint-Germain, Montreal Canadiens, plus advertising deals with sports stars such as LeBron James.

Every UK Premier League club was in bed with a cryptocurrency trading partner. Manchester United agreed a $25 million per year deal with the cryptocurrency Tezos to sponsor their training kit. Watford wore the proudly useless cryptocurrency Dogecoin on their sleeves. Players themselves had also been involved endorsing NFT collections while passing on all the financial risks to their fans. The former Chelsea captain, John Terry, started the trend endorsing ape-related NFTs at the end of 2021. Some of these images sparked controversy when they appeared to include the Chelsea badge, Chelsea kits and the Premier League's trophy – all registered trademarks – the use of which required licensing agreements. Terry then had another go with a revised collection featuring baby gorillas in football strips, called the 'Ape Kids Football Club'. They were listed with an average price of around $800. Within days they plummeted in value by 90 per cent, of course, leaving angry fans out of pocket. At the same time that Terry's project was tanking, the English Premier League signed a $30 million NFT gaming deal with Paris-based crypto start-up Sorare. Despite a US federal judge ruling that a similar basketball-themed NFT game, NBA Top Shots, were likely to be unregistered securities, the English Premier League seemed to believe their fans were worth the risk.[24]

Not all fans were happy. After Socios, another fan engagement platform, tried flogging NFT tokens to Crystal Palace supporters, huge banners were unfurled at matches reading: 'MORALLY BANKRUPT PARASITES SOCIOS NOT WELCOME'. Sports Journalist Joey D'Urso told me:

> People buying these fan tokens, which are all endorsed by legitimate major English clubs, are doing it because they come with an implicit understanding that these tokens will appreciate in value. But these are actually very high-risk investments. The companies providing these tokens claim the fans can be involved in decision making on important aspects of the clubs' management. But really, [the tokens] don't come with any meaningful utility. Holders might get

to vote on their team's Instagram banner, or the colour of the bus. But that's it.

To avoid a government-imposed ban, in 2022 the Premier League asked clubs to support a deal phasing out betting company shirt sponsorships. As none of the top teams had betting sponsors, the deal only hurt hard-up clubs sitting further down the league table. With few alternatives, many of these clubs turned to shady crypto companies. In April 2023, a BBC investigation revealed that 40 per cent of top English clubs had endorsed crypto investment platforms known by regulators to be scams. Unregulated crypto-trading apps are bad. But unregulated gambling apps offering punts with crypto are what D'Urso described as 'a double whammy of risk'. In the summer of 2022, online casino company Stake.com became Everton FC's Main Partner. Besides their football team affiliations, Stake.com also brought in punters using live video-streaming platforms such as Twitch. But Twitch moved to ban Stake.com streamers reportedly due to concerns over their business model. It was suggested the streamers were marketing to minors in countries where it would require virtual private networks or Tor browsers to use the service.

Stake.com was one of 450 online casinos registered in the tiny South American island nation of Curaçao. Despite locating the business in what seems like an actual shed with several other online casino companies, Strike's CEO, Australian Edward Craven, was reported to be the owner of the most expensive residential property in Melbourne Australia: a $38 million mansion. Matt Zarb-Cousin, director of UK pressure group Clean Up Gambling, told me that Stake.com supposedly 'don't even hold a full UK Gambling Commission license but are able to advertise and sponsor in the UK through a white label arrangement with TGP Europe, based in Malta, a tax haven'.

As well as English football, Stake.com had sponsorship deals with Ultimate Fighting Championship, Formula One and the Canadian rap artist Drake. According to Craven, he and Drake shared 'the same love for crypto, gambling and community and are like-minded fans of the technology and culture at the forefront of this movement'. Despite his love of gambling, Drake appeared cursed, outside of his own online crypto casino that is. Drake reportedly lost $210,000 dabbling on the Spanish Grand Prix, before losing $655,000 on Barcelona beating Real Madrid. He was far more successful sat at Stake.com's online roulette table. In October 2022 Drake won $14 million on a single spin. And, lucky for Stake.com, they caught the very moment on camera before sharing the convenient PR with national newspapers. 'There's no transparency around [Stake.com's] commercial relationship with Drake', says Zarb-Cousin. 'It is utterly mad this company has been able to sanitise itself in the Premier League.'

CHOOSE YOUR PILL

Crypto is far more likely to promote violent misogyny than gender equality or emancipatory feminism. A 2019 survey showed that nearly 70 per cent of self-described incels, or 'involuntary celibates' – men who struggle to form romantic relationships with women – were considering suicide. But a tiny minority of incels are being radicalised towards murder.[25] And there is an increasingly clear pipeline between incels, far-right white supremacist extremism and crypto. According to the US charity Hatewatch,[26] many violent followers of inceldom are as much part of the far-right ecosystem as they are misogynists. They become dangerous at the nexus of intent and capability. Crypto is proving an enabler of both.

Incels are part of a loose network of online subcultures, known as the 'manosphere'. They're a broad and dysfunctional church, but each element is united in their conservative, anti-feminist views. For the most extreme fringe of the manosphere, a social revolution involving direct action is promoted to balance the odds back into men's favour by sexually subordinating women.[27] White supremacist and orange-pilled incel Kyle Davies was committed to such direct action. In 2019, he was found guilty of planning a mass shooting in Gloucester, UK. He used Bitcoin to procure a fully operational Glock pistol and ammunition. Davies' weapon was intercepted by police in the post. But thanks to crypto, far-right extremists can build their own DIY firearms. These 'ghost guns' are exploding in popularity among libertarian gun owners. In the USA the number of seized guns without a serial number has increased tenfold between 2016 and 2020. Kit guns can be put together by a novice in roughly the same amount of time it takes to build an IKEA cabinet.

Guns n' Bitcoin are one of many new online groups sharing designs and parts for building untraceable firearms. The group promotes new ways to develop and purchase guns that are 80 per cent complete. These so-called 80 per cent kits or paper weights come with the instructions and materials needed to build a 100 per cent deadly firearm. Purchased only with crypto, they're untraceable and account for a growing number of guns used in crimes. Guns n' Bitcoin also provide a forum for right-wing anti-government enthusiasts, both online and off. In the USA, the group hosts in-person Bear Arms N' Bitcoin conferences to share the latest technology, tips and improvements on gun part manufacturing. They also discuss ways to further anonymise cryptocurrency transactions, offering a handbook for far-right extremists who want to operate completely under the radar.

Building ghost guns out of entirely 3D-printed parts is an increasingly popular option. Crypto transactions enable the trade to take place in broad daylight, with offers promoted on YouTube and Twitter. The US-based Ghostgunkit.com provides users with instructions on how to buy crypto using Coinbase and other exchange apps. Live in Australia or UK? No problem. Just send a short-lived encrypted message and payment details to the company's Wickr address and they'll sort you out.

According to evidence submitted during his trial, Kyle Davies was inspired by the far-right terrorist Anders Breivik, who murdered 77 people, mostly teenagers, in Norway in 2011. Breivik himself straddled multiple extremist camps. His 1,500-page manifesto rants about feminism as 'the most destructive and fanatical element of modern liberalism'. The online spaces these far-right extremists occupy are characterised by intermingling between various factions. From the Boogaloo Boys to the Proud Boys, the intersecting dimensions of anti-feminist, anti-state, pro-Bitcoin hate are clear.[28] Languages, cultures and jokes have all intermingled. And they are all radically conservative in their moorings.

For misogynist hate groups, women's empowerment is seen as something that is eroding the rights of white men. For them, feminists are an enemy and an outgroup. Empowered women, they believe, deny men their dominant positions which they feel is not only natural but essential for their happiness.[29] Although incels are widely considered the most dangerous and violent part of the manosphere, the connection between violence and the incel community has led to sweeping generalisations about incels, dubbed in the USA as 'an emerging domestic terrorism threat'. But, according to Julia

Ebner, author of *Going Dark: The Secret Social Lives of Extremists*, they've not always been like that. Incels were originally a forum on Reddit set up for lonely young men struggling to find a romantic partner. 'There was a positive goal behind incels in the beginning', says Ebner. 'But that goal has been hijacked.' Incels have become a key recruiting ground for the far right. And their motive is often crypto.

Right-wing activists created crypto, while white supremacists continue to take a shine to it, with Bitcoin in particular reshaping the racist right in radical ways. According to a 2021 Hatewatch report, many prominent racist terrorists were also crypto early adopters. Patrik Hermansson, of the Hope Not Hate watchdog in the UK, told me:

> In the UK, most far-right activists were quick to start taking crypto donations, from Tommy Robinson to Patriotic Alternative. This was often for practical reasons. They're de-platformed from other payment rails, like PayPal and Stripe. They may have their bank accounts frozen. Crypto effectively solves this problem. And extra anonymity is also useful. The risk of being publicly exposed as a financial supporter for a violent far-right cause usually deters other donors.

Roosh Valizadeh was one of the most prominent misogynists and manosphere pick-up artists. Valizadeh's meet-up tours featured hours of female fat-shaming while seemingly celebrating the non-consensual filming of sex acts. He appeared to advocate for the legalisation of rape (on private property). 'No does mean no. Until it means yes!' is one of Valizadeh's favourite catchphrases. Despite seemingly not having a problem with women being attacked, in 2016 he cancelled 165 meet-ups in 45 countries due to concerns for his own safety. Shortly after, he was banned from entering the UK by then Home Secretary Amber Rudd. Valizadeh has threatened to bring a legal claim against the EU after UK MP Mary Honeyball asked Brussels to ban him following his repeated attempts to spread 'deplorable and violent' messages about women.

Valizadeh has been a Bitcoin devotee since the early years. His online chat forum has displayed crypto threads for over a decade. But Valizadeh's Bitcoin appreciation peaked shortly after his string of cancellations. 'The events surrounding the meetup outrage this year made me realise that our community is not as anti-fragile as I would like', read one of his posts in March 2016. 'We are vulnerable to attacks that attempt to reveal our identities.' Bitcoin would supposedly enable him and his followers to be 'immune from witch-hunts'.[30] Pick-up artists such as Valizadeh appear to operate with a profit-driven playbook, radicalising young men with alt-right rhetoric as a marketing tool to sell crypto.

SAD LONELY GUYS

The pornographer and pick-up artist Andrew Tate has become one of the most famous far-right misogynists and Bitcoin devotees. He reportedly made millions from a Romania-based erotic webcam business. Models were employed by Tate as part of an apparent crypto 'pig butchering' scam,[31] sharing sob stories while getting men to part with cash and crypto. He reportedly once claimed the reason for relocating from the UK was his belief that police in Romania were less likely to pursue rape and sexual assault allegations against him.[32] But in April 2022 his home was raided by Romanian police amid reports he had abducted two women. He was released. But in

January 2023, while making crypto-trading tutorial videos for his followers, he was taken into police custody again.

Tate rose to fame in 2016 when he was removed from TV show *Big Brother* over a video depicting him attacking a woman. He went on to gain notoriety following a Twitter ban. 'Women should bear responsibility for being sexually assaulted', he said. In another video, Tate talked about hitting, choking and kidnapping women. 'Bang out the machete, boom in her face and grip her by the neck. Shut up bitch', he says in one video, acting out how he'd attack a woman if she accused him of cheating. By August 2022, Tate was banned from TikTok too, where videos of him had been watched 13 billion times. He refused to abandon his crypto fans though, framing his censorship as a feminist conspiracy requiring cryptocurrency as the fix. He claimed that by enrolling in his private online academy, known as Hustlers University, 'any sad lonely guy' could be as rich as he is. According to Tate's website, 168,000 active students had signed up to his crypto-investing and NFT courses.

'Any one of you can retire from your Matrix job, in three years from now guaranteed', explained Tate, shortly before his arrest in January 2023. He claimed Bitcoin would help his students 'escape the work/consume/die cycle. You must escape the Matrix. We can show you how.' Michael Conroy, whose organisation Men at Work trains school staff on talking to boys about sexism, suggested influencers such as Tate were 'grooming' young men in a similar way to terrorist groups or gangs. Their image of 'conspicuous success' woos boys desperate for a connection.[33] A secondary school teacher in Nottinghamshire, UK told me:

> During [students] lunch breaks, they'll all be comparing their Coinbase apps. It's never the girls who are bothered about [cryptocurrencies]. It's the boys thinking they're like

the Wolves of Wall Street. And they're the same boys who you just know aren't in a good place financially at home, to be wasting money on Dogecoins. [...] These influencers aren't teaching them about money. Like how to budget or get a job. It's all just gambling tips. And being rude to girls.

Puertopian YouTuber Logan Paul used his influence over a young male audience to sell NFTs. In January 2023, investigative journalist Stephen Findeisen, exposed Paul's 'CryptoZoo' collection – a set of crudely drawn eggs – as a giant NFT rug pull, defrauding investors for millions of dollars.[34] Paul is currently facing a class action lawsuit.[35] Following in the footsteps of Brock Pierce, Paul ditched his career as a teenage Disney star to start his own media company, working with influencers to build their brands. Funding for Paul's project came from another prominent crypto-influencer and men's self-help guru, Gary Vaynerchuk, more popularly known as Gary Vee. In May 2021, Vaynerchuk launched 'VeeFriends': another collection of hand-drawn zoo animals minted as NFT's. The images also functioned as access passes for 'VeeCon': a three-day hyper-capitalist life-coaching conference hosted by Vaynerchuk.

It wasn't just angry middle-aged men taking advantage of vulnerable boys. Layah Heilpern's anti-feminist views towards 'the war on masculinity' attracted hundreds of thousands of young men. Much of Heilpern's YouTube content revolved around her support for misogynist Bitcoin believers cancelled due to what she described as 'the clown world of LGBT woke insanity'. She self-published the short book *Undressing Bitcoin: A Revealing Guide to the World's Most Revolutionary Asset*. Heilpern was frequently invited to promote her thoughts on feminism and fintech (financial technology) as a guest on *BBC News*. Her crypto outreach to manosphere misogynists and beyond was sponsored on YouTube by the 'effective altruist' Ben Delo's BitMEX. And then there's Myron Gaines. His 'Fresh and Fit' podcast also set out to showcase the benefits of crypto investing to overcome what he called the femoids' hypergamic mindset. His podcast usually featured seemingly intoxicated OnlyFans models insulted repetitively with sexual slurs and misogynist hate until they either leave the recording studio or, more often, are thrown out for answering back. As well as hate-filled misogyny, Gaines and his co-hosts offer their viewers the opportunity to escape the feminist state with their crypto literacy courses.

James Gallagher shot to unexpected fame after a BBC documentary on incels featured the 31-year-old from County Down, Northern Ireland. He was a self-identifying orange pill and KHHV (a Kissless Handholdless Hugless Virgin), perhaps the lowest rung on the manosphere ladder. He's a likeable man, battling anxiety, depression and cystic acne. Struggling with limited job opportunities, Gallagher admitted to having gambled half his income on crypto. 'I threw all my money away. Scammers have it. [They] can take it. Take your dirty money. Take your blood money. I don't care', he says. 'These scammers make millions from people. From poor people, through these courses that cost thousands of pounds.' Gallagher was introduced to crypto investing through online forums and YouTube videos aimed at young men like him. 'At first, I was really careful with my investments in crypto. Then I started buying into all these little ones, branching into possibly the next 100X or 1,000X coins. But I just get rug pulled. Money gone. All gone.' Gallagher admits to losing around $400 just on Ethereum gas fees paid for failed transactions when trying to buy into what turned out to be shitcoin rug pulls.

Besides Bitcoin and Ethereum, Gallagher explained he has limited understanding of the projects taking his money. But for him, Bitcoin and Ethereum were his gateway drugs into what he described as a 'gambling addiction on shitcoins'.

In Scotland, the first cryptocurrency addiction clinic was set up to help those like Gallagher get clean. The Castle Craig clinic, better known as Crypto Castle, had been providing a refuge to crypto addicts since 2017. Castle Craig therapist Tony Marini said that inquiries for admission to his crypto rehabilitation programme had increased tenfold between 2021 and 2022. The need for therapeutic approaches to crypto-gambling addiction were boosted by lockdown isolation and a Bitcoin bull market. Marini believed that crypto trading was very similar to other forms of gambling. The journey to addiction goes from occasional trades and frequent wins, which feed a dopamine craving, leading to fantasies of even bigger wins, through to prolonged losing episodes and a loss of face which results in isolation and withdrawal. The risk of self-harm and suicide are then increased, especially when young men are already battling depression.

In June 2020, after borrowing $500,000 from his wife's parents and then losing $3 million on crypto investments, one man in China decided to take his own life by jumping from the Xinghaiwan Sea Bridge in Dalian. He survived. But he and his wife had agreed to 'keep the family together in death'. After murdering his own daughter, he jumped into the sea with his wife. His wife also perished.[36] With massive losses and mounting debt, an amateur crypto trader in India killed his wife and two children before shooting himself in October 2020.[37] Then in March 2021, after thousands fell victim to a $2 billion Turkish cryptocurrency fraud, another man who suffered heavy losses killed his family before killing himself. A month later an Indian man drank rat poison and died after losing $13,600 in yet another crypto scam.[38] London Bitcoin trader Stefano Reale was 23 when he lost his crypto fortune and took his own life.[39] South Korea appears to be a hotspot for tragedies; there are too many to list here. Unsurprisingly, the number of young men dying for crypto also seems to jump whenever markets crash. The Terra/Luna Reddit forum was full of suicidal posts from young men when that crypto fraud collapsed in May 2022.[40] The pattern of desperation was repeated six months later, following the collapse of FTX.[41]

The diehard commitment of some men towards crypto is part of a deeper struggle of capitalist masculinity, exemplified by memes circulated in crypto forums. Possibly the most common set of crypto meme stock imagery comes from the 2006 testosterone-fuelled fantasy film *300*. There's even several shitcoins that take direct influence from the film. Spartan Token has a maximum supply of 300, for example. The *300* memes, like the film, epitomises the Bitcoin subculture that celebrates hypermasculinity and traditional gender roles.

Mithu Sanyal explains how gendered Western capitalist conceptions of honour are shaped mainly by classical antiquity. The mass suicide of Spartan warriors following their loss at the Battle of Thermopylae exemplifies ideas of masculinity as something that must be negotiated on the battlefield or on the job.[42] Once a man has honour, it can only be lost through avoiding work or desertion. Or in crypto by selling. Conversely, antiquated ideas about woman's honour saw it located in her body: in her virginity or in her state as an honourable wife or widow.

Honourable masculinity in liberal capitalism relates to a man's employment and economic production. But with the rise of digital automation and the gig economy, opportunities for young men to negotiate their masculinity, and keep it, has never been more precarious. And digital platforms are not as easily smashed as the Luddite's looms. Applying this struggle to the crypto age, Dan Olsen hits the nail on the head in his film *Line Goes Up*,[43] showing how young men investing in crypto suffer a potent anxiety about their future:

It goes without saying that they're fixated on money, and they principally understand the technology as a means of making money. Ultimately the driving forces underlying this entire movement are economic disparity. And that's how it draws in the bottom: people who feel their opportunities shrinking, who see the system closing around them, who have become isolated by social media and a global pandemic, who feel the future getting smaller, people pressured by the casualisation of work as jobs are dissolved into the gig economy and want to believe that escape [from it] is just that easy.

Taking advantage of this crisis of capitalist masculinity were crypto influencers – the only guaranteed winners from shitcoin gambling and NFTs – offered huge amounts of cryptocurrency to dump on fans and followers. Crypto influencers often presented themselves as good ol' Mr Brownlows, fighting to free poor Oliver Twist. But really, they were Bill Sykes. Vulnerable boys were preyed upon, taught scamming skills and indoctrinated – often with far-right violent misogyny – to promote and sell cryptocurrencies. Crypto is not a definitive calling card or precursor for violence. But young people with limited opportunities and seemingly little to lose are easy prey for crypto con artists using the sirens' call of hate for profit.

6

For Betterverse or Metaworse

In September 2021, Traci and Dave Gagnon made history and headlines as the first couple in the world to tie the knot in the metaverse. While an average wedding in the USA would cost between $10,000 and $20,000, their metaverse marriage would reportedly come in at around $30,000. 'I think it shows that the world has changed', Traci said.[1] 'It is a very exciting thing.' Meanwhile, Brock Pierce's daughter, Aurora Rose Pierce, supposedly became the first baby launched in the metaverse. Aurora's tiny body was given a full-body scan under a dome of 160 high-powered cameras, allowing Aurora to attend her parents' wedding celebrations in the metaverse.[2] Global overpopulation would soon be resolved, not via the costly fix of tackling the complex, poverty-related drivers of high birth rates across the Global South, but with tailored AI-powered metaverse baby subscriptions for the rich.[3] Palmer Luckey, who designed the first mass-produced VR headset, Oculus Rift, had his own metaverse fix for solving overpopulation. In November 2022, he unveiled his 'NerveGear headset, complete with death charges allowing the wearer to die gloriously in real life while doing battle in the metaverse'. From cradle to grave, in work rest and play, it appeared there was no need to ever leave the metaverse. Yet the 'massively scaled and interoperable network of real-time rendered, 3D virtual worlds that persist through time and across platforms and devices' – that metaverse, didn't exist.[4] But like everything in the wacky world of Web3, that didn't matter.

Despite not really existing, the metaverse was the logical next iteration of the web browser, representing what the WEF called 'a $5 trillion quantum leap forward' that was changing 'how we socialise, play, learn and shop' with 'opportunities to revolutionise the world of work everywhere'.[5] The digital foundations for our shared social lives were being talked into existence. Despite the headlines, Traci and Dave had a relatively normal wedding in front of 100 guests in Manchester, New Hampshire. No VR headsets. The event was simply live streamed using a teleconferencing app called Virbella. Neither did Aurora wear a headset to her parents' wedding party. And anyone foolish enough to wear Luckey's death headset would probably just be dead. In lieu of an actual $5 trillion experience, crypto scammers were ready to serve up whatever bargain basement alternatives they could get away with.

Referring to any old website as a metaverse was like calling any old house a skyscraper. Back in 1919, Wichita Falls in Texas was similarly pumped as an up-and-coming boom town. With big coal and oil money flowing in, and sensing an opportunity, a local businessman, J. D. McMahon, proposed the construction of a skyscraper to house incoming energy tycoons. From the building's plans it seemed this would be among the tallest in the world at that time. McMahon shared the proposed dimensions with prospective investors and collected millions of dollars. Construction started but questions soon followed. The skyscraper was not as 'Texas-sized' as promised. The investors eventually received a skinny four-storey tower with no elevator or stairs. They accused McMahon of fraud, but after reviewing the approved plans, which showed a 480" (inch) building, as opposed to the expected 480' (foot) tower, a judge couldn't see a problem.

Just like Wichita Falls, the overpromised and barely delivered metaverse offerings from the crypto industry not only looked terrible; they were dangerous, especially for younger guinea pigs roped in like canaries in a coal mine.

Massively oversold metaverse experiences, suggesting the existence of a bold leap forwards, had a striking resemblance to the crypto-utopian affinity frauds of Chapter 2. For example, with the launch of the metaverse world known as the Free Republic of Liberland, all persecuted libertarians had a place to call home and live in peace without paying tax. The republic was originally meant to lie on a parcel of swamp forest on the western bank of the Danube, between Croatia and Serbia. Liberland's self-appointed president was Czech politician Vit Jedlička. Despite frosty relations between Serbia and Croatia following wars, accusations of ethnic cleansing and border disputes, both Serbia and Croatia had agreed that the territory, locally known as Gornja Siga, was not worth any more bloodshed, but it was not a no-man's land either.

Police forces from the two nations were also united in their belief that Jedlička was a pest. In 2015, police stations were set up on both sides of the border. Patrol boats would prevent Jedlička illegally hopping the border to reach the island's only shed, or Capitol building as Jedlička called it. In the summer of 2022, after reportedly processing 700,000 Liberland residency permits, Jedlička decided to plant the republic's flag where government tyrants couldn't remove it: in the metaverse. In November 2022, Liberland's 3D renderings were drawn up by Zaha Hadid, the same architect influencing the design of Akon's illusive crypto cities in Senegal and Uganda. 'The biggest improvement is that, in Liberland, taxes are voluntary, and people are rewarded when they pay them', Jedlička said. But despite the slick renderings, the Liberland metaverse was still just a fantasy.

The term 'Web3' is often used interchangeably with 'the metaverse'. That's probably because all of crypto comes together in the metaverse, including the linguistic tricks. As with everything in Web3, redefining commonly used words is key to changing people's perceptions of reality while obfuscating what's really happening. Land, property and real estate language were used to make people believe they were getting a skyscraper, when what they were really getting was conned.

ROBUX, ZUCK BUCKS AND LINDEN DOLLARS

Think of the metaverse and you're probably imagining a virtual meeting featuring floating cartoon avatar torsos. In October 2021, Mark Zuckerberg bet the Facebook farm on creating such a world. He changed the company's name to Meta and reportedly committed to throwing more than $100 billion into metaverse research and product development.[6] Adjusted for inflation, that's four times more than the US government spent on the Manhattan Project (which is five Eurotunnels or 150 Golden Gate Bridges). It's 20 times more than Sony spent on research and development in the same year. But for Zuckerberg, the implications of not securing the company's early dominance of whatever it was would be catastrophic. He understood Timothy O'Reilly's Web 2.0 'dominate or die' ethos. In *Zero to One*, Zuckerberg's mentor and his company's first private investor, Peter Thiel, wrote the book on how network effects make monopoly the only sustainable Silicon Valley business model. With Meta steering things, Zuckerberg would always be king of the metaverse, thanks to the dual-class structure of the company's shares. Meta's 'Class B' shares were controlled by a tiny circle of insiders. And every Class B share imbued the holder with ten times more voting power than a regular 'Class A' share. Zuckerberg would never be dethroned.

At the WEF's Davos meeting in 2023, Meta's chief product officer, Christopher Cox, seemed to argue that Meta's monopoly was essential to ensure safety and privacy in a centralised metaverse. But the statement left many in the audience perplexed.

Meta's algorithms were accused of amplifying hate speech, leading to genocide, including that of Rohingya Muslims in Myanmar. Nearly every day, mass murders, self-harm and suicide were streamed in real time to whoever cared to tune in via Facebook Live.[7] And whenever viewers stopped tuning in, the company's pioneering 'behavioural design' ideas poked them back online, leading to addictive dependencies among users. Thanks to Meta's algorithms, social media platforms generally grew more addictive than cigarettes.[8] Children in the UK and USA reportedly spent more time scrolling than eating, walking and watching TV combined. With every swipe, post and like, users gave away personal data for optimised advertising. Meta was trusted with the personal data of nearly three billion platform users, or 'dumb fucks' as Zuckerberg referred to them.[9] As far as Meta's founder was concerned, privacy was 'no longer a social norm'.

In 2012, Meta apologised after conducting covert psychological tests involving the manipulation of 700,000 users' posts 'to see what would happen'. Another 'sorry' came after the company allowed fake news to circulate during the 2016 US presidential election, including stories that Hillary Clinton was performing satanic rituals and sexually abusing children in the basement of Comet Ping Pong pizza restaurant in Washington, DC. The posts inspired Edgar Maddison Welch to take action with his AR-15 semi-automatic rifle, a handgun and a folding knife. There were no captive children in the basement. The restaurant didn't have a basement. Then, in 2018, Meta apologised for selling data connected to 87 million users to Cambridge Analytica. By sharing photos with Meta, users could also be sharing them with ClearviewAI, a company selling biometric facial data to law enforcement agencies world wide. Clearview reportedly collected more than 20 billion images of people's faces from Meta in 2022. Police forces globally no longer bothered filling out forms or asking judges for warrants when needing to access people's browsing history or track their real-time locations. They simply purchased user data from Meta. The company was apparently under no obligation to inform users of data sales, or about who they sold the data to.

As well as advertising revenue, Meta also planned to make money from a crypto-powered metaverse marketplace. Selling everything from digital wigs to land parcels as NFTs would net the platform a fortune. Meta planned to take a 47.5 per cent cut on virtual asset sales; far more lucrative than Google or Apple's app stores, which take between 15 per cent and 30 per cent. Buying Meta's digital accessories was to be even more lucrative for the company with a purpose-built Zuck Buck.

In June 2019, Meta planned to launch their own digital currency. Libra, as it was called, was to be a cryptocurrency whose exchange rate was pegged against a basket of other currencies including the US dollar. It had the backing of the world's major payment networks and tech companies, including MasterCard, Visa, PayPal and Stripe. Big names in crypto, including Coinbase and Mercy Corp, were also on the list. Together they would form the Libra Association, a Swiss-based non-profit that would oversee the running of everything. To get off the ground, Libra needed the approval of US regulators: a big ask given the number of times Meta had its knuckles rapped by lawmakers for broken privacy promises. Meta had just received a Federal Trade Commission fine for breaking a previous 2011 settlement over privacy issues. US Senator

Sherrod Brown explained: 'Facebook has burned down the house over and over. And called every act of arson a learning experience.' They referred to Libra as Zuck Bucks, and for US lawmakers, Zuck was not a safe pair of hands. 'The Russians have tried to disrupt elections on Facebook. Now Facebook wants to control the money supply?' asked Senator John Neely Kennedy. 'What could possibly go wrong?'

David Gerard suggested regulators were going after Libra because the project posed systemic risks.[10] 'When regulators use the word 'systemic', it means they're setting off the air raid sirens', he told me. 'It means, "this could break things". The Libra reserve plan would have caused another 2008 financial crisis.' Regulators were convinced the company would use people's personal financial data for advertising purposes. If it failed, it would break things. If it were successful, Libra could undermine the global dominance of the US dollar and make it impossible for the US government to impose economic sanctions or prevent money laundering, terrorism and financial crimes. Once it was clear Zuckerberg had failed to impress US regulators, eBay, Visa, MasterCard and Stripe jumped ship. But in December 2020, Libra shed its skin, renaming itself Diem.

Instead of acting as a single global currency from the get-go, Diem would initially act as a suite of stablecoins, all independently pegged to national currencies. Then, if Diem didn't break anything, they would take over all the money. Instead of being 'permissionless' – open to anyone, like Bitcoin – the job of deciding who gets access would fall on the desk of 26 tech companies, many of whom were at that moment defending themselves in courts globally for various privacy and rights infringements, including Spotify, Coinbase and Uber. These companies would be charged with performing all the anti-money-laundering/know your client checks expected of banks and money transmitters. Facebook expected Diem to attract billions of users spending trillions of Diem dollars daily, all backed one-to-one with a vault full of real cash. According to economist Francis Coppola, the opaque institutions behind Diem would be managing a reserve fund easily big enough to move markets and hold central banks to ransom. But, according to the Diem Association's chief economist and MIT blockchain professor, Christian Catalini, Diem would not be required to manage the reserve for long. 'The moment Central Bank Digital Currencies (CBDCs) become available, we can stop operating the reserve and start operating at digital speed', he said.

Jay Powell, who headed the US Federal Reserve, was not massively against moving fast or breaking things. He was willing to give the go-ahead for a Diem trial. He knew the Treasury had concerns. But on balance, he believed the project could be useful for setting industry standards on crypto.

In 2022, after weeks of deliberation, the US Treasury Secretary Janet Yellen was still unconvinced. Yellen told Powell it was his decision to make, but she would not protect him from any political fallout. Powell ordered Facebook to call it a day. The project was sold to Silvergate Bank for $182 million and subsequently written off. Silvergate was the real-money banker for most of the US crypto industry. A bank run in March 2023 forced the bank to announce its voluntarily unwinding and liquidation.[11]

The Zuck Bucks dream was dead, but Meta still planned for users of their metaverse to be shopping for various digital things using tokens controlled by Meta. The company is continuing to look for the most unregulated way to offer payments, digital IDs and asset management.[12]

As of mid-2022, there were around 160 companies building unique digital worlds, 20 of which were active metaverse projects. Many sold digital things using only their own purpose-built digital currency. This isn't a new thing. The earliest life simulation platforms featured in-game currencies. Second Life, a game developed by Linden Labs in 2003, required players to use digital Linden dollars to buy stuff. For acquiring illicit drugs and guns on the dark net, Second Life was the best conduit for purchasing crypto anonymously. Using the Virtual World Exchange, or Virwox website, children of any age could swap their US dollars for Linden dollars, and exchange those for Bitcoin, and back again. Second Life dropped in popularity when regular crypto exchanges grew to dominate the world's money-laundering markets. Facebook Credits were launched in 2009 as a virtual currency that enabled users to make in-app purchases, typically in games such as FarmVille.

Roblox, another centralised take on the metaverse idea, also had an in-game currency called Robux. The platform was used by over half of all US children in 2022, who netted the platform around $2 billion. One Australian six-year-old handed over 8,000 of his parents' dollars to buy in-game digital hats and shoes. The company was valued at $42 billion.

PLEASURE ISLANDS

Zuckerberg's metaverse was not a new idea. The sci-fi writer Neal Stephenson gave birth to it in *Snow Crash*, a 1992 novel about an immersive virtual world accessible via a VR headset. Stephenson was easily the most influential novelist among billionaire businessmen since Ayn Rand. Just as the internet was getting started, Stephenson was imagining its next iteration, where users could choose avatars, go shopping with friends, attend concerts and work from anywhere.

Google Earth and Xbox Live were platforms inspired by *Snow Crash*. Stephenson's 1995 novel, *The Diamond Age*, inspired many of Jeff Bezos' big ideas. Amazon Prime, Amazon's kindle digital reading device and Amazon's labour outsourcing platform to poor countries known as The Mechanical Turk all take influence from the book. In 1999, the idea for Blue Origin, Bezos's commercial space company, was reportedly launched after Bezos and Stephenson went to the cinema together to watch *October Sky*. After the film, Bezos employed Stephenson to envision novel approaches to space travel. But because Bezos insisted on using boring old rockets, Stephenson resigned.[13]

Bill Gates, Peter Thiel, Sam Altman, LinkedIn's Reid Hoffmann and Google's Sergey Brin were among the many other Silicon Valley billionaires citing Stephenson's work as their major creative influence. Many in the crypto space believed Stephenson was the first to come up with the idea of cryptocurrency, ten years before Bitcoin. In his 1999 book, *Cryptonomicon*, Stephenson discusses a distributed and untraceable electronic cash system developed by cryptographers. Whether Bitcoin was Stephenson's idea or not, *Cryptonomicon* did inspire PayPal. And many of today's Bitcoin billionaires include early PayPal founders and investors.

In February 2023, dozens of for-profit Silicon Valley start-ups were reportedly itching to release clouds of chlorinated iron particles into the atmosphere, thanks to inspiration from Stephenson's book, *Termination Shock*.[14] In it, Stephenson describes a longtermist tech billionaire battling against incompetent governments and systemic snowflake-ism to bravely launch a geoengineering company. If the book's influence is as infectious as Stephenson's other ideas, we're doomed. *Termination Shock*, like his other works of speculative fiction, holds libertarian capitalism as the mother of all Swiss army knives, able to fix any social or environmental problem that society or the environment can throw at it.

In 2023, Stephenson launched his own metaverse called Lamina1 with fellow Bitcoin billionaire Peter Vessenes. Vessenes co-founded the Bitcoin Foundation in 2012 as a centralised non-profit governing body to help legitimise Bitcoin after countless scandals involving dark web drug markets and fraud. While Zuckerberg's take on the metaverse idea relied on centralised control resting in Meta's unsteady hands, Lamina1 proposed a decentralised approach with a purpose-built blockchain. The project would join a growing list of similarly structured crypto metaverses, including The Sandbox, Decentraland and Somnium Worlds.

While centralised metaverses such as Roblox and Meta's nascent 'Horizon Worlds' attempt relied on harvesting user data for tailored advertising, blockchain metaverses provided open fantasy game worlds without collecting personalised behavioural data. Blockchain-based metaverses relied on digital landlords doing all the development work. But, as with everything in Web3, 'decentralisation' meant that if things went wrong, no one could easily be held accountable.

In October 2022, the supermarket chain Walmart devised its first metaverse experiment in The Sandbox. The platform's terms of use stated that players must be aged 18 or older. Yet Walmart's Universe of Play was, according to the company's press release, 'designed with the next generation of shoppers in mind'. Players could chase a blimp dropping digital toys, join a pop music festival, and collect virtual coins to spend in a virtual store of virtual merchandise or 'verch'. The verch brands included LOL Dolls, Jurassic Park and Paw Patrol. Other retailers explained how they were targeting teen gamer audiences, including Raving Rabbids and the Nikeland experience. In Nikeland, teens could participate in a dunk contest while wearing the company's gear. Gucci Garden wanted teens to imagine owning limited edition designer outfits as virtual items.

HSBC and JP Morgan occupied plots of land in Decentraland's crypto-gaming spaces to complement their marketing strategies geared towards tomorrow's crypto-capitalists. Stella Artois, Budweiser and the brandy brand Martell also had blocky Minecraft-style games. Once time had been called at Maison Martell, users of any age could visit the Lego lady bunny girls of Playboy Mansion or Lovehoney's pop-up space for 'sexual explorations'. A metaverse horseracing tournament called Zed Run was designed to 'attract a younger audience' to sports gambling. And gambling was by far the biggest reason most kids visited. A single virtual casino accounted for over a third of all Decentraland's daily footfall in 2022. Most of the gambling venues were unregulated. In May 2022, a Russia-based outfit set up a metaverse poker hall called Flamingo Casino Club. It was labelled by US regulators as simply 'a high-tech scam'.

As with anything related to crypto, it was near impossible to know if wash trading or other shenanigans were artificially poking up prices. But of the 90,601 NFT plots of land available for sale in Decentraland, many appeared to have sold for at least $10,000 each. The Metaverse Group, a Canadian 'virtual real estate company', purchased a basketball court-sized digital space for around $3 million. PricewaterhouseCoopers bought a plot for an undisclosed sum.

In June 2021, Sotheby's opened an NFT gallery and auction house in Decentraland where on busy days they welcomed up to ten visitors. Meanwhile, internal statistics showed that only 9 per cent of Meta's virtual worlds ever received more than 50 visitors. Most were never visited at all. To increase footfall, in February 2023, Meta agreed to open its doors to children as young as 13. To protect them from adult content and weirdos, Meta's global affairs president and former UK deputy prime minister, Nick Clegg, explained the companies pub landlord approach to child safety: 'We wouldn't hold a bar manager responsible for real-time speech moderation in their bar, as if they should stand over your table, listen intently to your conversation, and silence you if they hear things they don't like', Clegg said.[15] If a child were to be confronted by 'an uncomfortable amount of abusive language', they should leave, rather than expect the busy publican to intervene. But children aren't generally allowed in pubs. And US regulators weren't happy. In a letter to the company sent in March 2023, two US Senators wrote:

With a documented track record of failure to protect children and teens, Meta has lost parents', pediatricians', policymakers', and the public's trust. Your plans to imminently pull these young people into an under-researched, potentially dangerous virtual realm with consequences for their physical and mental health is unacceptable.[16]

Other metaverse platforms were very lonely pubs indeed. In October 2022, The Sandbox was ushering in around 500 punters per day. Decentraland was valued at $1.3 billion. But on most days, fewer than 40 users signed in. The real reason behind the ten-digit valuations of crypto-metaverse platforms was not the number of kids coming through the digital doors, it was speculation. To encourage more of it, in December 2022, Decentraland launched a virtual property renting feature for NFT plot holders. With zero upkeep costs for landlords, tenants could pay to host temporary events in prime spots. For example, Parcel 2787 – located close to where visitors to Decentraland first spawn – would set you back $7,000 per day. Brands such as MasterCard and Heineken rented plots for their events. But as of January 2023, only around 40 plots were temporarily occupied by tenants.

The justification for needing to integrate blockchains and NFTs into metaverses was to ensure interoperability between virtual worlds. Users buying digital swag on one platform could then use it on another. But it doesn't work like that. Take Decentraland for example. NFTs purchased on its platform exist as entries on the Ethereum blockchain. Yet the associated land, shoes and hats worn by avatars in their metaverse exist only on centralised private servers. All visual and functional aspects of metaverse digital assets – the very features that give NFTs any value – are not on the blockchain at all. These features fall under the complete control of the metaverse platform developers. Because of their terms of service, platforms can legally delete or copy them, or delink any digital asset features from their associated NFT blockchain entry. Landlords may 'own' an entry on the Ethereum blockchain, but they legally own none of the associated utility in Decentraland. Law Professor João Marinotti explained the not-so-decentralised Decentraland paradox like this:

> On one day you might own a $200,000 digital painting for your apartment in the metaverse, and the next day you may find yourself banned from the metaverse platform, and your painting, which was originally stored in its proprietary databases, deleted. Strictly speaking, you would still own the NFT on the blockchain with its original identification code, but it is now functionally useless and financially worthless.

Concurrency issues often meant 3D renderings were terrible. But in other ways, experiences in the metaverse were too real. 'Within 60 seconds of joining, I was verbally and sexually harassed', Nina Jane Patel wrote in her *Medium* newsletter that chronicled an attack she suffered in a metaverse experience:

> Three or four male avatars, with male voices essentially gang raped my avatar and took photos. As I tried to get away, they yelled, 'don't pretend you didn't love it', and 'go rub yourself off to the photo'. A horrible experience that happened so fast and before I could even think about putting the safety barrier in place. I froze.[17]

After posting about the ordeal, comments from other users varied from, 'just don't choose a female avatar, it's a simple fix', to 'don't be stupid, it wasn't real', and 'a pathetic cry for attention'. Patel believed the reason she found the experience so affecting was due to the Proteus effect: a tendency for people to connect their behaviour to the experiences of their digital representations, such as avatars, dating site profiles and social-networking personas. Psychologists sometimes refer to the illusion as 'embodiment'. Mel Slater, a researcher in the psychology of virtual environments, suggested that as far as our brains are concerned, 'the overwhelming evidence is that this [avatar] is your body'. The virtual environment doesn't have to look particularly realistic for this to happen. For this reason, as far as Patel was concerned, her avatar's virtual rape was her own.

According to the US-based Cyberbullying Research Centre, 'age play' and child grooming through the exchange of pornography is common in open online worlds, despite platforms being endorsed and legitimised by toy brands and trusted high-street retailers. But where regulation does exist, metaverse spaces are legally defined as marketing and social media platforms. New laws, or updates to old ones, to protect children will likely require platforms to share the legal burden when people get hurt.

Users of the metaverse are not just visiting because they're too lazy to visit places in real life. Visitors call into virtual worlds to transcend traditional norms and values. The whole purpose of privacy-preserving and censorship-resistant metaverses is to escape mediated content and centralised control. They are unsafe by design. There are no age assurances and few protections because that's how you build a libertarian utopia. For their developers and sponsors, they are sandboxed. For everyone else, blockchain metaverses are Pleasure Island donkey worlds of Carlo Collodi's *Pinocchio*, with trauma inflicted on children that could persist long after the headset is removed.

Advanced VR headsets and hardware make consensual and non-consensual metaverse experiences feel more real. Full-body haptic suits with vibration motors and linear actuators distributed across the body can accurately simulate online experiences in real life. Even temperature changes could be simulated using thermoelectric diodes. The pain of a zombie attack, a gentle stroke or a rain shower could feel quite real. They start at around $300, but high-end wearables, like the ultra-immersive Teslasuit and gloves with realistic tactile interaction, go for around $15,000. Elon Musk's Neuralink is also working to make digital experiences more immersive. 'In the long term, a sophisticated Neuralink could put you fully into virtual reality', Musk said. The company intends to offer visual prosthetics channelling an electronic feed directly to someone's visual cortex via a smartphone. The company's wireless 'N1 implant' is implanted onto a moving brain using their R1 surgical robot. Once a hole in the wearer's skull has been drilled, the process of stabbing 64 wires into the brain takes around 15 minutes.[18]

The founder of the original Oculus VR headset, Palmer Luckey, reportedly created a wearable capable of killing the wearer in real life. Luckey launched Oculus in 2012 off the back of some very early Bitcoin investments. He bought his first batch of Bitcoins in 2011 at 18-years-old for just $2.54 each. In the 2013 *Forbes Magazine* 30-under-30 edition, when asked what advice he would give to other young founders, Luckey replied simply, 'buy more Bitcoin'. He sold Oculus a year later to Facebook for $2 billion. Luckey stayed on as an employee of Zuckerberg's but left six months later when it was revealed Luckey had been running a pro-Donald Trump campaign group dedicated to 'meme magic and shitposting' about Hillary Clinton, in Luckey's words. Luckey was a hardcore Republican. He'd teamed up with Peter Thiel to sell spy-tech to the Trump administration. Luckey's Anduril start-up had developed autonomous drones and surveillance towers used for intercepting would-be asylum seekers. Like Thiel's spy-tech company Palantir, Anduril was also named after a mythical weapon from *The Lord of the Rings*. Together, their hi-tech cameras and AI systems were used to identify, detect and track 'objects of interest'. The objects included women and babies to be detained separately as part of the US 'zero tolerance' deterrence policy towards Central American refugees.

'The idea of tying your real life to your virtual avatar has always fascinated me', Luckey wrote in a 2022 blog post. 'You instantly raise the stakes to the maximum level and force people to fundamentally rethink how they interact with the virtual world and the players inside it'. Luckey's death headset was connected to three explosive charges, each tied to a photosensor. 'When an appropriate game over screen is displayed, the charges fire, instantly destroying the brain of the user', he said.[19]

Luckey's device appeared to take influence from another Bitcoin-powered death machine called the Sarco Pod. Once inside the biodegradable pod, users could blink twice to trigger their own suffocation. Death would occur in less than a minute according to the Australian founder of the company, Philip Nitschke, more popularly known as 'Dr Death'. Prospective users were offered a dry run using a VR headset to experience the comfort of the Sarco Pod, minus the fatal hypoxia. With laws in many countries prohibiting assisted suicide, Dr Death's services are commonly requested and paid for using encrypted messages and Bitcoin. For elderly folks less savvy with crypto, the company offered 'euthanasia and suicide for dummies' workshops, focusing on using Bitcoin to 'safely obtain the best end of life care'.[20]

'PERFECT EMPATHY MACHINES'

VR is an egocentric experience. 'Mirrors are the go-to place in almost all metaverse worlds', the popular VR vlogger known to his followers as Twice told me. Mirror dwellers, as they're called in the metaverse, 'spend hundreds of dollars on full-body tracking, so they can just lay down in front of mirrors. The most popular worlds get listed in the "hot section". And these all have LOTS of mirrors.' According to Twice's research, 85 per cent of VR users with body trackers do nothing but sit in front of mirrors. 'I remember the first time I used VR using a headset. Seeing myself as someone else was such a surreal feeling, I couldn't help myself just looking in the mirror and bobbing left and right', he says. 'It was like magic.'

Back in 2014, film maker Chris Milk, in collaboration with the UNDP, created an immersive VR experience called *Clouds over Sidra*. The film followed Sidra, a twelve-year-old girl living in a tent in the Za'atari Refugee Camp in Jordan, home to some 130,000 Syrians, mostly children. Milk's film was put together for the 2015 WEF meeting in Davos: 'a group of people who might not otherwise be sitting in a tent in a refugee camp in Jordan', Milk said during his hit TED talk entitled 'How Virtual Reality Can Create the Ultimate Empathy Machine'. 'They suddenly all found themselves there. And they were affected by it'. A slide behind him read, 'VR is a machine – that makes us more human'.

In 2022, after conducting a rigorous empirical study on whether 360-degree videos like Milk's increased charitable donations,[21] psychologist Alison Jane Martingano realised that it very much didn't. 'Given the cost of creating 360 videos – approximately $10k per minute – charitable organisations may well question their investment in this VR technology', she told me. 'Donors are unlikely to support the use of their gifts for the creation of VR, since it diverts the funds away from the cause itself, without any apparent increase in charitable donations.'

But as with every Web3 project that fails to fix a problem, the UN-funded experiment with refugees was lauded as a success. However, within a few weeks of removing the headsets at Davos, it seemed the policymakers had learnt little in the way of empathy. The horror of human tragedy unfolding on the shores of Europe didn't require a VR headset. Images of a lifeless three-year-old Alan Kurdi represented one of the nearly 3,000 Syrian asylum seekers to drown in the Mediterranean that year. Policymakers took to prosecuting those charitable organisations empathetic enough to fish survivors from the water. Meanwhile, Sidra – our young guide through the Za'atari camp – just wanted a home. Yet in 2016 she became a UN guinea pig once again, this time for their 'eyeballs for crypto scheme', otherwise known as the Building Blocks experiments.

'I don't like this "empathy machine" thing', said documentary film maker Amaury La Burthe. 'Stealing someone's shoes is a bit weird and ineffective.' Game developer Robert Yang published an essay against the term 'empathy machine', arguing that these experiences offered only 'the illusion of empathy'. 'If you won't believe someone's pain unless they wrap an expensive 360 video around you, then perhaps you don't actually care about their pain', Yang wrote. An earlier essay by Kathryn Hamilton also criticised *Clouds over Sidra*, which she said 'invites the user into a visual and aural immersion, without the user facing any of the consequences of being immersed in that space'. VR allowed passive viewers to consume the lives of others from the comfort of their offices or living rooms, killing empathy in even the well-intentioned.

Microsoft's augmented reality headsets could block out user empathy altogether, making the US military a more effective killing machine. Samuel Marshall, a US army general, described in his 1947 book, *Men Against Fire*, how in almost all contexts, three-quarters of men with guns aimed at the enemy refused to kill. The average soldier was a natural born lover, according to Marshall. But thanks to a $22 billion US government contract, Microsoft set out to change all that. Body-count tallies, thumbs up emojis or just dehumanising filters could all make it easier to park the soldier's love of fellow man. VR was as likely to turn you into a human as it was a monster, depending on which filter you chose. After all, as one soldier said in a *Black Mirror* episode, also called *Men Against Fire*: 'It's a lot easier to pull the trigger when you're aiming at the boogie man.'

A METAVERSE FOR GOOD?

In 2016, researchers at Stanford University suggested that VR could help people become 'more aware of their impact on nature' by forcing them to 'feel the pain of climate change'. Stanford's immersive experience, called Virtual Ischia, allowed the user to fully connect their daily lives with coral bleaching by 'becoming the coral'.[22] Virtual Ischia would arrive pre-installed on widely available commercial headsets. But such VR experiences inspire no meaningful solutions to ocean acidification. They simply remove the capitalist context surrounding it. The ecological destruction caused by producing, using and disposing of digital devices is commodified as an enjoyable VR experience and sold back to us, resulting in more ecological destruction. The purpose of the VR techno-fix was not to encourage empathy with nature but to divert responsibility for the destruction of it away from the gears of consumer capitalism.

VR projects were popping up claiming to prevent climate change, protect nature and support charities with their fundraising goals. Meta launched VR for Good, a fund to 'foster and promote immersive storytelling, focused on social impact'. Betterverse was a 'virtual world to save our own'. Donations to charities who'd acquired land and relocated to the Betterverse generated NFTs representing trees, fungi and other features. These could be held to certify a company's philanthropy, or resold on third-party marketplaces.

In collaboration with Ray Kurzweil's Singularity University, South African Bitcoiner Mic Mann developed a metaverse called Ubuntuland. It was essentially an NFT gallery developed as an Africa-inspired version of Decentraland. Much of the artworks for sale inside Ubuntuland were 3D versions of pieces produced in the 1970s by popular South African artists Norman Catherine and Walter Battiss, known as Fook Island. Fook was created by Battiss as a fantasy island far from the realities of racism and homophobia in apartheid South Africa. Back then, the make-believe island had its own written language, stamps, currency, passports, driving licences and 'fooklore'. It was a tool for fighting racism and inequality. Meanwhile, Ubuntuland was selling political struggles as a consumer spectacle. But by encouraging visitors into the site's vaguely Africa-themed spaces, the project claimed to offer sustainable 'digital tourism' and opportunities to 'democratise access to nature'.

Far from acting as alternatives to international travel, virtual experiences act as advertising for real destinations. One need only look at the so-called corporate land rush to snap up advertising space in metaverse worlds. In buying land in The Sandbox, Martell weren't interested in quenching one's thirst with a free immersive experience. They wanted people to buy and drink their real bottles of brandy. Immersive experiences are not designed to satisfy our consumer interests. They're designed to drive our capitalist consumption of products and places.

In November 2022, the Pacific nation of Tuvalu threw their flag into the metaverse. As a response to the existential threat of rising sea levels, Tuvalu minister Simon Kofe addressed world leaders at COP27 explaining his nation's plan for dealing with a 'worst case scenario'. Tuvalu would create a 'digital twin' of itself preserved forever in the metaverse. When life in real Tuvalu eventually becomes unliveable, the culture, sovereignty and territory of the nation would continue in the cloud. But the Tuvalu metaverse was a head-in-the-sand solution to the actual problem. According to Nick Kelly, a professor in interaction design, the idea of a metaverse nation as a response to climate change, though possible, is exactly the kind of thinking that got humanity into our current mess. The language that gets adopted around new technologies – such as cloud computing, VR and metaverse – comes across as both clean and green. 'Such terms are laden with technological solutionism and greenwashing', said Kelly. 'They hide the fact that technological responses to climate change often exacerbate the problem due to how energy and resource intensive they are.'

At the 2023 meeting in Davos, the WEF pitched its own metaverse mission ostensibly designed to fix global challenges, calling it the Global Collaboration Village. The WEF's metaverse was developed by Microsoft and Accenture. And despite the many shortcomings of blockchain-based metaverses, the WEF's attempt would integrate digital assets and artificial scarcity using cryptocurrencies and NFTs.[23] One WEF project leader explained why:

> The blockchain industry are [WEF's] members and they get to participate in our work and attend Davos. And the WEF blockchain platform has multiple members who are big crypto companies. They are the ones incentivised to pay and participate. And they exert their influence over our projects. There's usually a project manager who filters that influence. But most are not well-versed on blockchain topics. And they're usually under pressure from these private companies to allow the hype through in our work.

Some WEF project managers were very well versed in crypto. Sheila Warren founded the WEF's blockchain and digital assets team and WEF's Centre for the Fourth Industrial Revolution. She oversaw crypto policy strategies across 14 countries and regularly briefed ministers, big tech CEOs and heads of state. Warren is now the CEO of the Crypto Council for Innovation, a 'global alliance formed to demonstrate the transformational promise of crypto and educate policymakers, regulators, and people around the globe'. The group comprises the most influential crypto industry leaders, including exchanges such as Coinbase and Gemini and VC firm A16z.

METAVERSE U

While spiralling student debt threatens to make higher education unaffordable to all but the wealthy, Meta promised to invest $150 million to develop ten virtual university campuses in the metaverse. Students signing up to a professional masters programme at Vienna University of Economics and Business could complete the entire course – attending lectures, meeting their classmates for a coffee and so on – by just logging in via a laptop. New Mexico State University announced that from 2027 all of their students would be able to take all of their classes in VR. While rich kids could learn, network and experience life away from home at real universities, poor kids could enrol at Decentraland U, receiving their certificates as NFTs. The WEF's metaverse also appeared keen to provide poor doors for people with bodies considered too problematic for the real world:

> The metaverse holds promise to improve educational and social access for people with disabilities. An immersive environment offers young adults with special needs, autism, and social interaction issues the ability to improve their interpersonal and job skills, such as visiting a mall or grocery [shopping], shelving products at a store, or loading goods in a truck. Through VR apps, they can practice skills and interact with others in a safe environment.[24]

By manipulating sets of dropdown boxes, users of Meta's Horizon Worlds could present themselves as their preferred age. Users could pick from a list of 58 gender options (and three pronouns). They would be free to create their avatar representation however they wished, so long as they didn't want a wheelchair. But, according to Legacy Russell, author of *Glitch Feminism*, these categorisations are an essential spoke in the wheel of capitalism. Diverse race, gender and other bodily options in the metaverse were not radical or liberating gestures but rather neoliberalism at its finest. The dropdown options were there for better marketing outcomes, not for the user's emancipation. Our differences and vulnerabilities would be disguised in the metaverse, not supported or nurtured.

As far as the WEF's membership were concerned, barriers to education would be smashed with Web3. One of the WEF's metaverse steering group members was the VC firm Animoca Brands. The company was behind the hugely popular play-to-earn metaverse experience Axie Infinity, designed to make online gaming a full-time job. At its peak, Axie had around 2.9 million active monthly users, most of whom were based in the Philippines. To get started, players needed to buy (or borrow) three unique NFT characters: furry blobs with a face. Some had tails too. They didn't look like much, but entry-level characters were around $300 each. Special ones came with equally special price tags. The renowned Axie #2655 – also known as Sir Gregory – with a rainbow-coloured turnip on its back and a shiba inu tail was purchased in July 2021 for $800,000. Once assembled, one's team of Axie blobs could complete challenges in return for Smooth Love Potion (SLP): a cryptocurrency and Axie aphrodisiac. SLP was required to breed new characters that could then be sold or deployed within the game. It could also be swapped for other cryptocurrencies via an exchange. By breeding Axies and selling SLP, top players were reported to earn up to $500 per day.

In typical Web3 metaverse fashion, to keep players interested, the game's developers introduced a scholarship system allowing Axie owners, or 'managers', to rent them out to 'scholars' elsewhere in the world. Scholars would then play on their manager's behalf and take up to 30 per cent of their own winnings. Managers often set exploitative daily minimum quotas of SLP before their scholars could take a cut. There were also big problems in the game's economics. Sweatshop-style gaming outfits popped up. There were reports of young people having to send nude pictures of themselves before being signed up as scholars.[25] And Axie blobs and SLP tokens only retained their value if a constant supply of investors were entering the ecosystem. Axie was a Ponzi scheme.

As of February 2023, the number of active users had dropped from nearly three million to around 300,000. Trading volumes for Axies dropped by 98 per cent, meaning that many investors who paid upwards of $1,000 for three blobs had likely lost money. Yet many managers in the Global North understood what they were doing as charity. 'Axie is a gateway for Filipinos to be educated about crypto, which I believe will help advance them in the future', one US manager said.[26] 'I've set up crash courses for them about the basics of crypto – how to create wallets, trade, and how to avoid scams – basically making them literate in the crypto world.'

In April 2022, Animoca Brands teamed up with A16z-funded Yuga Labs to announce another metaverse job/game, where players could own land and turn their existing Bored Ape NFTs into playable characters. Yuga Labs initially sold 55,000 NFTs linked to virtual land ownership, reportedly raking in about $1 billion.[27] In preparation for the game's unveiling, Yuga Labs launched the NFT game Dookey Dash, a three-week-long endurance race through a sewer pipe. Like in Axie, many NFT holders established teams of poor people to race on their behalf.[28] Despite being referred to by the usual Silicon Valley suspects as metaverse games, play-to-earn worlds weren't immersive or collaborative, nor did they elicit any sense of connection. This was the WEF's world of work in the metaverse: a bizarre crypto Ponzi game where only WEF's members win.

An NFT project called Pixelmon launched in early 2023 with a slick-looking promotional demo to entice prospective investors. The YouTube scam sleuth Stephen Findeisen explained, 'you have to understand in the world of NFT games, even the smallest amount of effort makes you seem like you're the next Mark Zuckerberg, which is why it basically sold out'. The one-minute teaser video netted Pixelmon's 21-year-old developer $70 million. The funds were meant to be used to develop the triple-A-rated, professionally produced metaverse game that he'd promised. What was eventually delivered included a selection of slightly modified stock images, including an egg and a baby dragon minted as NFTs. These so-called immersive Web3 experiences epitomised the metaverse mantra: overpromise, barely deliver.

The metaverse never really began. Yet aside for a plethora of NFT scams, it already seems over. In February 2023, Microsoft closed their metaverse development arm. Disney eliminated its entire metaverse division in March. The same month, Meta reined their VR efforts back to focus on 'a new top-level product group at Meta, focused on generative AI to turbocharge our work in this area', Zuckerberg said.[29] Even NFT support on Meta's existing platforms was ditched. The case of the missing metaverse would probably have been forgotten had Zuckerberg not rebranded the entire company around the idea. With the concurrency issues, real-time rendering limitations and lack of a universal protocol to allow for interoperability across 3D worlds, we might never get the singular and seamless metaverse of Neal Stephenson's dreams. Building such a world depends on a Web3 *Field of Dreams* fallacy: no matter whether virtual worlds could be built in the future, most normal people don't care and wouldn't come. But even if that changed, and all the techy issues got ironed out, the metaverse would still be fully optimised towards Silicon Valley's interests, not ours.

7

A World without Web3

In 2019, after a few years of researching so-called blockchain for good projects, I suggested in the journal *Nature Climate Change* that it would be too hasty to 'throw the blockchain baby out with Bitcoin's bathwater'.[1] Today, the writing is on the wall: blockchain is a rotting fruit bowl of bad ideas thrown hurriedly together to solve made-up problems. To explain how we should engage Web3 problem solving, computer scientist Nicholas Weaver devised what he called the 'Iron Law of Blockchain': when somebody says you can solve x with blockchain, they don't understand x, and you can ignore them. Without exception, the problem with all Web3 projects is that they have little interest and/or capacity to solve real problems. They merely reframe problems. In doing so, Web3 fixes create new sets of crises as an opportunity to launch yet more techno-fixes for profit. Cryptocurrencies are terrible. And we should not cling on in hope that the 'underlying blockchain technology' could come in handy for socialists, any more than we should cling to polystyrene balls or mustard gas.

The left-wing Canadian magazine *Adbusters* – the unofficial organisers of the Occupy movement – once suggested that 'Bitcoin was the story of what capitalism did to a good idea'. But Bitcoin was never an anti-imperialist technology that was somehow co-opted by free market fundamentalists. Bitcoin and blockchain were designed for and by right-wing anarcho-capitalist libertarians to weaken democratic government. This last chapter considers the many challenges of archiving the blockchain scam in the back of a museum some-where, and how we might change course away from Web3 thinking towards real digital innovation. But there are pow-erful vested interests with political backing, keen to keep the innovation illusion of blockchain going.

CRYPTOGANDA: THE MYTH OF ANTI-CAPITALIST BLOCKCHAIN

Ridding the web of Web3 will be tricky due to an enduring myth that free market capitalism can emancipate the poor from free market capitalism. This myth is epitomised in the book *Bitcoin and Black America*, in which Isaiah Jackson argues that cryptocurrencies are levelling the economic playing field, allowing poor Black communities the opportu-nity to enrich themselves and catch up with wealthy, mostly white, political elites.[2] But this narrative, according to Jared Ball, is 'cryptoganda'.[3] Ball argues that the mythology of 'Black capitalism' implies that the rich acquired their compounding wealth, not through violence, but through the same modes of investment that Black communities are now being advised to use in order to get ahead. Even if some poor Black investors do strike it rich from crypto, their personal investment strat-egies in no way benefit their wider communities. 'There is no investment pathway to collective revolutionary change or closing the material inequality gaps that exist between Black and white or any other group', Ball tells me. 'No technology has ever changed social relationships. They exacerbate and intensify them and allow for a consolidation of power and we're already seeing that happen in the cryptocurrency space.' Even if some Black communities had successfully enriched themselves by collaboratively investing early in a cryptocurrency, this on its own doesn't change the nature of a broader dog-eat-dog playing field.

Some academic literature has argued that blockchain technology can bring about a more equal society and is therefore useful for promoting something that resembles socialism. The Marxian economist Richard Wolff argues that digital platforms run by DAOs could be useful within a post-capitalist economy as part of a wider revolutionary agenda.[4] Steve Huckle and Martin White suggest that 'there is much about blockchain technology and its development that is directly applicable to various forms of socialism'.[5] Burning as much energy as a medium-sized-country to play guess the number, they argue, is much the same as workers toiling to produce something of value in the industrial economy. They argue that Bitcoin supports a socialist paradigm because it could be used by socialists, and that the organising principles that exist between blockchain coding teams have many similarities to anarchism.

There are plenty of political causes where anarcho-capitalists and socialists see eye to eye. Self-sovereignty over our personal data, for example. Data activists, such as Edward Snowden, Chelsea Manning[6] and Julian Assange, have all taken big personal hits to uphold the values shared by anti-imperialists the world over. Their activism tends to attract funding from crypto donors. Brittany Kaiser was a key whistle-blower in the disgraced Facebook snooping outfit Cambridge Analytica. But she also chairs a large Bitcoin-mining company and was an early Puertopian disciple of Brock Pierce. She was his presidential campaign manager in 2020. Similarly, the self-described anarcho-communist Alexandra Elbakyan has single-handily slapped the academic publishing industry that traps knowledge behind paywalls. Her Sci-Hub website offers access to millions of research papers and books. She has achieved what George Monbiot described as something 'more effective than any government to tackle one of the biggest rip-offs of the modern era: the capture of publicly funded research that should belong to us all'. Yet, all her work and legal fees are funded through crypto donations.

Julian Assange has always claimed that crypto saw WikiLeaks through its extra-legal banking blockade unscathed. A few months after the blockade, images of state brutality were beaming live across the globe as Occupy Wall Street protestors were seen bloodied and pepper sprayed while peacefully protesting in New York's Zuccotti Park. #FeedTheProtest, a website claiming to support the protestors, solicited for donations in Bitcoin. This came after PayPal again blocked donations to accounts associated with the 'illegal activities'. There was no strong link between Occupy and Bitcoin, just as there was no apparent link between Bitcoin and the right-wing Tea Party movement. But it felt, at the very least, like Bitcoin and Occupy were products of the same moment in history. 'Bitcoin is the real Occupy Wall Street', Assange said. His wife, Stella Assange repeated the claim at the Bitcoin Amsterdam Conference in 2022, while Julian was fighting extradition to the USA on charges of espionage. In April 2023, Julian's fight for freedom and Bitcoin was celebrated as the front cover of *Bitcoin Magazine*.

Vitalik Buterin founded *Bitcoin Magazine* during the Occupy protests. It was the first dedicated print magazine covering Bitcoin and digital currencies. Bitcoin's activist connections were made clear when the cover of the magazine's first issue depicted an Occupy protestor wearing an Anonymous mask. Buterin was not an anti-imperialist *per se*. He was driven to crypto after his World of Warcraft avatar was 'cruelly cancelled'.[7] 'I happily played World of Warcraft during 2007–2010, but one day [software developers] Blizzard removed the damage component from my beloved warlock's Siphon Life spell', Buterin said. 'I cried myself to sleep, and on that day, I realised what horrors centralised services can bring.' Nevertheless, Buterin appreciated Occupy for inflating the potential of crypto. With data activism, it's the journalism and activism bit that's subversive, not crypto. Similarly, Robin Hood was a virtuous character, not because he robbed the rich but because he gave to the poor. Just converting and holding your money as Bitcoin is no more subversive than converting your savings to Amazon gift vouchers. Crypto was never a sincere anti-capitalist uprising, because without a political struggle, nothing changes.

For most users, crypto is a slapstick acting out of stakeholder capitalism. A few weeks before the Occupy protests in 2011, much of where I lived in Clapham, south London, was going up in flames following several nights of looting and rioting. But in the mayhem, some young people were reportedly trying on clothes in the fitting rooms of looted sports shops, before taking the merchandise away (without paying), sometimes making a trip to the tills to collect a carrier bag.[8] Despite years of austerity following the global financial crisis, and the unlawful shooting of Mark Duggan by police, for some looters, the London riots were not part of an anti-racist insurrection or a protest against consumer capitalism. As Zygmunt Bauman explained, more than anything else, the riots were a manifestation of a consumerist desire violently enacted when unable to realise itself in the 'proper' way.[9] Similarly, cryptocurrencies were a response by defective and disqualified consumers: 'You called on us to be good capitalists, while simultaneously depriving us of the means to do it "properly" – now here we are, doing it with crypto.' As Slavoj Žižek argues in *The Relevance of the Communist Manifesto*:

At this point we reach the supreme irony of how ideology functions today: it appears precisely as its own opposite, as a radical critique of ideological utopias. The predominant ideology today is not a positive vision of some utopian future but a cynical resignation, an acceptance of how 'the world really is', accompanied by a warning that, if we want to change it (too much), only totalitarian horror can ensue.

Crypto is not a challenge to capitalist realism: the crises of imagination that Mark Fisher describes as leaving us with no alternatives to free market capitalism.[10] Crypto is free market capitalism in its most violent form.

Yet Bitcoin has acquired the aura of saviour in nominally socialist countries such as Cuba and Venezuela, suffering under external sanctions and hyperinflation. Antulio Rosales, a Venezuelan researcher at the University of New Brunswick, suggests that crypto is a last resort for many young people who have no jobs and no land. 'Since 2013, the Venezuelan economy has shrunk by around 80 percent. That's unprecedented outside of a warzone', Rosales tells me. Since 2006, US sanctions have prevented Venezuelans from accessing the US financial system. According to Rosales:

Young people were stuck. They're skilled and bright, but underutilised. So, they were either forced to find jobs outside Venezuela, or they find alternatives in digital finance. They know crypto is not going to solve the erosion of the economy. It's not a long-term option for them. And we can see that because as soon as Venezuelans were allowed to use US dollars again since 2019, crypto became far less popular. Once the crisis was gone, so was crypto.

Converting Bitcoin into anything remotely useful requires trust in a global system of shady shadow intermediaries. But when people are desperate, they will trade illicit things to survive. Some will even sell their own body parts. That doesn't mean human organs work as money. Using cryptocurrencies for something other than speculation – just like cocaine, kidneys and blood diamonds – is nothing more than a measure of duress and/or desperation. And crypto could never be more than that. Given the extremes of inequality in the currently existing Bitcoin economy, Jon Danielsson argues that Bitcoin's success in supplanting other mainstream means of exchange would never be widely tolerated, even by anarcho-capitalists.[11] Bitcoin has a Gini Index rating of 0.88, while Ethereum's sits at 0.90.[12] No country on earth has a higher level of income inequality than exists in Cryptoland.[13] As well as the inevitable environmental crises and resource conflicts that would quickly ensue under Bitcoin, enormous inequality would fuel social division and political instability. Most socialists (who care about this sort of thing) would baulk at a technology designed to bring about a libertarian fantasy featuring such extreme social disparity and waste.

Yet the left-wing Spanish activist Enric Duran has made cryptocurrencies his centrepiece for disobedience in the hope of enabling radical economic alternatives to flourish. Duran is more popularly known as Robin Banks in the newspapers. He's a Catalan activist who between 2006 and 2008 defrauded several Spanish banks of nearly half a million euros. He used the money to help set up the Catalan Integral Cooperative, a loose network of cooperative financial ventures. In 2014, Duran bought ten million FairCoins, roughly 20 per cent of the entire supply of that cryptocurrency, and set up the FairCoop. He chose the coin because he liked the name and judged it to be the most suitable for building an ethical currency system.[14] 'The FairCoop ecosystem was not just a currency network', Duran said. FairCoop was 'an alternative society'. The project grew steadily as members convinced local artisans and merchants in different territories to accept and trade with it. But after a few years of growth, the use of FairCoin came to a screeching halt. Xavier Balaguer Rasillo, a researcher of alternative economies at University of Zurich, told me: 'The project's dynamic governance structure, articulated around recommoning and degrowth values, was just a façade for speculative investments. There was limited transparency or communication in terms of the project's internal workings and, just like many other collapsing crypto organisations, there were stark examples of strategic mismanagement.'

FairCoin was a degrowth currency in much the same way that Dogecoin had something to do with dogs. Degrowth was a logo that failed to translate to radical economic alternatives.[15] Meanwhile, Jackson Palmer, the co-creator of Dogecoin, revealed his epiphany about the inherent conservatism of all crypto projects, from degrowth to dog money: 'After years of studying it, I believe that cryptocurrency is an inherently right-wing, hyper-capitalistic technology built primarily to amplify the wealth of its proponents through a combination of tax avoidance, diminished regulatory oversight and artificially enforced scarcity.'

There is a strong argument for big tech platforms to be broken up and/or regulated as 'natural monopolies'. James Muldoon suggests we should be treating the internet for what it really is – a public service – and creating the organisational structures that make it run in all our interests.[16] But crypto has no potential public service role. Cryptocurrencies and blockchain applications can't form a legitimate part of our digital economy, run in all our interests. We should treat crypto for what it is: a digital car boot sale, manned by unscrupulous salesmen keen to sell all their defective money-like things before the police show up. There is nothing of any value on the crypto stall. Making the stall appear more legitimate will not change its wares. In regulating crypto, our only question should be: how do we get rid of it?

CRACKING DOWN ON CRYPTO

If the political will exists, then controlling the most destructive aspects of crypto is straightforward. Cryptocurrencies don't produce anything with inherent value. Their market price can, and often does, fall to zero. For Proof of Work cryptocurrencies such as Bitcoin, the higher their price, the more prolific the problem. Likewise, if the costs of winning new coins outweighs the rewards for producing them, the resources going into them also falls. Should the market stagnate for long enough, then Proof of Work cryptocurrencies start to see an increasing number of miners capitulate. Miners with the highest costs sell off their Bitcoin holdings first as profitability drops, creating even more selling pressure in the market. Short-term capitulation among smaller mining outfits with high costs, using intermittent energy sources, is normal. But a domino effect with major mining firms closing down one after another would cause crypto prices, and the network's carbon emissions, to drop rapidly towards zero. This earth-saving event in crypto-speak is called a 'Bitcoin death spiral'.

The sensible fix to make sure we see a spiral effect would involve crypto holders dumping their stash ASAP. But markets don't work like that, and crypto prices are also subject to intense manipulation by exchanges and stablecoin issuers such as Tether. The funny business carried out on these platforms provides the appearance of bullish market sentiments to ward off the necessary selling pressure. Meaningful action will need the input of the state.

Nicholas Weaver argues that all crypto assets, including NFTs, are securities – as defined by the Howey test – and should be regulated as such.[17] But the US SEC, which would then need to oversee the regulation of most token releases, has generally taken a hands-off approach to crypto unless the release of tokens fails in spectacular fashion.[18] The SEC's remit, after all, is primarily to facilitate orderly capital formation. The lack of widespread proactive prosecution so far has meant crypto Ponzi promoters are simply playing the odds, which have so far tended to remain in their favour. The crypto scam has left millions penniless while a tiny elite have made off with fortunes. But for law makers there are tried and tested ways to rebalance things. As of early 2023, a US Justice Department Victims' Fund successfully recovered nearly 90 per cent of investments in Bernie Madoff's multi-billion dollar Ponzi scheme. The damage perpetrated by Madoff 'reverberates around the world, devastating thousands of victims', Assistant Director Luis Quesada of the FBI's Criminal Investigative Division said. Recovering the funds shows the government's 'unwavering commitment to bringing justice to the victims of Madoff's greedy crimes.[19] There are trillions of dollars in crypto markets, so Bitcoiners say. And so, there should be plenty of cash spare to claw back and compensate victims of the biggest scam in human history. As well as token offerings, regulators could crack down on exchanges and stablecoins. Weaver's *Digital Future Whitepaper* offers a thorough breakdown on what that should look like in practice.[20] But a continued light-touch approach risks an implied regulatory stamp of approval. A phased-in 30 per cent tax on electricity used for cryptocurrency mining has been proposed by US President Joe Biden for his 2024 fiscal year budget.

But as discussed in Chapter 3, if this is a standalone fix, the issue may simply be offshored while potentially worsening the climate impacts of the network as a whole.

A continuing light-touch regulatory relationship not only gives fraudulent crypto projects legitimacy, it also throws retail investors to the lions. Following the collapse of FTX, regulators in Japan secured the return of all Japanese customer funds totalling approximately $50 million. Meanwhile, customers in other countries got $0. According to the crypto blogger John Paul Koning, this was all thanks to the crypto lobby: 'Japanese FTX users were saved by a set of regulatory protections that US lobbyists had successfully fought off.' Left to its own devices, the industry will carry on the greenwash and wash trades and/or rebrand itself. The WEF's head of blockchain and digital assets, Brynly Llyr, has suggested that to rebuild public confidence, Web3 should become 'decentralised systems'.

While the crypto market crumbled in late 2022, the Nobel Prize-winning economist Paul Krugman saw 'uncomfortable parallels' between crypto and the subprime mortgage bubble, the precursor to the 2008 global financial crisis. The cause of Krugman's discomfort was not the abandoned communities left holding bags of magic crypto beans but the possible contagion routes between the wild west world of crypto and the regulated world of Wall Street. Like many liberal economic commentators, for Krugman the predatory nature of crypto was not the problem. After all, *caveat emptor*, and all that. Regulation that avoided upsetting the crypto sandbox, allowing continued fintech innovation and experiments, would require insulating the legitimate part of the economy from the unregulated and illegitimate part. But the world is a far dirtier and more dangerous place with crypto in tow, no matter how well the rich are insulated.

North Korean hackers had a bumper year in 2022, pinching somewhere between $630 million and $1 billion worth of crypto. According to a UN Security Council committee, the stolen crypto was being used to fund North Korea's nuclear weapons programmes.[21] In October 2021, a couple in West Virginia were arrested by FBI agents after hiding blueprints of nuclear-powered warships inside their sandwiches, before attempting to sell them in exchange for $100,000 worth of cryptocurrency.

Ordinary Americans lost $10.3 billion to online scammers in 2022,[22] while two out of every three businesses in the USA were hit with ransomware attacks.[23] Criminals forced 98 per cent of their victims to pay ransoms in Bitcoin. Around 25 per cent of US hospitals were hit by crypto ransom attacks since 2020, resulting in sharp increases in patient deaths in their aftermath.[24] Cryptocurrencies and ransomware are now so entwined that many experts claim the only way to fight the latter is to ban cryptocurrencies altogether.

Fixing problems with crypto requires a globally coordinated crackdown. This will be challenging. But while public scepticism towards crypto is growing, now is the time to do it. In 2021, a YouGov poll showed that nearly half of all Brits were in favour of banning crypto on climate change grounds alone. In December 2022, a poll in the USA found that just 8 per cent of Americans had a positive view of cryptocurrencies.[25] In September 2022, I was invited to be part of the first crypto sceptics conference of concerned academics, data activists and industry bosses.[26] Rhodri Davies told me: 'The mood music for crypto has changed. It's gone from innovative, to pyramid scheme. And, unless the music changes back again, risk averse businesses, charity trustees and marketeers are mostly going to steer clear of it.'

By late 2022, with every new business or charity jumping on the blockchain bandwagon, another was jumping off again. Most high-profile NFT drops or crypto schemes for good causes all faceplanted. A prompt backlash followed WWF's NFT fundraiser for critically endangered species. A David Bowie-inspired art project backfired when fans agreed 'Bowie On The Blockchain' betrayed the artist's futurist tendencies. 'Don't do this', read one tweet. 'Bowie was ahead of his time on so many things, not just musically – the early days of the internet, etc. THIS isn't novel or new. Not even interesting.' Even big games industry players were taking a pass on businesses with a blockchain. *Games Industry* magazine had nothing positive to say: 'Above and beyond the plentiful scams and schemes that still define the blockchain world, we have repeatedly seen that immutable and permanent digital ownership – the crucial thing advocates tout as the key innovation that NFTs offer people – is an illusion.'[27] When the cryptocurrency exchange FTX collapsed, it wasn't just FTX customers and ambassadors who were upset. All the 'immutable' functionality of the NFTs minted on the FTX Solana platform were lost forever. That included lifetime passes to Tomorrowland festival in Belgium and California's Coachella music festival, which had sold as NFTs for $1.5 million. When American NFL stars were paid to take part of their salaries in Bitcoin, they were blasted by fans for participating in 'crypto money laundering'.

In April 2023, the Texas Senate unanimously passed a bill to cut out Bitcoin miners' participation in the state's energy grid demand–response programmes. The bill still needs the sign-off from the House of Representatives where opposition could be intense. Conservative politicians and lobbying groups, including Dennis Porter's Satoshi Action Fund, have launched campaigns against the bill, which they say is 'anti-competitive'. But if approved, Bitcoiners could be gone from

Texas within a year. The growing upswell of opposition to Bitcoin mining in Texas all started with the pressure group Concerned Citizens of Navarro County, set up by the energy and environment activist Jackie Sawicky in opposition to Riot Blockchain's mining centre. 'We've been arranging town hall meetings and block walking every weekend', Sawicky tells me. 'There's a real sense of hope and momentum. This is people power indeed.' Bitcoin was born to subvert corrupt governments. But today, in the face of mounting people power opposition, the enthusiasm of these governments seems to be what's keeping crypto afloat.

BUYING LEGITIMACY

In an age of individual responsibility, the Web3 narrative remains especially alluring for conservative policymakers. Crypto has always been bad news for the little guys, but the narrative fits neatly into neoliberal ways of engaging global challenges. Despite always causing greater crises, Web3 innovations make problem solving profitable. But these neoliberal fixes are part of a broader market-based indifference towards life. The UK government, for example, has invested in a range of Web3 innovations to lower public health costs, such as the blockchain-based 'walk-to-earn' app Sweatcoin. The project was developed by a Portugal-based company and funded through a sizeable Innovation Grant from the UK government's Health Innovation Network. The app was designed to incentivise walking outdoors. Anyone with a smartphone and a data plan could download the Sweatcoin app, walk two miles and net themselves around 20 cents worth of sweatcoins. The project followed the same rug pull trading trajectory as almost every other crypto token. But Sweatcoin's tokenomics also worked by selling subscription packages. For $80 per year,

National Health Service (NHS) users could remove the app's arbitrary daily earnings limit. Users could also earn crypto by recruiting 30 or more new subscribers. The tokens could then be traded on a decentralised exchange app called Uniswap. But 97.7 per cent of all tokens launched on Uniswap were rug pulls. According to David Gerard: 'There's a simple and obvious heuristic to apply here: if you assume all [Uniswap tokens] are scams, you'll be right 97.7 per cent of the time.' And yet, Sweatcoin was considered by the UK government as something to do with healthcare. Perhaps a reason for this delusional approach was a revolving door between right-wing politicians and the crypto lobby.

In the USA, the total value of political donations from crypto companies in 2022 was greater than all defence and big pharma lobbying combined.[28] According to OpenSecrets, a research group that tracks political donations, crypto firms and their employees invested $73 million into the US 2022 elections, up from the $13 million contributed during the 2020 cycle. Sam Bankman-Fried made the largest donation among crypto industry representatives, totalling $39.8 million. He was the third largest total contributor for the 2022 elections. In the UK, the overlaps between conservative politics and the crypto industry is just as murky.

Tory donor Richard Sharp was reportedly an early investor in Swiss crypto business Atomyze, which was established by Russian oligarch Vladimir Potanin, once considered Russia's richest man. Sharp allegedly used an offshore Cayman Islands company to invest in Potanin's crypto outfit. Sharp was a former member of the Bank of England's financial policy committee before being appointed as chairman of the BBC after giving hundreds of thousands of pounds to the Conservative Party.[29] His lengthy career in the City included a 23-year stint at Goldman Sachs, where he employed Rishi Sunak, who would later become the UK's captain crypto and prime minister. Sunak famously addressed a debate on the cost-of-living crisis by ordering the Treasury to start minting an 'NFT for a Digital Britain'. The idea (whatever it was) was quietly mothballed a year later.

High-profile Tories such as Tom Tugendhat used Commons debates to explain how excited they were about their speculative investments in magic internet money. In 2021, former chancellor and Tory peer Philip Hammond joined the cryptocurrency firm Copper, helping the company win regulatory approval to operate in the UK. Hammond reportedly held 'growth shares' in Copper worth up to $15 million.[30] Even ex-Prime Minister Boris Johnson managed to slip awkwardly through the revolving door of the crypto industry. In December 2022, Johnson was invited as a keynote speaker at the International Symposium on Blockchain Advancements in Singapore. Johnson described the room of blockchain enthusiasts as 'pioneers at the cutting edge of a new and still infant technology'. He also urged them to 'come to London, come to the UK', while he argued that technology was 'morally neutral' and scepticism about its uses were 'generally wrong'. As well as receiving a $1 million personal loan facilitated by his crypto-crony Richard Sharp, new disclosures also suggest Johnson received $1.2 million from Bitcoiner and Brexiteer Christopher Harborne, in order to help stablecoin operator Tether circumvent a block on access to the US banking system.[31]

Disgraced ex-Minister for Health Matt Hancock pushed hard to make the UK 'the world's most crypto-loving economy'. Hancock also continued to extol the virtues of his magic beans that year as a guest speaker for Crypto Club dinners in London. He explained how the Conservatives had used blockchain to solve international development challenges for Africa and how crypto was helping refugees fleeing war in Ukraine.

In February 2022, Hancock set up 'From Ukraine with Love', a collection of images to be sold as NFTs to raise money for the war effort.[32] His commitment to crypto went down a treat among London's NFT enthusiasts. For Ukrainians, it was hard to swallow.

Using major exchange apps, such as Kucoin and Huobi, Russians were continuing to evade international sanctions with crypto. Crypto was enabling the Wagner Group to pay their mercenaries recruited from central Africa.[33] Even Ukraine's government had banned Bitcoin purchases on the grounds that they were undermining economic stability. In the spring of 2022, Hancock hosted Binance boss Changpeng Zhao who, despite pleas from the Ukrainian government, refused to block Russian crypto accounts on its platform. Binance and Zhao were under investigation for money laundering and criminal sanctions violations by the US Department of Justice. Binance's arguments against the filing of criminal charges included the claim that '[a] prosecution would wreak havoc on a blockchain industry already distressed from criminal activities'. Despite all the criminal shenanigans, for Hancock, Sunak and the other Tory Crypto Bros, the poor should not be sheltered from volatile crypto markets rife with grift and insider trading. Instead, they should be aggressively included. Hancock continued his march to become the master of the metaverse, urging Parliament to make the UK a hotbed for metaverse innovation.

For the Tories, the City of London remains the engine of the UK economy. Over the years, despite the many promises of 'levelling up' and a 'northern powerhouse', industrial production outside the City has continued to take a back seat to financial speculation and tax evasion with nothing of much value produced for society. Cryptocurrencies, NFTs and metaverse apps, whose economic valuations were being calculated based on an arbitrary 'Fear and Greed Index' based purely on popular sentiment, relied solely on a steady influx of new suckers to keep the market moving. And if they all lost their money to blockchain developers? They only had themselves to blame. As Bitcoiners say: 'do your own research'.

The UK's crypto lobby stepped up its influence in Westminster with the launch of an All-Party Parliamentary Group (APPG) made up of MPs and peers, including long-time Bitcoin champions Ed Vaisey, John Glen and Phil Davies. The 753 active groups outnumber sitting MPs and have a huge influence in UK public debate. All groups are externally funded but, like official select committees, they're still allowed to carry out meetings in Parliament and brand themselves with the UK Parliament logo. $25 million was funnelled into them in 2022. Chris Bryant, chair of the Commons Standards Committee, said in March that year: 'It feels as if every MP wants their own APPG, and every lobbying company sees an APPG as an ideal way of making a quick buck out of a trade or industry body.' A committee report warned that they could represent the next great parliamentary scandal.

The Crypto and Digital Assets group was one of three APPGs dedicated to Web3 and blockchain. But big crypto interests were also bankrolling other groups, including the APPGs representing a Central Bank Digital Currency and digital IDs. The Crypto and Digital Assets group was set up by CryptoUK, a trade association for the blockchain industry. Its membership included Hammond's Copper, Binance, Coinbase, Crypto.com and many other big crypto industry donors.[34] The other two groups – The Metaverse, and The Blockchain APPGs – were administered by the UK International Innovation Centre, otherwise known as the UKIIC Accelerator. Despite many MPs fearing China as an increasing threat to UK security, UKIIC was based in China. Their published remit involved 'upgrading China's soft power and international influence'.[35] To achieve this objective, in 2021 UKIIC purchased Magna Carta Island in Berkshire. At a cost of $5 million, the property would be used to host events promoting Chinese interests in the UK blockchain industry. The island hosted the forced signing of the Magna Carta by King John I in 1215. The island's name was convenient for UKIIC who also aimed for UK MPs to sign a Magna Carta for the Metaverse, or 'The Metacharter'. The project involved promoting blockchain-based digital IDs and smart cities, as well as record management systems for government and charities.[36]

In July 2022, Magna Carta Island played host to the crypto groups' MPs and corporate interests, including founding member and US-based crypto outfit Phoenix Community Capital. Phoenix was responsible for launching a rug pull token known as Fire. Then, in September 2022, the company vanished leaving their 8,000 or so investors in the lurch. Some investors claimed to have lost tens of thousands of dollars. The company reportedly pulled off the scam by promoting their links with UK parliamentarians.[37] UKIIC was affiliated with the Big Innovation Centre think tank, which sold access packages to other crypto companies needing to push crypto projects and tech agendas to parliamentarians with little transparency. Big Innovation Centre reportedly facilitated donations of over $600,000 in 2022, making it the sixth largest APPG donor.

THE NEXT BIG RIGHT-WING CONSPIRACY AND WEB3 SCAM

To counsel the many downhearted victims of crypto scams, there will be a Web3 industry ready to ensure what Erving Goffman referred to as their 'adaptation to failure'. Today's loss would be reframed as tomorrow's big win.[38] Victims can expect to hear cries of, 'one Bitcoin is worth one Bitcoin', 'buy the dip', 'diamond hands, not paper hands', 'HODL for dear life' and 'scared money doesn't make money'. These are all designed to keep crypto suckers captive.[39] In the aftermath of failed fundamentalist projects throughout history there have been zealots encouraging another go. Žižek notes that following the final days of the Soviet Union's collapse in 1989, zealots of the communist system blamed the crises as caused by a deficit of fundamentalist faith in communism. Similarly, following the 2008 global financial crisis, fundamentalist free market ideologues blamed Keynesian thinking for interfering in the beautiful self-regulating market system that was busy cleansing itself with 'creative destruction'.[40] Today, 'cooling out'[41] the victims from failed blockchain experiments involves fundamentalist calls for more decentralised automation, not less, with yet another set of Silicon Valley moonshots and pump projects.

Blockchain has been promising to revolutionise every industry for years. Today, generative AI is jumping on the same hype train. Sam Altman and Elon Musk's ChatGPT, for example, just like Google's Bard and Microsoft's Bing, generate uncanny human communication styles by rehashing human work usually without acknowledging it. They are in effect multi-billion dollar plagiarism engines. Like blockchains, these AI language models are prone to the same 'garbage in, garbage out' dilemma, which in AI circles is referred to as 'hallucinating'. For example, you could ask ChatGPT a basic maths problem: 'When I was 6 my sister was half my age. Now I'm 70. How old is my sister'. ChatGPT will, after a long explanation, confidently respond with an answer that's completely wrong. 'Garbage in, garbage out' hallucinations were causing problems for smart contract security too. Where the

AI feeds off bug-ridden garbage, the regurgitated smart contract also has the same features. Despite its clumsiness, many creative industries have turned to ChatGPT as an alternative to employing skilled humans. In March 2023, an open letter petitioning for an immediate moratorium on AI training attracted tens of thousands of signatures from concerned scientists. The letter was written by the longtermist group bankrolled by Elon Musk, the Future of Life Institute. '*Should* we automate away all the jobs, including the fulfilling ones? *Should* we develop nonhuman minds that might eventually outnumber, outsmart, obsolete and replace us? *Should* we risk loss of control of our civilization?', the letter asked.[42] In developing advanced language models some have likened Altman to J. Robert Oppenheimer, the coordinator of the Manhattan Project.[43] ChatGPT is indeed a potential 'destroyer of worlds', but not because of its intelligence. The real danger with these language models is that they offer a mechanical Turk parlour trick dressed as trustworthy, cutting-edge technology. Web3 word-hacks are used to suggest the box of tricks has brain-like qualities. Words such as 'neural nets' and 'hallucinations' give the appearance of unfathomable complexity to a search engine stealing other people's work.

In a lengthy 2021 essay, Altman used the observation of Moore's law to suggest the inevitability of engines such as ChatGPT rendering many creators redundant. But the unemployment crises could be resolved as follows:

Each of the 250 million adults in America would get about $13,500 every year. That dividend could be much higher if AI accelerates growth, but even if it's not, $13,500 will have much greater purchasing power than it does now because technology will have greatly reduced the cost of goods and services. And that effective purchasing power will go up dramatically every year.[44]

The proposed compensation would probably be paid in Altman and Musk's Worldcoin cryptocurrency. But how unemployment would be tackled outside of the USA is not explained.

A resurgence of interest in crypto is also likely with the introduction of CBDCs. These are essentially e-money systems – like the kind of money issued by M-Pesa or PayPal – controlled by a central bank. CBDCs are often pitched as a kind of cryptocurrency. They're cryptographically secured digital tokens with payment cards and online wallets. But they rarely rely on open blockchains or distributed validator networks.[45]

As of February 2023, 114 countries, representing over 95 per cent of global GDP, were exploring a CBDC. Eleven had already launched. But CBDCs are not a new thing. The Bank of Finland launched the first one back in 1993. It worked like a pre-payment smart card that could be topped up (for a fee) and used in some shops. Ecuador's followed in 2014, Uruguay's in 2017, Bahamas and the Eastern Caribbean in 2020. The Marshall Islands' Sovereign (SOV) was the first CBDC with a blockchain.[46] In a standard crypto-colonial power punch, the SOV was launched as an ICO pushed on the country in 2018 by Israeli fintech firm Neema. The Marshallese Declaration and Issuance of the Sovereign Currency Act 2018 set out a plan for the Marshall Islands to get twelve million SOVs, while Neema would get the same amount to sell (dump) on the global retail market.[47] The US Geological Survey predicted that due to climate change the Marshall Islands will start to disappear due to rising sea levels by 2035 and drinking water aquifers will be contaminated with saltwater. As a result, the Marshallese would be forced to migrate away from their homeland. Yet, minting new SOVs would require highly energy-intensive crypto mining and lots of carbon emissions. Neema's development of a decentralised Proof of Work blockchain for a centrally administered bank token left some believing the company had no idea what they were doing.[48]

The level of control governments have to programme their CBDC varies between each project. Most governments already have powers to freeze people's bank accounts. In February 2022, for example, the Canadian government ordered a freeze on more than 206 bank accounts as part of Prime Minister Justin Trudeau's Emergencies Act crackdown on anti-vaccine mandate protests. Private banks can already refuse to make unlawful or unusual payments based on their personalised modelling of a customer's normal spending habits. But as plans to develop CBDCs accelerate, so has the pushback against intermediated banking, while cryptocurrencies are being pitched as viable workarounds.

High-profile Bitcoiners have keenly peddled conspiracy theories to boost the value of their own crypto stash. Michael Saylor suggested that CBDCs were 'unstable and certain to fail'. Popular Bitcoin YouTuber and founder of Standard American [Bitcoin] Mining, Anthony Pompliano, told his followers:

Nasty shit is coming to money. Ultimately the central bankers will be able to say who you can transact with, what you can purchase, when you can purchase. Maybe they think you're fat and you shouldn't buy candy. This is totalitarian control over your financial life. If you don't have the freedom to transact, you're not free.

El Salvador's Bitcoin Ambassador, Max Keiser, shared his perspective at the 2022 Bitcoin Conference:

[A CBDC] gives the state greater powers of surveillance. They'll introduce things like currency that expires after a certain amount of time. They'll airdrop money into your government account and if you don't spend it in six months it expires. Everything becomes like a freaking Flyer Mile. And the ability to save money will be gone. The surveillance of everyone through their transactions will be pervasive and global. As we see in countries in Asia this is going to be used for a social credit score where if you spit on the sidewalk suddenly your social credit score goes down and you can't get on an airplane. It's social control. It's everything in a dystopian nightmare novel that we've read, like 1984 and Brave New World. All wrapped up into one neat digital fuckwickery.

As discussed in previous chapters, cryptocurrencies depend on right-wing anti-government conspiracy theories to give them a use case. In an interview with anti-feminist Bitcoiner, Layah Heilpern, in February 2022, the ex-UK Independence Party leader, Nigel Farage, explained: 'I'm thinking to myself, if we move towards [CBDCs] and I don't want government to control potentially every aspect of my life, this could be the biggest thing that's ever happened to Bitcoin and other crypto coins'.

To dispense similar narratives more efficiently, many crypto companies are writing their own news. 'Every tech company should go direct to their audience and become a media company',[49] Brian Armstrong opined in 2021 while announcing Coinbase Fact Check: his personal quest to 'decentralise truth in the age of misinformation'. While Twitter algorithms filter the news, Elon Musk has partnered with the trading app eToro to allow users a ramp onto cryptocurrencies.[50] CBDCs are excellent news for the crypto industry, but for all the wrong reasons. When right-wing crypto 'truth tellers' have vested interests in public distrust of state-backed money, CBDCs will likely add fuel to the conspiracy theory fire, reducing trust in governments while driving adoption of Bitcoin and other cryptocurrencies.

Most retail CBDCs will demand digital ID systems, which will integrate with a digital wallet to meet KYC requirements. The IMF, World Bank UN and the WEF have all committed to the development of digital IDs in almost every country by 2030. The target's been around since 2015, at the dawn of the UN SDGs, specifically SDG 16.9: 'Legal identity for all, including birth registration.' Under international human rights law, everyone already has the right to everything SDG 16.9 promises, whether or not they have a document to prove it.[51] But digital IDs are more than just a PDF of someone's birth certificate. SDG 16.9 has been widely interpreted as meaning a digitally documented proof of identity linked to a biometric database and issued to citizens from birth.

The goal's original spirit was to prevent statelessness. But digital IDs generally don't guarantee someone a nationality. As digital ID projects expand into other areas, including education and healthcare records, banking and tax information, the global goal has spurred the private sector to sniff out opportunities for profitable data harvesting. Many digital ID platforms, such as Sam Altman's Worldcoin, IOHK's Cardano project in Ethiopia and self-sovereign ID platforms in India, use blockchain to avoid the need for national-level mediation, even though the professed purpose of SDG 16.9 was to give people a nationality.

In September 2019, the birth of Brazilian 'Baby Álvaro' was the first in the world to be exclusively certified on an IBM blockchain. Álvaro's biometric data is today immutably stored with many others, shared with a network of private companies and government agencies. The plan for this brave new crypto citizen is to connect his unique blockchain entry to a crypto wallet and digital ID, which will then be linked indelibly to every notable event in Álvaro's life: vaccinations, college courses, salary, hip operations, death – everything. In April 2022, New York's crypto-friendly mayor, Eric Adams, confirmed his allegiance to blockchains, allowing IBM to store everything from New York citizens' birth certificates to property deeds. 'The stagnation, the inability of government to have these partnerships between corporate entities and government is what's keeping us back from solving so many problems', Adams said. 'Blockchain is the way of the future and we're excited about it.'[52]

In poorer countries, centring the development of digital IDs around the commercial interests of crypto companies exemplifies what Shoshana Zuboff calls *Surveillance Capitalism*.[53] States think they're getting a good deal on their digital infrastructure development, while companies grab private human experiences from citizens to be used as 'behavioural data' for their 'prediction products'. According to Laura Bingham from the Open Society Justice Initiative:

> States have low technical capacity. And so commercial vendors are dominating this space. They're approaching states with techno-utopian solutions for everything. But they end up being extremely costly and poorly designed. The vendors lock-in their position with states so that if [the state] ever wants to update anything, they're stuck. And they don't train government employees how to implement the systems.

Like CBDCs, digital IDs offer no clear benefits to citizens, while the obvious risks for a public who are already weary of government surveillance will push many towards crypto alternatives.

In the UK, the NHS Covid app was essentially a state-issued digital ID. And unbeknownst to most users, Amazon was reportedly given free access to all healthcare information collected by the app. The company's Alexa devices targeted users with health-related ads in order to 'reduce pressure on our hard-working GPs and pharmacists', said Matt Hancock, who agreed the deal.[54] In November 2022, Peter Thiel hired two senior NHS officials as well as former Labour cabinet minister Peter Mandelson, to acquire a $400 million data platform for England. The project would incorporate tens of millions of personal digital medical records into one of the biggest health data platforms in the world. Data could be used for targeted advertising and behavioural modelling, reportedly without obtaining explicit patient consent.[55]

From my many interviews with crypto fans around the world, the most popular motive for crypto-maximalism came from a perceived need to evade incoming government surveillance plans. The main source of evidence cited for this imminent full-spectrum control of our digital lives came from China's social credit system. This is understandable given the Western media coverage: the dystopian idea of Chinese government officials using algorithmic reputation scoring for every Chinese citizen based on real-time surveillance.

Former Vice President Mike Pence suggested that big data tools were controlling virtually every facet of human life in China.[56] *Wired* magazine suggested that one's place in Chinese society depended on your social credit score card. But according to Jeremy Daum, a senior researcher at Yale's Paul Tsai Centre, the Western media has created an idea of social credit that doesn't align with reality. 'The scoring mechanism gets so much traction and has become so popular because it resonates with a more global fear of emerging information technologies and surveillance', he said. Meanwhile, for Bitcoiners the only hedge against an impending grab for our privacy was Bitcoin, of course.

BACK TO THE FRYING PAN?

Putting out the fires from slapstick crypto capitalism doesn't mean jumping back in the frying pan of traditional market finance. In the frying pan, 'innovation', 'profit' and 'growth' are all used interchangeably. They are ends in themselves. Capitalist innovation, even of the 'green' variety, produces crises that ultimately call for further capitalist innovation for profit.[57] In the blockchain space, the favourite forum for launching capitalist innovations to solve crises of capitalism are developer competitions, hackathons and codefests. These time-bound and problem-focused events give small teams of experienced coders an opportunity to build digital applications to solve a global challenge. Several climate finance apps have launched off the back of the Elon Musk Foundation's XPrize. To get a look in for Prince William's Earthshot Prize,[58] climate change solutions should 'leverage the disruptive force of Web3'. As well as most UN agencies, we see similar gimmicks from crypto industry players themselves. Clawing itself out of the crypto 'bear market', the Solana blockchain company has organised a 'Grizzlython': a competitive coding challenge with a $5 million prize fund. The Grizzlython 'grand challenge' involves finding some practical use for the Solana blockchain. Adam Greenfield argues that these sorts of technical fixes often take the form of tetrapods: two-tonne spikey blocks of concrete used to prevent coastal erosion. Millions have been deposited at huge public expense along 55 per cent of the overall coastline of Japan. The problem is, they can accelerate erosion. They are worse than useless, yet they're still being produced in their thousands as a tacit state subsidy for the Japanese concrete industry.[59] Today, blockchain fits the same mould as the tetrapod. The industry has become a concrete feature on the landscape. Crypto courses are taught at most universities. Academic journals, incubators, conferences, 'climate warehouses', 'blockchain observatories' and other forums have all been pulled together at great expense. Policymakers and intergovernmental bodies often insist on blockchain because a blockchain has been built. But like the tetrapod, blockchains are worse than useless for solving any global challenge.

In challenging the crises–innovation spiral, it's tempting to reject digital innovation as something that ultimately capitalises on (or actively creates) crises. But capitalism is the problem here, not technology. Blockchain, like every techno-fix, embodies the political values shared by its design communities. Rather than understanding innovation as part of a wider growth imperative, we should recognise capitalism as an impediment to real digital innovation. Designing and building post-capitalist digital tools will require political struggles for post-capitalism. No app can take away from that fact. Only once developers embrace post-capitalist values can their digital innovations become untethered from the constraints and imperatives for economic growth and go about solving real human development challenges.

There are some successful examples of real digital innovations designed around human flourishing rather than growth for growth's sake. Wikipedia, the Internet Archive, Mastodon and the Mozilla Foundation together provide the backbone to what the internet can do best: spread knowledge at scale. They're not perfect. And while these projects depend on the good will of coders and charitable funders, they have all very publicly rejected cryptocurrencies and blockchain. This is because Web3 stands fundamentally at odds with their developers' free and open-source vision of the web.

Financial innovations will need a post-capitalist rethink too. Brett Scott argues that increasing our reliance on physical cash is our best shot at wrestling power from Wall Street and Silicon Valley. For Scott, the more that people rely on physical cash, the more inclined they'll be to spend money locally, free from surveillance capitalism.[60] Anitra Nelson suggests that localised economies may work just fine for people and planet at a local level. But when these money systems are drawn into competition with regional, national and global retailers, the whole thing quickly collapses. Nelson argues that we can't hope to establish a sustainable post-capitalist society without moving beyond money altogether.[61] 'Production for the sole purpose of trade is always going to be incredibly wasteful', she tells me. 'Instead of subordinating everything to systems of market pricing, we should use real values – actual social and ecological values whilst producing and allocating resources democratically.'

CONCLUSION

Cybercrime, terrorism, sanctions evasion, climate change and all the other social and environmental issues discussed in this book would be much easier to fix without cryptocurrencies. Crypto will always inhabit some dark corner of the internet, like ampules of smallpox in a Soviet-era bunker somewhere. As long as a handful of enthusiasts are validating transactions, crypto will live on. As with illegal pornography and snuff films, no amount of legislating will completely rid the internet of all traces of crypto. But banning crypto affects market confidence. And without confidence there is no con.

If pushed, crypto can be forced into some dusty back corner of the internet, like an old chess-playing automaton sitting in the back of a museum. At the dawn of the industrial revolution, Kempelen's chess Turk symbolised an unstoppable technological trajectory, a near-future where human ingenuity would be trounced by autonomous machines. One famous challenger of the Turk was Charles Babbage. He lost twice. Babbage apparently always suspected the Turk was a hoax. But playing and losing against it inspired Babbage to design with Ada Lovelace the world's first programmable computers: the Difference Engine and the Analytical Engine. These machines inspired Alan Turing's work on cryptography and AI. The Turk changed the world. The blockchain scam has too, but where shall we go from here?

Capitalists are not interested in decentralised and fully automated techno-fixes in order to free humanity from toil. For them, decentralisation and digital automation are part of the same quest to consolidate power rather than redistribute it. For example, in the aftermath of Covid, employees of McDonald's restaurants were demanding better pay and conditions before returning to work. But instead of a living wage, bosses developed the seemingly automated restaurant, circumventing pesky unionised workers. Some restaurants even embraced Bitcoin for a-political payments.[62] 'No more attitude at the counter: McDonald's has a fully automated restaurant completely run by MACHINES', read one UK newspaper headline.[63] Despite the restaurants' new cogs and gears, McDonald's was far from automated. Powerful humans with hands washed of any discernible accountabilities remained hidden behind the curtain. There is no such thing as full digital automation or a-political money. All digital innovations are developed with the interests and values of their developers in mind. Automated crypto restaurants, AI bots, blockchains and chess Turks all share the exact same fundamentals: underneath all their techno-blather, there are men pulling strings in their favour.

Notes

PREFACE

1. For example, in June 2022, a group of 26 technologists delivered an open letter to US lawmakers urging them to 'take a critical, sceptical approach toward industry claims that crypto-assets are an innovative technology that is unreservedly good'. See https://concerned.tech/.

INTRODUCTION

1. McKenzie, B. and Silverman, J. (2023) *Easy Money: Cryptocurrency, Casino Capitalism, and the Golden Age of Fraud*. Abrams, New York.
2. Like Satoshi Nakamoto, the mystery author(s) of the Bitcoin Whitepaper, the true identities of the chess master(s) operating the Turk during Kempelen's tour remain a mystery.
3. Some companies have experimented with building 'closed' or 'permissioned' blockchains, but these have a very niche set of uses, such as interbank lending platforms.
4. Howson, P. and de Vries, A. (2022) Preying on the poor? Opportunities and challenges for tackling the social and environmental threats of cryptocurrencies for vulnerable and low-income communities. *Energy Research & Social Science*, 84, 102394.
5. Gerard, D. (2017) *Attack of the 50 Foot Blockchain: Bitcoin, Blockchain, Ethereum and Smart Contracts*. Self-published, London.
6. Tully, S. (2021) How much Bitcoin comes from dirty coal? *Fortune*. 20 April. https://tinyurl.com/yhess6p5 (accessed: 2 March 2023).

7. Asmakov, A. (2022) Bitcoin hash rate suffers near 40% drop amid U.S. deadly winter storm. *Decrypt*. 26 December. https://tinyurl.com/2sjz9m82 (accessed: 2 March 2023).

8. Winner, L. (1980) Do artifacts have politics? *Daedalus, Modern Technology: Problem or Opportunity?* 109(1), 121–136.

9. Cypherpunk was a play on the science fiction genre cyberpunk. A cypher is a message written in a secret code.

10. Epstein, J. (2018) Tim May, father of crypto anarchy is dead at 66. *Reason*. 16 December. https://tinyurl.com/2nv46k9z (accessed: 2 March 2023).

11. Ibid.

12. Hayek, F. (1944) *The Road to Serfdom*. Routledge, London.

13. Phil Salin died of cancer in 1991.

14. These were neither smart nor contracts. They were a less sophisticated and less secure version of 'stored procedures', which have been around for decades.

15. Coindesk (2022) Edward Snowden on the long road to internet privacy. YouTube. www.youtube.com/watch?v=52l2lv33BkU (accessed: 3 March 2023).

16. Popper, N. (2016) *Digital Gold: The Untold Story of Bitcoin*. Penguin Books, London.

17. Golumbia, D. (2016) *The Politics of Bitcoin: Software as Right-Wing Extremism*. University of Minnesota Press, Minneapolis.

18. Ibid., 26.

19. Spencer, K. (2018) How bitcoin made right-wing conspiracy theories mainstream. *Salon*. https://tinyurl.com/3jnrubtk (accessed: 13 April 2023).

20. Farrow, R. (2019) How an élite university research centre concealed its relationship with Jeffrey Epstein. *The New Yorker*. https://tinyurl.com/2t32e52k (accessed: 13 April 2023).

21. MIT (2020) Faculty Gary Gensler. https://tinyurl.com/mtnsktkv (accessed: 13 April 2023).

22. Klein, J. (2022) Brian Forde: why Congress needs a crypto truth teller. *CoinDesk*. https://tinyurl.com/287ds8v8 (accessed: 13 April 2023).

23. Bloomberg (2018) Cryptoasset market coverage initiation: network creation. https://tinyurl.com/2c4d57er (accessed: 17 March 2023).

24. Coinbase (2022) A simple guide to the Web3 developer stack. Coinbase. https://tinyurl.com/4a62f9zc (accessed: 13 April 2023).

25. Morozov, E. (2013) The meme hustler. *The Baffler*. https://thebaffler.com/salvos/the-meme-hustler (accessed: 2 March 2023).

26. Sadowski, J. and Beegle, K. (2023) Expansive and extractive networks of Web3. *Big Data & Society*, 10(1), https://journals.sagepub.com/doi/full/10.1177/20539517231159629.

27. 'Web 3.0' was already being associated with Tim Berners-Lee's idea of the 'semantic web', so Wood went with 'Web3' instead.

28. Weaver, N. (2022) The death of cryptocurrency: the case for regulation. Yale Law School. https://tinyurl.com/2p8nys8r (accessed: 17 March 2023).

29. Mackenzie, S. (2022) Criminology towards the metaverse: cryptocurrency scams, grey economy and the technosocial. *The British Journal of Criminology*, 62(6), 1537–1552.

30. Ibid., 1545.

31. Swartz, L. (2022). Theorizing the 2017 blockchain ICO bubble as a network scam. *New Media & Society*, 24(7), 1695–1713.

32. Swartz, L. (2018) What was Bitcoin, what will it be? The techno-economic imaginaries of a new money technology. *Cultural Studies*, 32(4), 623–650.

33. Castillo, M. (2019) Secretary-general says United Nations must embrace blockchain. *Forbes*. https://tinyurl.com/mure29w4 (accessed: 13 April 2023).

34. Renieris, E. M. (2023) *Beyond Data: Reclaiming Human Rights at the Dawn of the Metaverse*. MIT Press, Cambridge, MA.

35. Howson, P. (2021) Cryptocurrencies like Bitcoin promise only false solutions for vulnerable communities. *Independent*. 20 September. https://tinyurl.com/cpfhwvv7 (accessed: 2 March 2023).

36. For example, Jamie Bartlett in *The Missing Cryptoqueen* exposes the fraudulent OneCoin cryptocurrency founded by Ruja Ignatova, who sold tokens without registering any transactions

on a blockchain, because there was no blockchain or cryptocurrency.

37. Smith, S. and Srivastava, L. (2022) Web3 and the trap of 'for good'. *Stanford Social Innovation Review*. https://tinyurl.com/3p3aycmb (accessed: 13 April 2023).

CHAPTER 1

1. Russo, C. (2020) *The Infinite Machine: How an Army of Crypto-Hackers Is Building the Next Internet with Ethereum*. Harper, New York.

2. Mackenzie, Criminology towards the metaverse.

3. Dale, B. (2017) Cryptocurrency has its potato salad moment with the useless Ethereum token. *The Observer*. https://observer.com/2017/07/useless-ethereum-token/ (accessed: 12 May 2023).

4. Wong, J. I. (2017) Eager cryptocurrency investors have sunk thousands of dollars into joke tokens. *Quartz*. https://qz.com/1023501/ethereum-ico-people-invested-thousands-of-dollars-in-useless-ethereum-token-uet (accessed: 12 May 2023).

5. Mackenzie, S. (2021) Inaugural lecture. YouTube. www.youtube.com/watch?v=IQv6RP8kh4A (accessed: 3 March 2023).

6. Song, J. (2022) Why Bitcoin isn't crypto. *Bitcoin Magazine*. https://Bitcoinmagazine.com/culture/why-Bitcoin-isnt-crypto (accessed: 3 March 2023).

7. Said, E. (1979) *Orientalism*. Vintage Books, New York.

8. Motiv (2022) Rich Swisher talks about Motiv with David Pingree on the whisky throttle show. YouTube. www.youtube.com/watch?v=iQa6c4OzRmY (accessed: 12 May 2023).

9. *Motiv* is the Romanian word for 'reason'.

10. Ibid.

11. Motiv.ngo.

12. Weiss, B. (2022) From El Salvador to South Africa, cryptocurrency evangelists are trying to persuade the world's poor to use bitcoin, not everyone is convinced they're helping. *Business Insider*. www.businessinsider.com/bitcoin-experiments-around-the-world-2022-8 (accessed: 12 May 2023).

13. Weiss, B. (2022) Christian crypto missionaries preaching Bitcoin in Latin America. *Gizmodo*. https://gizmodo.com/christian-crypto-missionaries-Bitcoin-lake-guatemala-1849508562 (accessed: 3 March 2023).

14. Melder, P. (2021) *The Christian Case for Bitcoin*. Self published.

15. Ibid.

16. 67Corvette (2022) Bitcoin Lake: The plan. *Medium*. https://tinyurl.com/mr3hebsx (accessed: 3 March 2023).

17. Vallis, J. (2022) Bitcoin Lake project in Guatemala with Patrick Melder. YouTube. https://tinyurl.com/4z9rna5y (accessed: 18 March 2023).

18. Self custodying involves holding cryptocurrency in a private wallet unconnected to a third-party exchange.

19. A seed phrase is a sequence of random words that stores the data required to access or recover cryptocurrency on blockchains or crypto wallets.

20. 67Corvette (2022) Lago Bitcoin. *Medium*. https://67corvette.medium.com/lago-Bitcoin-a2d4fad3797f (accessed: 3 March 2023).

21. Castor, A. (2021) Michael Peterson, El Salvador, and Bitcoin Beach. https://amycastor.com/2021/06/25/michael-peterson-el-salvador-and-Bitcoin-beach/ (accessed: 3 March 2023).

22. Fieser, E. (2021) World's biggest Bitcoin experiment is a surf town in El Salvador. *Bloomberg*. https://tinyurl.com/5xeevbab (accessed: 3 March 2023).

23. Munawa, F. (2022) Hyperbitcoinization is coming to an emerging market near you. *CoinDesk*. https://tinyurl.com/bdd5d7t9 (accessed: 3 March 2023).

24. Diehl, S. (2021) Bitcoin: The postmodern Ponzi. www.stephendiehl.com/blog/ponzi.html (accessed: 3 March 2023).

25. Nakamoto, S. (2009) Cryptography Mailing List. Satoshi Nakamoto Institute. https://tinyurl.com/52zrf8re (accessed: 18 May 2023).

26. Shevlin, R. (2021) The coronavirus cryptocurrency craze: who's behind the Bitcoin buying binge? *Forbes*. https://tinyurl.com/5xw4b32a (accessed: 3 March 2023).

27. Bloomberg Originals (2022) The dark side of microfinance, You-Tube. www.youtube.com/watch?v=N87PRcYuqkM (accessed: 12 May 2023).

28. Engel, S. and Pedersen, D. (2019) Microfinance as poverty-shame debt. *Emotions and Society*, 1(2), 181–196.

29. Pennock, L. (2022) Curse of the crypto whizz kids: missing millions, mysterious deaths and wild conspiracy theories. *Daily Mail*. https://tinyurl.com/4d2z5d45 (accessed: 3 March 2023).

30. Delfabbro, P. et al. (2021) Cryptocurrency trading, gambling and problem gambling. *Addictive Behaviours*, 122, 107021.

31. Pilgrim, K. (2021) Extra money, thanks to the student loan freeze. *College Finance*. https://tinyurl.com/yck9477y (accessed: 3 March 2023).

32. Brown, L. (2021) Student money survey 2021. *Save the Student*. https://tinyurl.com/47rcv7ab (accessed: 11 March 2023).

33. Chan, W. (2022) Jay-Z's Bitcoin School met with skepticism in his former Housing Project: 'I don't have money to be losing'. *The Guardian*. www.theguardian.com/music/2022/jun/17/jay-z-bitcoin-school-marcy-houses (accessed: 12 May 2023).

34. Onu, E. (2022) Nigeria SEC to avoid cryptocurrencies in Digital assets push. *Bloomberg*. https://tinyurl.com/4us5rhmj (accessed: 3 March 2023).

35. Hamacher, A. (2019) Jack Dorsey eyes Africa's Bitcoin market. *Decrypt*. https://decrypt.co/11417/jack-dorsey-eyes-africas-Bitcoin-market (accessed: 3 March 2023).

36. Mercy Corps Ventures (2022) Pilot launch: savings for low-income users in Cameroon through DeFi bond tokenization. *Medium*. https://tinyurl.com/36btx7a8 (accessed: 3 March 2023).

37. Wiedeman, R. (2022) How did SBF convince West Africans crypto was their future? *Intelligencer*. https://tinyurl.com/2p89jhe5 (accessed: 3 March 2023).

38. Ibid.

39. Adebayo, B. and Asher-Schapiro, A. (2022) Crypto collapse leaves Nigerian student ambassadors in lurch. *Context*. https://tinyurl.com/2tm879mh (accessed: 3 March 2023).

40. Armstrong, B. (2018) Introducing GiveCrypto. *Medium*. https://medium.com/givecrypto/introducing-givecrypto-org-fce707 dao3ee (accessed: 3 March 2023).

41. Schwartz, L. (2022) How coinbase's $1B crypto philanthropy ambitions left a trail of disappointment and workers in the lurch. *Fortune*. https://tinyurl.com/245432hz (accessed: 3 March 2023).

42. Ibid.

43. Nieva, R. and Sethi, A. (2022) Worldcoin promised free crypto if they scanned their eyeballs with the Orb. *BuzzFeed*. https://tinyurl.com/4wbsdxjk (accessed: 3 March 2023).

44. Ibid.

45. Guo, E. (2022) Deception, exploited workers, and cash handouts: how worldcoin recruited its first half a million test users. *MIT Technology Review*. https://tinyurl.com/y8ymdcaw (accessed: 3 March 2023).

46. White, O. et al. (2019) Digital identification: a key to inclusive growth. McKinsey & Co. https://tinyurl.com/5eb4h3au (accessed: 3 March 2023).

47. Travis, A. (2010) ID cards scheme to be scrapped within 100 days. *The Guardian*. https://tinyurl.com/4dka8m67 (accessed: 3 March 2023).

48. Venkataramakrishnan, S. and Wigglesworth, R. (2021) Inside the cult of crypto. *Financial Times*. https://tinyurl.com/mt7ut2xs (accessed: 3 March 2023).

CHAPTER 2

1. Fiat currencies are government-controlled money. The term tends to be used derogatorily in crypto subcultures.

2. Bitcoiners controlling more than 1 per cent of the total supply of Bitcoin are said to be members of the Vladamir Club.

3. Fyre Festival was a fraudulent luxury music festival founded in 2017 by Billy McFarland and rapper Ja Rule.

4. Luka Magnotta is probably a pseudonym. The real Magnotta is in prison for murdering a student and several cats.

5. Trader Cobb (2019) Brock Pierce's Smart City in Puerto Rico. YouTube. www.youtube.com/watch?v=D5I03_tqhqA (accessed: 12 May 2023).

6. Menn, J. (2014) Bitcoin Foundation hit by resignations over new director. *Reuters*. https://tinyurl.com/4rfx8hr7 (accessed: 12 March 2023).

7. Schreckinger, B. (2022) Bannon is helping a Vermont crypto bro get elected to the Senate. *Politico*. https://tinyurl.com/593nupcy (accessed: 12 March 2023).

8. Pelet, V. (2016) There's a health crisis on this Puerto Rican Island. *The Atlantic*. https://tinyurl.com/mu8bwp83 (accessed: 3 March 2023).

9. Valentín Ortiz, L. (2021) Puerto Rico Act 22 tax incentive fails. *Centro de Periodismo Investigativo*. https://tinyurl.com/3jxeraw5 (accessed: 3 March 2023).

10. Torres, A. (2023) New York businessman found guilty of shooting dog dead at a golf course in Puerto Rico. *Daily Mail*. https://tinyurl.com/4ndt9zse (accessed: 14 April 2023).

11. Glaze, V. (2021) Logan and Jake Paul under investigation after driving on beach during turtle nesting season. *Dexerto*. https://tinyurl.com/2uh25xd7 (accessed: 14 April 2023).

12. Crandall, J. (2019) Blockchains and the 'chains of empire': contextualizing blockchain, cryptocurrency, and neoliberalism in Puerto Rico. *Design and Culture*, 11(3), 279–300.

13. Paul, K. (2022) In balmy Puerto Rico, diehards shrug off the crypto winter. *The Guardian*. https://tinyurl.com/3ebfr2ez (accessed: 3 March 2023).

14. Nesheim, C. (2021) Vanuatu sets new CBI-revenue record for 2020 in 5th consecutive year of growth. *Investment Migration Insider*. https://tinyurl.com/bdfdxrek (accessed: 3 March 2023).

15. EC (2022) Vanuatu: council partially suspends Visa Waiver Agreement. https://tinyurl.com/mwt7zsjk (accessed: 3 March 2023).

16. PNG (2018) Finschaffen Special Economic Zone Bill 2018. https://tinyurl.com/5dsavn5k (accessed: 3 March 2023).

17. Sguazzin, A. (2022) Coinbase-backed Mara to help Central African Republic on Bitcoin. *Bloomberg*. https://tinyurl.com/36p9zrbj (accessed: 3 March 2023).

18. Valencia, R. (2023) Crypto barons get a diplomatic façade in El Salvador. *El Faro*. https://tinyurl.com/2wvdhy47 (accessed: 9 March 2023).

19. Crypto Critics' Corner (2023) Episode 108 – El Salvador and Bitfinex volcano token (feat. Domingo Flores). https://tinyurl.com/2p85evz3 (accessed: 3 March 2023).

20. Beijing Asia Pacific Xuan Hao (n.d.) Zona economica de libre comercio del Salvador. https://tinyurl.com/axbp6za7 (accessed: 3 March 2023).

21. Klein, N. (2007) *The Shock Doctrine*. Penguin, London.

22. Haskell is the 28th most popular programming language, used by less than 1 per cent of programmers on GitHub.

23. Renieris, E. (2021) Why a little-known blockchain-based identity project in Ethiopia should concern us all. *CIGI*. https://tinyurl.com/ptymwwnr (accessed: 3 March 2023).

24. Benjamin, R. (2020) Ruha Benjamin: how race and technology shape each other. *Emerson Today*. https://tinyurl.com/567b3d32 (accessed: 3 March 2023).

25. Marijnen, E. and Schouten, P. (2019) Electrifying the green peace? Electrification, conservation and conflict in Eastern Congo. *Conflict, Security & Development*, 19(1), 15–34.

26. Popescu, A. (2023) Gorillas, militias, and Bitcoin: why Congo's most famous National Park is betting big on crypto. *MIT Technology Review*. https://tinyurl.com/2p8nfuft (accessed: 3 March 2023).

27. Ryan-Mosley, T. (2022) He created an indigenous digital currency. *MIT Technology Review*. https://tinyurl.com/2f8eys9k (accessed: 3 March 2023).

28. Onu, E. (2022) Nigeria, Binance in talks for digital city to develop blockchain. *Bloomberg*. https://tinyurl.com/37wu2h2w (accessed: 13 March 2023).

29. Ellis-Petersen, H. (2019) US Bitcoin trader may face death penalty in Thailand over sea home. *The Guardian*. https://tinyurl.com/3mnua7f3 (accessed: 3 March 2023).

30. Doherty, B. (2019) How two Seasteaders wound up marked for death. *Reason*. https://tinyurl.com/m9ce48my (accessed: 3 March 2023).

31. Minicircle (2022) Access NFTs for a follistatin plasmid phase 1 clinical trial. *Minicircle*. https://tinyurl.com/4ex8jfsv (accessed: 3 March 2023).
32. Clarke, L. (2023) This biohacking company is using a crypto city to test controversial gene therapies. *MIT Technology Review*. https://tinyurl.com/5n6b7u98 (accessed: 3 March 2023).

CHAPTER 3

1. Market cap is defined by the value of one token multiplied by the total circulating supply of all tokens.
2. Paz, J. (2022) More than half of all Bitcoin trades are fake. *Forbes*. https://tinyurl.com/bdctkh28 (accessed: 13 March 2023).
3. Cong, L. W. et al. (2022) Crypto wash trading. *NBER*. https://tinyurl.com/27vtuape (accessed: 13 March 2023).
4. Based on Google averaging 63,000 search requests per second.
5. According to Chainalysis, merchant transactions account for 1.3 per cent of economic activity on the Bitcoin network, with speculation remaining the primary use.
6. Around 100–135 terawatt hours a year.
7. One Bitcoin is equal to 100 million satoshis (1 followed by 8 zeros). The block reward in 2023 was 6.25 Bitcoin.
8. De Vries, A. and Stoll, C. (2021) Bitcoin's growing e-waste problem. *Resources, Conservation and Recycling*, 175, 105901.
9. Ethereum requires users to stake a minimum of 32 Eth.
10. Bansal, D. (2020) Bitcoin astronomy. *Unchained Capital*. https://tinyurl.com/mwajwzcf (accessed: 5 March 2023).
11. Milman, O. (2022) Bitcoin miners revived a dying coal plant. *The Guardian*. https://tinyurl.com/5xf9waps (accessed: 5 March 2023).
12. Swaminathan, N. (2022) This power plant stopped burning fossil fuels, then Bitcoin came along. *Grist*. https://tinyurl.com/cnwzpnud (accessed: 5 March 2023).
13. Appleseed Inc. (2021) Greenidge Generation: economic impact statement. Greenidge Generation LLC. https://tinyurl.com/bcr998en (accessed: 5 March 2023).
14. Goodkind, A., Jones, B. and Berrens, R. (2020) Cryptodamages: monetary value estimates of the air pollution and human health

impacts of cryptocurrency mining. *Energy Research & Social Science*, 59, 101281.

15. US Department of the Interior (2022) Interior Department extends abandoned mine land program through 2034. https://tinyurl.com/yv8rxwj2 (accessed: 5 March 2023).

16. Monbiot, G. (2019) Britain's dirty secret: the burning tyres choking India. *The Guardian*. https://tinyurl.com/hyduxxs9 (accessed: 5 March 2023).

17. Williams, K. (2022) A neighbourhood's cryptocurrency mine: like a jet that never leaves. *Washington Post*. https://tinyurl.com/533ntdcx (accessed: 14 April 2023).

18. Lacey, A. and Hernandez, J. (2023) Trapped in their own home by Bitcoin mining's incessant din. Environmental Working Group. https://tinyurl.com/2p8a6nhr (accessed: 13 April 2023).

19. Satoshi Action Fund (2022) Orphaned Well Partnership Program Policy. https://tinyurl.com/jr9bty96 (accessed: 5 March 2023).

20. Howson and de Vries, Preying on the poor?

21. Lovgren, S. (2021) Two-thirds of the longest rivers no longer flow freely – and it's harming us. *National Geographic*. https://tinyurl.com/3adkur7p (accessed: 5 March 2023).

22. Plumer, B. (2020) Environmentalists and dam operators, at war for years, start making peace. *New York Times*. https://tinyurl.com/2p8u2cfp (accessed: 5 March 2023).

23. Aldhous, P. (2021) Texas winter storm excess deaths analysis. *GitHub*. https://tinyurl.com/4wm86rkr (accessed: 5 March 2023).

24. NOAA (2022) Navarro County conditions. https://tinyurl.com/2hr575cx (accessed: 5 March 2023).

25. Riot Blockchain rebranded as Riot Platforms in early 2023.

26. Barrett, E. (2022) Texas Bitcoin miners are getting paid to shut down amid heat wave. *Fortune*. https://tinyurl.com/2p983u5b (accessed: 5 March 2023).

27. Douglas, E. and Nguyen, A. (2023) Texas heat-related deaths reached a two-decade high in 2022 amid extreme temperatures. *Texas Tribune*. https://tinyurl.com/rf7rsyhw (accessed: 5 March 2023).

28. Quach, K. (2022) Bitcoin miner makes millions selling electricity to Texas. *The Register*. https://tinyurl.com/36xndzea (accessed: 5 March 2023).

29. Wright, L. (2022) Bitcoin mining company Compass Mining loses facility for not paying electricity bill. *CryptoSlate*. https://tinyurl.com/ytpuzz8z (accessed: 5 March 2023).

30. AFP (2022) Kosovo Serbs block road to main border crossings in volatile north. *The Guardian*. https://tinyurl.com/3srrpse7 (accessed: 5 March 2023).

31. Enegix Mining (2020) Opening our 2nd Bitcoin mining data centre with Kazakhstan PM. Twitter. https://tinyurl.com/yc8yw476 (accessed: 5 March 2023).

32. Segal, D. and Nechepurenko, I. (2021) The crypto capital of the world. *New York Times*. https://tinyurl.com/3wdmtpmd (accessed: 5 March 2023).

33. De, N. (2021) Michael Saylor: Mining Council will defend Bitcoin against uninformed and hostile energy critics. *CoinDesk*. https://tinyurl.com/2p9dhmyk (accessed: 5 March 2023).

34. De Vries, A. et al. (2022) Revisiting Bitcoin's carbon footprint. *Joule*, 6(3), 498–502.

35. www.coindesk.com/business/2022/04/21/flared-gas-bitcoin-miner-crusoe-energy-raises-350m-series-c/.

36. Sigalos, M. K. (2022) Exxon is mining Bitcoin in North Dakota as part of its plan to slash emissions. *CNBC*. https://tinyurl.com/tswxfhxs (accessed: 13 April 2023).

37. Milman, O. (2023) Revealed: Exxon made breathtakingly accurate climate predictions in 1970s and 80s. *The Guardian*. https://tinyurl.com/4rzhhjm8 (accessed: 5 March 2023).

38. Aronoff, K. (2018) Shell Oil executive boasts that his company influenced the Paris Agreement. *Intercept*. https://tinyurl.com/bdeatehr (accessed: 5 March 2023).

39. Howson, P. et al. (2019) Cryptocarbon: the promises and pitfalls of forest protection on a Blockchain. *Geoforum*, 100, 1–9.

40. UNEP (2022) In battle against Climate Crisis, don't overlook the Blockchain. https://tinyurl.com/yc67wnn9 (accessed: 5 March 2023).

41. Watt, R. (2021) The fantasy of carbon offsetting. *Environmental Politics*, 30(7), 1069–1088.

42. Howson, P. (2018) Slippery violence in the REDD+ forests of Central Kalimantan, Indonesia. *Conservation & Society*, 16(2), 136.

43. Song, L. (2019) An (even more) inconvenient truth: why carbon credits for forest preservation may be worse than nothing. *ProPublica*. https://tinyurl.com/kkw2uwsy (accessed: 5 March 2023).

44. Howson, Cryptocarbon, 1–9.

45. Lang, C. (2022) Toucan's crypto layer on top of carbon offsets is expanding the market for toxic hot air. *Redd Monitor*. https://tinyurl.com/24ytdpj9 (accessed: 5 March 2023).

46. Ibid.

47. KlimaDAO (2022) Response to Verra's comments on crypto instruments and tokens. *KlimaDAO*. https://tinyurl.com/ycxabncw (accessed: 5 March 2023).

48. Camilleri, M. (2022) How billionaire Mark Cuban got revenge on DeFi with KlimaDAO. *Protos*. https://tinyurl.com/36c777md (accessed: 5 March 2023).

49. Howson, P. (2020) Building trust and equity in marine conservation and fisheries supply chain management with blockchain. *Marine Policy*, 115, 103873.

CHAPTER 4

1. Vanian, J. (2022) Melania Trump put an NFT up for sale. *Fortune*. https://tinyurl.com/bdf47kup (accessed: 11 March 2023).

2. Davis, B. (2021) I looked through all 5,000 images in Beeple's $69 million magnum opus, what I found isn't so pretty. *Artnet News*. news.artnet.com/opinion/beeple-everydays-review-1951656 (accessed: 13 May 2023).

3. Castor, A. (2021) Metakovan. https://tinyurl.com/2p88p2yc (accessed: 7 March 2023).

4. White, M. (2022) Tax loss harvesting service emerges to help collectors unload their worthless NFTs. *Web3 Is Going Just Great*. https://tinyurl.com/2zbxm27p (accessed: 7 March 2023).

5. Shin, L. (2019) How donating crypto can help you save on taxes – Ep.94. YouTube. https://tinyurl.com/5xx7uj45 (accessed: 7 March 2023).

6. Cammaerts, B. et al. (2013) The myth of youth apathy. *American Behavioural Scientist*, 58(5), pp. 645–664.

7. Milmo, D. (2022) Elon Musk denies he sexually harassed attendant on private jet in 2016. *The Guardian*. https://tinyurl.com/muyznj4f (accessed: 7 March 2023).

8. As defined by US Department of the Treasury's Financial Action Task Force and Office of Foreign Assets Control.

9. Mollersen, J. (2013) Using human rights for right-wing politics. *Truthout*. https://tinyurl.com/ysnhrfwa (accessed: 7 March 2023).

10. Gillet, K. (2017) Romanian UNESCO site proposal may be halted to allow gold mining. *The Guardian*. https://tinyurl.com/2jkenamv (accessed: 7 March 2023).

11. Wilser, J. (2022) Garry Kasparov: Bitcoin will remain as a standard. *CoinDesk*. https://tinyurl.com/m7dbr8j6 (accessed: 7 March 2023).

12. Blumenthal, M. (2017) Oslo Freedom Forum founder's ties to Islamophobes. *The Electronic Intifada*. https://tinyurl.com/ypesck39 (accessed: 7 March 2023).

13. Bostrom, N. (2019) The vulnerable world hypothesis. *Global Policy*, 10(4) 455–476.

14. Bostrom, N. (1996) Re: offending people's minds. *Extropians*. https://tinyurl.com/55sc79ah (accessed: 7 March 2023).

15. Andersen, R. (2023) Elon Musk puts his case for a multi-planet civilisation. *Aeon*. https://tinyurl.com/5f4n9sx4 (accessed: 7 March 2023).

16. Al-Sibai, N. (2022) Elon Musk hired a professional gambler to manage his philanthropic donations. *Futurism*. https://tinyurl.com/c45ud2ey (accessed: 19 March 2023).

17. Alter, C. (2023) Effective altruism has a sexual harassment problem, women say. *Time*. https://tinyurl.com/4cnxyy2w / (accessed: 7 March 2023).

18. Ibid.

19. UN (2021) Our common agenda. https://tinyurl.com/4wayxuw3 (accessed: 7 March 2023).

20. Piper, K. (2019) Britain's youngest self-made billionaire is giving away his fortune – to people who don't exist yet. *Vox.* https://tinyurl.com/2p8csa62 (accessed: 15 April 2023).

21. State of California (2020) Courtlistener. Case No: CGC-19-581267. https://tinyurl.com/zcvawky6 (accessed: 7 March 2023).

22. Ibid.

23. *Business Insider* (2021) Inside the college years of the 29-year-old crypto billionaire Sam Bankman-Fried. https://tinyurl.com/233vw3ch (accessed: 13 April 2023).

24. Alter, C. (2023) Effective altruist leaders were warned about Sam Bankman-Fried years before FTX collapse. *Time.* https://tinyurl.com/bdhb5suy (accessed: 16 March 2023).

25. Department of Justice (2022) FTX founder indicted for fraud, money laundering, and campaign finance offenses. https://tinyurl.com/k9px3cs3 (accessed: 18 May 2023).

26. Ibid.

27. Srinivasan, A. (2021) Stop the robot apocalypse: the new utilitarians. *London Review of Books.* https://tinyurl.com/44vsfy6v (accessed: 7 March 2023).

28. Cundy, A. (2023) Oxford University stuck with Sacklers as opioid deaths led others to cut ties. *Financial Times.* https://tinyurl.com/39zzxkkr (accessed: 7 March 2023).

29. Mance, H. (2022) Louise Richardson: I do wish our students were more resilient about nasty remarks. *Financial Times.* https://tinyurl.com/5n8ns4fz (accessed: 7 March 2023).

30. Bercovici, J. (2016) Peter Thiel is very, very interested in young people's blood. *Inc.* https://tinyurl.com/4fyemzum (accessed: 7 March 2023).

31. Tangermann, V. (2021) Billionaire launches startup to reprogram human gene expression. *Futurism.* https://futurism.com/neoscope/billionaire-launches-startup-epigenetic-reprogramming (accessed: 12 May 2023).

32. Fong, T. (2022) sam Bankman-Fried's first interview after FTX Collapse. YouTube. https://tinyurl.com/bp8v9x8j (accessed: 7 March 2023).

33. Lee, M. (2022) Oath keepers, anti-democracy activists, and others on the far right are funding Canada's Freedom Convoy.

The Intercept. https://tinyurl.com/5fyabffm (accessed: 7 March 2023).

34. Malik, H. (2022) Canadian trucker protest raises over $900,000 in Bitcoin after GoFundMe blocks millions of dollars in donations. *Business Insider.* https://tinyurl.com/yav2wbyz (accessed: 15 April 2023).

35. www.theguardian.com/news/2018/feb/15/why-silicon-valley-billionaires-are-prepping-for-the-apocalypse-in-new-zealand.

36. Holiday, R. (2018) *Conspiracy: Peter Thiel, Hulk Hogan, Gawker, and the Anatomy of Intrigue.* Portfolio, New York.

37. Howson, P. (2020) Crypto-giving and surveillance philanthropy: exploring the trade-offs in blockchain innovation for nonprofits. *Nonprofit Management and Leadership*, 31(4), 805–820.

38. May, M. (2021) Oxfam sees aid funding suspended over DRC abuse allegations. *UK Fundraising.* https://tinyurl.com/z8n5tn6r (accessed: 7 March 2023).

39. Warren, T. and Baker, K. (2019) WWF funds guards who have tortured and killed people. *BuzzFeed News.* https://tinyurl.com/5xajn96y (accessed: 7 March 2023).

40. Safronova, V. (2022) A party crawl with pussy riot's Nadya Tolokonnikova. *New York Times.* https://tinyurl.com/58xzxxtu (accessed: 7 March 2023).

41. *Kyiv Post* (2023) Money disappearing from major charity to help Ukraine – is there a scam? https://tinyurl.com/4h8vheew (accessed: 12 May 2023).

42. Muldoon, J. (2022) Web3 can't fix the internet. *Jacobin.* https://tinyurl.com/5pu2tkew (accessed: 15 March 2023).

43. Golumbia, *The Politics of Bitcoin.*

44. Giftcoin (2017) Giftcoin White Paper. https://tinyurl.com/yym3j2a4 (accessed: 18 May 2023).

45. Howson, Crypto-giving and surveillance philanthropy.

46. Cryptocurrency donations were converted locally to Ugandan shillings before being transferred either using mobile money services or a traditional bank transfer.

47. GiveDirectly (2019) GiveDirect RCT Overview 20110616. https://tinyurl.com/yawr5u9r (accessed: 7 March 2023).

48. HRW (2021) UN shared Rohingya data without informed consent. Human Rights Watch. https://tinyurl.com/dn6sjk2v (accessed: 13 March 2023).
49. Howson, P. (2020) Climate crises and crypto-colonialism: conjuring value on the blockchain frontiers of the Global South. *Frontiers in Blockchain*, 3, 1–6.
50. Cheesman, M. (2022) Blockchain for refugees. *Data & Society: Points*. https://points.datasociety.net/blockchain-for-refugees-a46b41594eee (accessed: 9 March 2023).

CHAPTER 5

1. For his promotion of Dogecoin, Elon Musk is currently being sued in the US federal court of Manhattan for $258 billion.
2. In October 2022, the promoters were charged by the US Securities and Exchange Commission (SEC) for touting EthereumMax without disclosing the $250,000 payment's they received for doing so. Kardashian agreed to pay $1.26 million in penalties and was banned from endorsing crypto products for three years.
3. Henshaw, A. (2022) Women, consider crypto: gender in the virtual economy of decentralized finance. *Politics & Gender*, 1–25, https://doi.org/10.1017/S1743923X22000253.
4. Lagarde, C. (2010) Women, power and the challenge of the financial crisis. *New York Times*. www.nytimes.com/2010/05/11/opinion/11iht-edlagarde.html?dbk (accessed: 12 May 2023).
5. Palmer, D. (2021) Ex-Enron CEO leaves jail to plot possible blockchain venture. *CoinDesk*. https://tinyurl.com/28dvjb9c (accessed: 9 March 2023).
6. Jack, J. (2014) Autism and Gender: From Refrigerator Mothers to Computer Geeks. University of Illinois Press, Champaign, IL.
7. Mac, R. and Baker, K. (2018) A cryptocurrency pioneer wrote about sex with a preteen girl. *BuzzFeed News*. https://tinyurl.com/ycdpbpn5 (accessed: 9 March 2023).
8. Okcoin (2021) Okcoin announces $1M commitment to bring more women into crypto. https://tinyurl.com/3epv8kjy (accessed: 14 March 2023).

9. USDJ (2022) Former employee of NFT Marketplace charged in first ever Digital Asset Insider Trading Scheme. https://tinyurl.com/4nev8a9t (accessed: 14 March 2023).

10. Gamergate was a loosely organised misogynistic online harassment campaign and a right-wing backlash against feminism in the videogame industry, which occurred mainly between 2014 and 2015.

11. Hayward, A. (2021) Sorry for the lie: Ethereum NFT fraud fame Lady Squad comes clean. *Decrypt*. Available at: https://tinyurl.com/3hxdxm95 (accessed: 14 March 2023).

12. Kwan, J. (2021) An artist died, then thieves made NFTs of her work. *Wired*. https://tinyurl.com/2be23fyc (accessed: 14 March 2023).

13. Sung, M. (2022) Anna Sorokin plans to launch an NFT collection. *NBC News*. https://tinyurl.com/bdcujfnx (accessed: 9 March 2023).

14. Vogel, L. (2016) Fracking tied to cancer-causing chemicals. *Canadian Medical Association Journal*, 189(2), www.ncbi.nlm.nih.gov/pmc/articles/PMC5235941/.

15. Clabots, B. (2019) The darkest side of fossil-fuel extraction. *Scientific American*. https://tinyurl.com/3wf7pd4p (accessed: 11 March 2023).

16. Henshaw, Women, consider crypto.

17. Cornwall, A., Harrison, E. and Whitehead, A. (2007) Gender myths and feminist fables: the struggle for interpretive power in gender and development. *Development and Change*, 38(1), 1–20.

18. SpankChain (2017) Introducing SpankChain. YouTube. https://tinyurl.com/2p85ymhb (accessed: 3 March 2023).

19. Consensys (2019) World Wide Fund for Nature and consensys launch blockchain platform. Available at: https://tinyurl.com/29hstw8h (accessed: 9 March 2023).

20. UNOICT (2018) Consensys wins #Blockchain4Humanity Challenge. *UN Press*. https://tinyurl.com/34jr5b4t (accessed: 9 March 2023).

21. Tran, K. (2019) What is SpankChain? The guide to the adult crypto. *Decrypt*. https://tinyurl.com/bddpbvhc (accessed: 9 March 2023).

22. A 2019 study carried out by the National Centre on Sexual Exploitation found that 88 per cent of PornHub videos contained physical violence towards women, with 15 per cent depicting rape.

23. Kristof, N. (2020) The children of Pornhub. *New York Times.* https://tinyurl.com/wa89a2wh (accessed: 14 March 2023).

24. Cohen, A. (2023) Sorare NFTs should be regulated under new category, CEO says. *Decrypt.* https://tinyurl.com/2fx5f8ur (accessed: 9 March 2023).

25. Daly, S. E. and Laskovtsov, A. (2021) Goodbye, my friendcels: an analysis of incel suicide posts. *Journal of Qualitative Criminal Justice & Criminology.* https://tinyurl.com/2c2ej3rm (accessed: 9 March 2023).

26. Hayden, M. and Squire, M. (2021) How cryptocurrency revolutionized the white supremacist movement. Southern Poverty Law Center. https://tinyurl.com/5e9xvdwd (accessed: 9 March 2023).

27. Bates, L. (2021) *Men Who Hate Women.* Simon & Schuster, London.

28. Hayden and Squire, How cryptocurrency revolutionized the white supremacist movement.

29. Bates, *Men Who Hate Women.*

30. Roosh, V. (2016) *How To Make Your First Bitcoin Purchase.* https://tinyurl.com/558z4b9r (accessed: 18 May 2023).

31. The pig-butchering scam, also known as a romance scam, is a long-term fraud that combines investment schemes, romance scams and cryptocurrency.

32. Tahsin, J., Shea, M. and Hume, T. (2023) I love raping you: what Andrew Tate told woman who accused him of rape. *Vice.* https://tinyurl.com/5wpjxy8z (accessed: 9 March 2023).

33. Fazackerley, A. (2023) Vulnerable boys are drawn in: schools fear spread of Andrew Tate's misogyny. *The Guardian.* https://tinyurl.com/bdde4u2r (accessed: 9 March 2023).

34. Marshall, C. (2023) Logan Paul's crypto drama and pet pig fiasco, explained. *Polygon.* https://tinyurl.com/yj6xptrn (accessed: 9 March 2023).

35. State of Texas (2023) Courtlistener. No:1:23-cv-110. https://tinyurl.com/ysspch39. (accessed: 9 March 2023).

36. TBS (2021) Chinese couple kills daughter, commit suicide due to loss in Bitcoin. *Business Standard*. https://tinyurl.com/2nxs85fp (accessed: 9 March 2023).

37. www.timesnownews.com/india/article/punjab-cryptocurrency-trader-shoots-wife-two-kids-dead-before-ending-his-own-life-after-threats/671545.

38. Tribune News (2020) Man into online trading shoots dead wife, children before killing himself in Bathinda. *Tribune India*. https://tinyurl.com/yck46c9d (accessed: 9 March 2023).

39. Evans, H. and Sharman, L. (2022) Bitcoin trader, 23, takes own life after break-up and losing all his money. *Mirror*. https://tinyurl.com/2m5wz5pd (accessed: 9 March 2023).

40. Hood, L. (2022) Suicidal posts spike after crypto project crashes. *Futurism*. https://tinyurl.com/mrehut5k (accessed: 9 March 2023).

41. Singh, M. and Mattackal, L. (2022) Cryptoverse: forget crypto winter, this is a Bitcoin bloodbath. *Reuters*. https://tinyurl.com/nhj8amku (accessed: 9 March 2023).

42. Sanyal, M. (2019) *Rape: From Lucretia to #MeToo*. Verso, London.

43. Olson, D. (2022) Line goes up – the problem with NFTs. YouTube. https://tinyurl.com/mr4uazb4 (accessed: 9 March 2023).

CHAPTER 6

1. Gissen, L. (2021) Couple who met online holds virtual wedding in metaverse. *Daily Mail Online*. https://tinyurl.com/4w6zak8w (accessed: 11 March 2023).

2. Rose, C. (2019) Thanks to DNA block and a dome of 160 high powered cameras. Twitter. https://tinyurl.com/b44mmd42 (accessed: 11 March 2023).

3. Campbell, C. (2022) *AI By Design: A Plan for Living with Artificial Intelligence*. CRC Press, Boca Raton, FL.

4. Ball, M. (2023) Framework for the metaverse. https://tinyurl.com/mty66vdj (accessed: 11 March 2023).

5. Beaulieu, V. (2023) 6 world of work challenges the metaverse will help address. World Economic Forum. https://tinyurl.com/y5knwmur (accessed: 11 March 2023).

6. Rose, S. (2022) The metaverse will be our slow death! *The Guardian*. https://tinyurl.com/2c9fjr9h (accessed: 11 March 2023).

7. Grygiel, J. (2022) Livestreamed massacre means it's time to shut down Facebook Live. *Conversation*. https://tinyurl.com/2j2jranm (accessed: 11 March 2023).

8. Hady, L. (2022) Opinion: it's time we treated social media as the addiction machine it really is. *Independent*. https://tinyurl.com/4w8wpfbm (accessed: 11 March 2023).

9. Raphael, L. (2018) Mark Zuckerberg called people who handed over their data 'Dumb f****'. *Esquire*. https://tinyurl.com/4z-rh7yy3 (accessed: 11 March 2023).

10. Gerard, D. (2020) *Libra Shrugged: How Facebook Tried to Take Over the Money*. Self-published, London.

11. Castor, A. (2023) Crypto collapse: good night Silvergate Bank. https://tinyurl.com/42444b54 (accessed: 11 March 2023).

12. Murphy, H. (2022) Facebook owner Meta targets finance with Zuck Bucks. *Financial Times*. https://tinyurl.com/bp87fheu (accessed: 11 March 2023).

13. Foust, J. (2018) A changing shade of blue. *The Space Review*. https://tinyurl.com/3pvbbeup (accessed: 11 March 2023).

14. Temple, J. (2023) These startups hope to spray iron particles above the ocean to fight climate change. *MIT Technology Review*. https://tinyurl.com/mtm5nc2z (accessed: 11 March 2023).

15. Clegg, N. (2022) Making the metaverse: what it is, how it will be built, and why it matters. *Medium*. https://tinyurl.com/5f7yx3k6 (accessed: 11 March 2023).

16. Markey, E. (2023) Sens. Markey, Blumenthal urge Zuckerberg to halt plan to bring young teens into the metaverse. https://tinyurl.com/4x6nvdvn (accessed: 11 March 2023).

17. Patel, N. J. (2022) Fiction vs. non-fiction. *Medium*. https://tinyurl.com/4hwd635f (accessed: 11 March 2023).

18. Neuralink (2022) Show and tell, fall 2022. YouTube. https://tinyurl.com/wy3438wn (accessed: 11 March 2023).

19. Huet, N. (2022) Game over: the VR headset designed to kill you if you die in a game. *Euronews*. https://tinyurl.com/583vdrth (accessed: 11 March 2023).

20. Exit International (n.d.) Euthanasia Workshop for ACT Elderly to teach eMail encryption & Bitcoin use. *Exit*. https://tinyurl.com/2wweutth (accessed: 11 March 2023).

21. Martingano, A. J. et al. (2022) The limited benefits of using virtual reality 360° videos to promote empathy and charitable giving. *Nonprofit and Voluntary Sector Quarterly*, https://journals.sagepub.com/doi/10.1177/08997640221125804.

22. Rieland, R. (2016) How virtual reality can help us feel the pain of climate change. Smithsonian Institution. https://tinyurl.com/y6rpnxb6 (accessed: 11 March 2023).

23. Li, C. and Collins, K. (2023) Interoperability in the metaverse. World Economic Forum. https://tinyurl.com/2s3nvrx5 (accessed: 11 March 2023).

24. Jagannathan, S. (2022) How could the metaverse impact education? World Economic Forum. https://tinyurl.com/3xdvmn6j (accessed: 11 March 2023).

25. Delfabbro, P., Delic, A. and King, D. L. (2022) Understanding the mechanics and consumer risks associated with play-to-earn (P2E) gaming. *Journal of Behavioural Addictions*, 11(3), 716–726.

26. Ongweso Jr, E. (2022) The metaverse has bosses too. *Vice*. https://tinyurl.com/3krdd3ec (accessed: 11 March 2023).

27. Perper, R. (2023) Yuga Labs otherside metaverse to launch. *CoinDesk*. https://tinyurl.com/46rrd3f5 (accessed: 11 March 2023).

28. White, M. (2023) Yuga Labs' 3-week-long 'Dookey dash' game tournament ends. *Web3 is Going Just Great*. Available at: https://tinyurl.com/43fw5nbu (accessed: 11 March 2023).

29. Zuckerberg, M. (2023) Mark Zuckerberg. Facebook. https://tinyurl.com/yc3m4s2b (accessed: 11 March 2023).

CHAPTER 7

1. Howson, P. (2019) Tackling climate change with Blockchain. *Nature Climate Change*, 9(9), 644–645.

2. Jackson, I. (2019) Bitcoin and Black America. Self-published.
3. Ball, J. A. (2020) *The Myth and Propaganda of Black Buying Power*. Palgrave Macmillan, Cham.
4. McGleenon, B. (2022) Karl Marx would see Bitcoin as a revolutionary tool to upend capitalism. *Yahoo News*. https://tinyurl.com/3v4hzk4k (accessed: 15 March 2023).
5. Huckle, S. and White, M. (2016) Socialism and the blockchain. *Future Internet*, 8(4), 49.
6. Smith-Meyer, B. (2022) Chelsea Manning dances with the crypto devil. *Politico*. https://tinyurl.com/2p8mkpex (accessed: 12 March 2023).
7. Good, O. S. (2021) NFT mastermind says he created Ethereum because Warcraft nerfed his character. *Polygon*. https://tinyurl.com/2p8kj8nc (accessed: 12 March 2023).
8. Morrell, G. et al. (2011) The August riots in England – DMSS. UK Cabinet Office. https://tinyurl.com/2rx3hrcy (accessed: 12 March 2023).
9. Žižek, S. (2019) Shoplifters of the world unite. *London Review of Books*. https://tinyurl.com/y24kt6tt (accessed: 12 March 2023).
10. Fisher, M. (2009) *Capitalist Realism: Is There No Alternative?* Zero Books, Alresford.
11. Danielsson, J. (2022) The beginning of the end for cryptocurrencies. *CEPR*. https://tinyurl.com/3suwjera (accessed: 15 March 2023).
12. A Gini Index rating of 1 signifies that 1 individual has 100 per cent of all wealth, while a rating of 0 signifies absolute equality. The USA has a Gini Index rating of 0.49. South Africa – considered by the World Bank to be the most unequal country on Earth – has a Gini Index rating of 0.63.
13. Guo, M. et al. (2020) Gini index based initial coin offering mechanism. Preprint. https://tinyurl.com/wt9j7ecd (accessed: 12 March 2023).
14. Seth-Smith, N. (2018) Do we have the right to financial rebellion? *OpenDemocracy*. https://tinyurl.com/4r4schpj (accessed: 12 March 2023).
15. Dallyn, S. and Frenzel, F. (2020) The challenge of building a scalable postcapitalist commons: the limits of Faircoin as a commons-based cryptocurrency. *Antipode*, 53(3), 859–883.

16. Muldoon, J. (2022) *Platform Socialism: How to Reclaim Our Digital Future from Big Tech*. London: Pluto Press.

17. Weaver, The death of cryptocurrency.

18. Ibid.

19. Department of Justice (2022) Justice Department announces total distribution of over $4 billion to victims of Madoff Ponzi scheme. https://tinyurl.com/57t8z2cr (accessed: 18 May 2023).

20. Weaver, The death of cryptocurrency.

21. Nichols, M. (2023) Record-breaking 2022 for North Korea crypto theft. *Reuters*. https://tinyurl.com/bdhuhdka (accessed: 12 March 2023).

22. Vipers, G. (2023) Americans lost a record $10.3 billion to online scammers last year. *Wall Street Journal*. https://tinyurl.com/5n6sy98d (accessed: 17 March 2023).

23. Patel, R. (2022) Ransomware attacks hit two out of three organizations in 2021. *Forbes*. https://tinyurl.com/266ph3v8 (accessed: 17 March 2023).

24. Wetsman, N. (2021) Hospitals say cyberattacks increase death rates and delay patient care. *The Verge*. https://tinyurl.com/3refwyhr (accessed: 12 March 2023).

25. Licsman, S. (2022) Just 8% of Americans have a positive view of cryptocurrencies now. *CNBC*. https://tinyurl.com/mr3s9bn9 (accessed: 12 March 2023).

26. Diehl, S. (2022) Crypto policy symposium. YouTube. https://tinyurl.com/4285nnt3 (accessed: 12 March 2023).

27. Sinclair, B. (2022) Why we're still passing on blockchain pitches. *Games Industry*. www.gamesindustry.biz/why-were-passing-on-blockchain-pitches (accessed: 12 May 2023).

28. Versprille, A. and Allison, B. (2022) Crypto bosses flex political muscle. *Bloomberg*. https://tinyurl.com/2z6ndj67 (accessed: 12 March 2023).

29. Waterson, J. (2022) Offshore firm links BBC chair to sanction-hit Russian. *The Guardian*. https://tinyurl.com/yc5ar2bf (accessed: 12 March 2023).

30. Davies, R. (2022) Cryptocurrency firm linked to Philip Hammond still lacks UK approval. *The Guardian*. https://tinyurl.com/5n9ahrpr (accessed: 14 April 2023).

31. Amery, P. (2023) Dark money concerns over Boris Johnson donor. *New Money Review*. https://tinyurl.com/mj3zmsdt (accessed: 12 March 2023).

32. Hancock, M. (2023) Matt Hancock. Twitter. https://tinyurl.com/4xkx4wcp (accessed: 12 March 2023).

33. Shoaib, A. (2022) African former rebels recruited as mercenaries by the Kremlin-linked Wagner Group have been abandoned in Ukraine. *Business Insider*. https://tinyurl.com/yc6etzvr (accessed: 12 March 2023).

34. CryptoUK (2023) Members. https://tinyurl.com/7rhvar4t (accessed: 12 March 2023).

35. UKIIC (2022) Introduction to Magna Carta Island International Innovation Center. UKIIC Accelerator. https://tinyurl.com/bdz68dt6 (accessed: 12 March 2023).

36. PCC (2022) A magna carta for the metaverse. *Medium*. https://tinyurl.com/5y29r9xn (accessed: 12 March 2023).

37. Mason, R. (2023) Crypto firm with links to parliamentary groups appears to have vanished. *The Guardian*. https://tinyurl.com/yds332vx (accessed: 17 March 2023).

38. Goffman, E. (1952) On cooling the mark out. *Psychiatry*, 15(4), 451–463.

39. Mackenzie, Criminology towards the metaverse.

40. Žižek, S. (2019) Post-wall: neo-anti-communism. *London Review of Books*. https://tinyurl.com/2xjsa4yu (accessed: 17 March 2023).

41. Goffman, E. (1952) On cooling the mark out. *Psychiatry*, 15(4), 451–463.

42. Future of Life Institute. (2023) Pause giant AI experiments: an open letter. https://tinyurl.com/49cycjxc (accessed: 18 May 2023).

43. Nosta, J. (2023) Is Sam Altman today's Robert Oppenheimer? *Medium*. https://tinyurl.com/59d7c9ht (accessed: 18 May 2023).

44. Altman, S. (2021) Moore's law for everything. https://tinyurl.com/26er6nj6 (accessed: 12 March 2023).

45. The so called eAUD pilot in Australia was built using Ethereum. Palau is experimenting with Ripple.

46. Gerard, *Libra Shrugged*.

47. RMI (2018) Sovereign Currency Act 2018. https://tinyurl. com/2a252x7n (accessed: 12 March 2023).

48. Gerard, *Libra Shrugged*.

49. Armstrong, B. (2021) Announcing Coinbase fact check: decentralizing truth in the age of misinformation. *Medium*. https://tinyurl.com/5b7s4r4u (accessed: 12 March 2023).

50. Browne, R. (2023) Twitter partners with etoro to let users trade stocks, crypto as Musk pushes app into finance. *CNBC*. https://tinyurl.com/mwhfudvw (accessed: 16 April 2023).

51. Article 7 of the UN convention on the rights of the child (birth registration, name, nationality, care) states that every child has the right to be registered at birth, to have a name and nationality, and, as far as possible, to know and be cared for by their parents.

52. Wayt, T. (2022) Eric Adams: using blockchain for birth certificates, deeds 'way of the future'. *New York Post*. https://tinyurl.com/5n7e6zwp (accessed: 12 March 2023).

53. Zuboff, S. (2019) *The Age of Surveillance Capitalism: The Fight for a Human Future at the New Frontier of Power*. Profile Books, London.

54. Walker, A. (2019) NHS gives Amazon free use of health data under Alexa advice deal. *The Guardian*. https://tinyurl.com/y5n42hn5 (accessed: 12 March 2023).

55. Ungoed-Thomas, J. (2022) Controversial £360m NHS England data platform lined up for Trump backer's firm. *The Guardian*. https://tinyurl.com/3skbuwer (accessed: 12 March 2023).

56. Matsakis, L. (2019) How the West got China's social credit system wrong. *Wired*. https://tinyurl.com/ycykbmw7 (accessed: 12 March 2023).

57. Howson, P. (2021) Distributed degrowth technology: challenges for blockchain beyond the green economy. *Ecological Economics*, 184, 107020.

58. Earthshot Prize (2022) Roadmap. https://tinyurl.com/3hcsfk6h (accessed: 17 March 2023).

59. Greenfield, A. (2017) *Radical Technologies: The Design of Everyday Life*. Version, London.

60. Scott, B. (2022) *Cloudmoney: Cash, Cards, Crypto, and the War for Our Wallets*. Bodley Head, London.

61. Nelson, A. (2022) *Beyond Money: A Postcapitalist Strategy*. Pluto Press, London.
62. Amick, S. (2023) McDonald's accepts Bitcoin Payments in Lugano, Switzerland. *Bitcoin Magazine*. https://tinyurl.com/mpw3mwej (accessed: 14 April 2023).
63. Gissen, L. (2023) McDonald's new fully-automated restaurant completely run by machines. *Daily Mail*. https://tinyurl.com/3pbkyh3b (accessed: 12 March 2023).

Index

For topics related to Bitcoin and cryptocurrency, *see* the topic,
e.g. children; environment

The Pluto Press Newsletter

Hello friend of Pluto!

Want to stay on top of the best radical books
we publish?

Then sign up to be the first to hear about our
new books, as well as special events,
podcasts and videos.

You'll also get 50% off your first order with us
when you sign up.

Come and join us!

Go to bit.ly/PlutoNewsletter

Thanks to our Patreon subscriber:

Ciaran Kane

Who has shown generosity and
comradeship in support of our publishing.

Check out the other perks you get by subscribing
to our Patreon – visit patreon.com/plutopress.

Subscriptions start from £3 a month.